I0822606

ONE WITH A PAPER

SELECTED WORKS

2010–20

CINCINNATI, OH

FIRST EDITION

Published by Praus Press

CONTENTS

INTRODUCTION

FOR MUCH OF THE NINETEENTH CENTURY, Cincinnati was the center of culture and learning throughout the Midwest. During this period, the residents of the city often founded organizations to sponsor cultural and educational activities. The Literary Club is one such organization. It was chartered on October 29, 1849, and is the oldest such club in the United States.

Since its founding, The Club has had no more than one hundred regular members at any given time. Traditionally, all of them have been men. Members have included many prominent Cincinnati residents, some historical figures, such as Presidents Rutherford B. Hayes and William Howard Taft. Today, membership is drawn from a cross section of many professions, including published authors. Members present papers at Club meetings, and occasionally famous writers have spoken to The Club's membership, as well. Among the guests have been Ralph Waldo Emerson, Booker T. Washington, Mark Twain, and Robert Frost.

Its members continue what is really the ancient Greek and Renaissance tradition of rhetoric as a form of entertainment. We should remember that the first great European literature was oral, beginning with the unknown author or authors whom we know as Homer. In this anthology, we present writing that may not quite equal The Odyssey; nonetheless readers will see in the twenty pieces included here, that our members produce a wide variety of quality writing in several exciting genres. These include remembrance, history, diary, essays, humor, and pieces on what makes for good writing.

Remembrances recount the deep senses of love, life, and loss that well up in us when a close family member or dear friend is taken by death. We are all touched by these sentiments roused at such times, and in sitting down to put deep feelings on paper with pen.

Histories inform, surprise, and entertain us in many ways. In this anthology, our members address events local, national, and international in concise fashion.

A diarist's contribution focuses on his reaction to the unanticipated news from his doctor that he had only a year of life left. Gratefully, his doctor was wrong, and the author's life continues, one of the few times when one is glad that the doctor's diagnosis is wrong.

Michel de Montaigne (1533-1592), a member of the petite nobility of France, wrote during the age of the European wars of religion, Catholic versus Protestant. He was what we might call today a "moderate," one who advocated tolerance. Montaigne devised a totally new genre of writing called the essay, in which the writer explores for understanding their own thoughts and feelings. This volume proffers our own fine example.

Several examples of humorous writing are also included. Humor makes us laugh and smile but humor can also highlight serious issues in a non-conflictual way. Other times humor just makes us laugh and relax, valuable in themselves.

Finally, we include an excellent piece on the important role of grammar in effectively expressing one's point of view. Correct grammar is often contested ground where the final resolution comes through a kind of armistice between the contesting parties.

We call upon the reader to browse through the collection, sampling whichever most appeals to them in the moment. The rewards will be rich and long-lasting.

{1}

THE CARD GAME

JOHN K. BRACKETT

ONCE A MONTH, right after the "eagle flies," if you know what I mean, a couple of my friends and I get together at my place in Avondale to play a little draw poker, an excuse really, to just shoot the shit. We have a lot more of that to throw around than we do cash. That is what true friendship is all about. Metaphorically, I mean. We aren't a bunch of sexually frustrated neurotic chimps in a cage with nothing else to do but play with our own crap. We're just a bunch of ordinary guys who have drifted together like loose branches in a stream.

Some of us are just as rough, too. Lonnie Bartell owns a medium-sized construction company that does a lot of work around town. Bartell Construction has a build going on downtown right now. But when it comes to money, Lonnie is one of the cheapest bastards I have ever met. For example, I heard from some of the crew he has working down there, that they had a bitch of a time getting him to supply port-a-potties, so the crew could relieve themselves in a civilized manner. But Lonnie did not permit that until the structure had reached a certain height. Until then, it was catch as catch can, or drip as drop could. Workers were running in and out of the Hamilton County Office Building and nearby businesses just to take a piss. Finally, they convinced him that this situation was slowing things down, so he finally had some of the blue/green potties delivered to the site. Except one thing — he had them modified so that they were coin operated!

Can you believe that?

He is a poor sport, too. If he ain't winning at cards, which he never does, we must keep playing until he at least breaks even.

Jim Powell is retired from the University up there on the hill. He retired from what used to be the College of Applied Science over on Victory Parkway, but its departments have been dispersed among others on the main campus. That land was too valuable to remain just a part of the University, despite its teaching and great placement success. The only graduates who did not get jobs were the ones who didn't want a job. James is the passive-aggressive type. He always has something to say under his breath, even if he wasn't in the argument. Like a lot of teachers, he tends to be long-winded when he does talk. You ask him a simple question, and you are liable to end up somewheres you don't recognize. Ask him how long it takes concrete to set, and he winds up telling you about how the Romans had it when the rest of the world did not. Now, that's some useful information. Who cares if there is a big old building in Rome with a huge concrete dome? What's that got to do with my life?

Bill Jones is coal black, the first thing you notice about him—other than he is six feet two, and two hundred and fifty pounds. He looks like the kind of guy you wouldn't want to piss off, and that is about right. Bill is a retired University of Cincinnati police officer. He retired early when his boss became a woman. I don't mean his boss used to be a man who had "the operation," but she was always a female. Bill said he could not work for no woman; should be the other way around, according to Nature and his Southern Baptist god. He is here because he is my brother-in-law. My older sister, Birdie, is the kind of woman who will bounce a lamp off your head if she gets riled up, so he spends most of the day out of the house. She say she don't need a man around in the daytime. She is the only person who has no fear of Bill.

Then there is me. My name is Oscar. I have always worked several different jobs, done different kinds of work. I get bored too easy, so when that happens, I just do something else: chauffeur, waiter, Uber driver, the kind of jobs that don't take all your time. Some folks say that I am just lazy. I say maybe so, but you ain't seeing me with high blood pressure. I would say that I am comfortable.

We usually start around 7:30 in the evening, sitting around the card table that I set up in the living room. Bill had a band aid on his head. I asked what happened, and before he could answer, Lonnie said, "He must have got home too early for Birdie's liking."

Bill bristled, “I ran into a doorway at home.”

“Who do you expect to believe that? What was you doing runnin’ in the house anyway? Do you mean Birdie slammed the door in your face?” I asked.

Bill said, “Ok, Oscar, try this: I slipped on the ice outside.”

I said, “Remember, we all know my sister.”

Bill said, “If you were my friends, you would have told me about her before we got married.”

I said, “Understand, we were desperate to get that woman out of the house.”

Lonnie said, “I can’t see why you would marry a woman like that when you can’t work for one.”

Bill replied, “That’s exactly why I retired. I get enough bossin’ at home.”

I said, “It’s more serious than that. You show up again lookin like you been beaned, and I’m going to call 911 to get you in concussion protocol.”

“Fuck you!” Bill said. “Let’s play some cards, man.”

I dealt a hand. Five cards down. Bill threw away three cards, took three more. Since he always did this when he was holding a pair of something, I knew what he likely had. But Bill folded. I didn’t have anything, but I threw in one card and took one, hoping to bluff a round. The pot was a dollar each with a betting limit of five dollars. I threw in two dollars and looked at Jim. He threw away four cards and took four more. That was as good as saying that he was hoping for divine aid for something, anything. Lonnie kept two and tossed three, then he saw my dollar and raised me fifty cents. Cheap bastard, I thought; he has a pair but is too cheap to bet to win. I raised him another dollar plus his fifty cents. Jim folded and that left me and Lonnie. My bet was too rich for his blood, so he folded. I won even though he had the better hand.

“Shit!” he proclaimed and threw down his cards. “What did you have?”

“That is the kind of question that you have to pay to have answered.”

“Goddamn it,” he said, taking out his wallet to count his remaining bank notes.

He sat hunched over as if he was afraid we would see what he had in there.

Bill said, “If it’s going to break the bank, maybe you shouldn’t play.”

“I will keep playing because I never lose.”

“That’s because we never let you lose,” Jim said.

"That's right," I said. "You whine like an old whipped dog when you get down in the betting."

Lonnie said, "Oscar, if you owned a business you would appreciate the value of a dollar."

"If you weren't such a skinflint maybe you would win this game every so often," I said. "Then you would appreciate the value of many dollars."

"I swear to god, sometimes I think you all are cheating me. I should be winning more often."

Bill chimed in, "How would you know if you were being cheated? You can't tell what's happening around the table anyway. You more afraid to lose than hope to win"

Jim said, "This is a bit more difficult than bossing around those Mexicans you hire on your work sites."

Turning red in the face, Lonnie said, "I did that to learn Spanish, you know from real Spanish speakers, right from the horse's mouth, so to speak."

I said, "If you were a horse, I'd say you were talking out of the other end."

Jim said, "You pick an odd moment to decide to learn the language of our brown brothers from south of the border."

Lonnie said, "Hell, they're taking over anyway. In Miami, you can't get a job unless you speak Spanish. Right here in our own country!"

Jim said, "You do know that the Spanish were here before the English by about one hundred years: Remember Christopher Columbus? Then you count the Vikings who came down from the north in the tenth century. The British were at least third in line in the seventeenth century. But, what the hell, I am just glad I don't have to learn Norwegian."

Bill said, "Deal another hand."

We played four or five more hands and I'll be damned if Lonnie didn't turn up ahead by a dollar fifty. "Who's cheating now?" I asked.

"Let's take a break. I want to relax and enjoy my winnings, "Lonnie said.

I went into the kitchen to bring out more beer and some snacks. You would not believe it, but the snacks provoked a harsh reaction. Usually, I served up the usual chicken wings, chips, pretzels, dip, etc. But I thought, why not try something different and even healthy for a change. When my friends cast their eyes on the food, you would have thought I had taken a knee with the flag passing by.

Lonnie looked over the kale chips, hummus, and flatbread arrayed on my table.

He said, "What are those green things?"

I said, "Those are kale chips. There is a sour cream dip there, too." There was also a dessert of stuffed kumquats, according to my grandma's recipe. (We used to be so poor. Stuffing kumquats is not easy!) Then he looked at me and, dripping sarcasm, said, "This is all the fault of political correctness."

Jim said, "When I was teaching, I might have told my students to eat this crap, but I would never do it myself."

Bill said, "What's wrong with the usual stuff we eat? Ain't it good enough for you all of a sudden?"

I was just about to set the quinoa bars on the table, but I decided not to.

I said, "I just wanted to change up, try something new and maybe even healthy, for a change. This don't have nothing to do with political correctness, either."

"Yes, it does," Lonnie replied. "It is the exact equivalent of when the mayor of New York a few years back — I can't remember his name — a fat little Jewish guy, tried to tell the people how big they could order their soft drinks and shit. Americans don't need no government agency telling them how much they can eat and drink, or what to eat and drink. Now you bring your friends this so-called 'health food.' Who is to say this stuff is healthier than a big fat nourishing cheeseburger?"

Jim said, "You know that eating meat is why our brains are so big."

I said, "Not to mention your gut."

Bill said, "Stop, you're making me hungry," and looking at the table, "I sure as shit ain't goin' to eat this stuff."

"Well fine. Starve to death for all I care."

Bill sighed and said, "We still got beer." That statement restored order in the room. Then he continued, "But I could sure use a chicken wing."

We played a few more stimulating hands of five card draw, and sure enough, Lonnie began to lose, and to whine about it. I decided to have a little fun busting his beignets. "As a white man, what do you feel your people do well in sports?"

Jim and Bill looked at me wide-eyed, as if they could not believe what had come out of my mouth. Lonnie said, "Well I guess all of them. What's your point?"

"I just was thinking that a way to measure worth is money. How much do pros make if you break it down along the Mason-Dixon line, you know. Who are the best players in the NBA, for example?"

Lonnie said, "I don't know. You tell me." His face began to redden.

I replied, "Certainly the black players are better because they get paid more. The former owner of the Los Angeles Clippers, a certain Mr. Sterling, was consulting with his GM and coach over whether they should sign J.J. Redick for a large sum of money. The coach and GM were in favor: He is a pretty good three-point shooter. Sterling, however, was dubious. He said, 'Are you sure this guy is worth all this money? He's not even black!' True story, I swear."

Jim said, "Is this the guy who the League forced to sell his team?"

I replied, "Yeah. And he had a black mistress, too. Sterling did not want her sitting with her black friends in the stands."

Lonnie, red in the face, said, "What does this have to do with anything? We're playing cards, and the only way you can beat me is to cheat."

Bill said, "Everybody knows that black and white are equal when it comes to cards."

"That's it," I said. "Lonnie is just delusional. I'd say he was bi-polar but he's cheap all the time."

Lonnie said, "I don't know why I hang out with you guys."

I said, "Who else would have you? Did you ever think about that?"

"Two washed up retirees, and a lazy bum" Lonnie said. "I'm the only one being a productive member of society. I work so you guys can lay around and cheat me out of my money. God only knows what you do with it."

Jim said, "It ain't really that much. We're playing with a five-dollar limit, after all. No one is going to vacation in Acapulco with their winnings or cheatings from this table."

"Let's cool down," I said. "I'll bring out the Jim Beam."

"Now you're talking," Jim said. "I'll get some ice."

I don't know why they call alcoholic beverages "refreshing." If the blurring of reality you find "refreshing," then you have a different idea of refreshment than I do. Refreshed means you stand up bright-eyed and bushy-tailed, not look around for the nearest chair to fall into. Well, whatever it is called, we all do it even if we don't know exactly why.

Some say that booze loosens the tongue, which is true for those already inclined to talk too much, but it also loosens the memory. Each of us was in Viet Nam back in the day, but at different times and places. That experience is part of what keeps us together as a group.

Lonnie said, "What are you muttering about over there?" Sure, enough we had all settled back into our chairs around the card table bourbon glasses in hand.

I replied, "I was just thinking about the 'bad old days,' Viet Nam."

Bill said, "Why would you want to rake through those coals again. They're dead, gone, and forgotten."

I said, "Yeah, but some of it was funny, even if not intentionally so."

Bill said, "That's the funniest kind of funny."

Jim said, "Agreed! Funny depends on your point of view, but basically it is a not very covert form of aggression."

I said, "Here goes the 'professor' again. Here is a true story that I witnessed. When I am finished, tell me why it is funny."

Lonnie chuckled, "Suppose it ain't funny?"

I said, "It's funny, motherfucker."

So, I began, "I was with the CBs in 1968 north of Hue and Quang Tri City, right after the TET offensive. I remember seeing Hue was really shot up. We were spread along the Quang Tri River as one of our perimeters. Camp was right across from the DMZ, so close that one afternoon when some of us were watching a movie while off duty, a short artillery round from friendlies landed in camp. It makes a characteristic ripping sound that I am happy to never have heard again. We cleared out of that tent fast, and rumors began to bubble up that the NVA had moved their artillery into the DMZ to fire on us. Our knees began to quake since this was also close to the time when Khe Sanh was under siege. Marines were sitting under daily artillery barrages for months, January to July 1967-68. When I was on base security sitting in a sand-bag bunker along the river, one of my mates was a red-haired Irish kid, who had been at Khe Sanh. Quietest Irishman I ever met."

Lonnie interrupted, "I ain't hearing anything funny. Except maybe you crappin' your drawers when that short round landed."

"I didn't say I crapped my pants, I said our knees shook. I just mention that stuff as context for the funny part. The prevailing mood was one of dread, so certain were we that the NVA was going to ultimately invade and run over us."

I continued, "While on base security, we rotated watches among three of us who basically lived in the bunker during our period of service. One nightshift that I had I sat atop the bunker staring out at the Quang Tri River quietly flowing past in the moon light. Then, I heard over the radio some guy in another bunker radio into the watch commander saying that he thought that he saw a periscope sticking up in the river. Radio central questioned him a couple of times asking if he was sure about what he was seeing. The guy swore up and down that he saw a submarine periscope in the river and asked for permission to fire his grenade launcher at it. Permission was granted! One or two rounds were fired at what had likely been a reed sticking up near the banks. I don't know what damage they believed that a grenade could have done to a sub."

"You can probably understand why normally we were not allowed to keep bullets in our guns, or presumably, grenades in our grenade launchers. Following the logic here leads you not only into the fog of war but also the fog in the human mind. Firing that grenade launcher was the product of supposedly rational procedures and logic. Think about it."

Jim said, "I was not aware that the North Vietnamese had a navy equipped with submarines, let alone submarines that were capable of submerging in a river. They would have been very small, the gooks being a small people, perhaps one-man affairs, with a reed for breathing, but not a periscope. In that case, it would have made sense to fire a grenade at it. In fact, there may have been a flotilla out there, and your man's shot scared them off."

I said, "Fuck you. And don't say 'gooks' around me."

Bill said, "We all said it often enough when we were over there."

"Fine," I said. "So, we haven't learned anything in forty-five years?"

Lonnie said, "We're getting pretty deep here. I suggest that we come up for air."

As the bottle of bourbon made its rounds, we got more "refreshed" as time passed, sinking further into our chairs. I picked up the deck of cards and dealt another hand.

I said, "You know there is a category of things that I never thought I would see."

Jim said, "If you live long enough a lot of things turn out like that."

"I thought I would never see the day when Compton's own Snoop Dog would become a game-show host."

Lonnie said, "Who the fuck is Snoop Dog? I thought the comic strip was over."

I said, "You're thinking of Snoopy the dog in the Peanuts comic strip. I'm talking about Snoop Dog, the gangsta rapper. It just seems odd to see this anti-establishment character now flowing in the mainstream."

I said, "The presentation is meant to hint at evil in that Snoop is dressed in a red jacket with black lapels that recalls the devil in some of his more sophisticated disguises. And, of course, there is some dirty language."

Jim said, "The possibility to commodify something, anything, even a rapper's odious persona, will always win out if it is believed there is money to be made." I said, "The most respected people, it turns out, are not always the safest."

Bill said, "Why are men, especially black men, called, call themselves, dogs?"

"Yeah," I said, "We used to be cats." I looked at Lonnie and said, "Which would you rather be?"

"Well, cats are kind of sneaky."

Jim said, "Historically, cats have been associated with women for precisely that reason. Women are weak, so they have to pursue their interests, not in the straightforward way of men, but slyly and from the side."

I said, "So, you're saying that when we were cats, we were actually reppin' ourselves as weak like women?"

Bill said, "There are a lot of dead musicians who would not agree."

"Hell, I don't agree!" I said.

Jim said, "Dogs are much more aggressive, much more in your face."

I said, "Depends on the breed of dog."

Lonnie said, "For the sake of peace among the brothers, let's stick with a generic category of dog who is big and bold, like a German Shepherd." We played another hand, and Bill started to chuckle.

Lonnie said, "Why are you laughing? Didn't get the cards you were expecting?"

Bill replied, "You ought to take a couple of Quaaludes and calm down."

"What are Quaaludes?"

I said, "Ask Bill Cosby. And don't tell me you don't know who he is." "I don't do drugs," Lonnie said.

Bill said, "Don't take it literally. I'm just sayin' to calm down, no one is cheating here."

"I have a question about your people. Perhaps you can answer," Jim said, looking at me. "What do you think it costs young black men to get their hair styled to look as though they forgot to comb it when they got out of bed in the morning?"

Bill said, "Did you ever stop and think it might not be a style?'

Jim said, "No. There are too many young dudes who look like that, including professional basketball players."

Since I had long been sporting the bald look, I began to wonder if the conversation wasn't meant to make fun of me. "Why do you pay so much attention to men's hair?" I said.

Jim said, "I am just trying to keep track of the changing styles and what they may mean."

I said, "Why don't you pay attention to women's hair, instead of men?"

Bill said, "Yeah. That's what men do. They don't look at other men. Black women have hair that is worth looking at."

I said, "That's right. Some of their styles are so elaborate they seem more like architectural designs and construction."

Jim said, "I'm just different, I guess. You two are overly macho. And I never said that I did not look at women, too."

Lonnie said, "Don't forget about me: I'm macho."

We all had a good laugh over that. I was relieved to see the free-floating paranoia in the room land on Lonnie. I wasn't worried any more about having my baldness be made fun of.

Jim said, "Well, I for one have enjoyed this exploration of black manhood."

I said, "Good. Now what about white manhood?"

Lonnie said, "White men are macho and smarter than anybody else."

Bill's eyes got wide, and he said, "You might have trouble backing that up."

Lonnie replied, "I don't think so. Ask any white person and if they are truthful, they will agree. If it weren't true, why is the world set up like it is?"

I said, "You all do have the money and the power."

Jim said, "Let's tread carefully here: we are friends and want to remain that way, right?"

Lonnie said, "I might have to reconsider unless we forget about healthy snacks.

I am not looking to find out what kale chips taste like. I'm not that macho."

Jim said, "Watch out, he'll have us doing shots of Jägermeister next."

I said, "Okay. I will get healthy, while the rest of you stay with the general trend of getting fat. If you must fly anywhere just know that airline seats are getting narrower. Last time I flew into CVG there was a fat woman that even the Sky Marshalls, two of them, could not pull out of her seat. They had to uninstall the whole seat and take it and her off the plane. The beautiful part is that she was threatening to sue them over her discomfort.

I don't know if it is true but I heard that this woman, an Italian American, was pretty hefty. They took her to a hospital where they tested her blood type as they routinely do. It came back marked ragu!"

Bill said, "I wonder what happened to the passenger who was scheduled to sit in her seat on the next flight and it ain't there?"

Lonnie said, "Oscar, I think it is time to put on the coffee, so we can drive out of here."

I said, "Okay. Should I bring the kumquat dessert?'

Jim said, "No. I think we can forget about that."

A little later my friends were "un-refreshed" enough to be trusted to drive home over the late-night streets. I cleaned up the place and threw out the healthy snacks. I poured myself a nightcap and flopped into my Lazy-boy in front of the TV to catch the 11 p.m. news. The routine description of car accidents, elderly abuse, and cruelty to animals stories I found strangely comforting, and I soon drifted off to sleep.

{2}

PRESCRIPTIVENESS PRESCRIBED

WILLIAM BURLEIGH

SEVERAL YEARS AGO, my tranquil retirement was interrupted with a surprise job offer: to teach writing to a pair of home-schooling grandchildren. Our daughter, their teacher, asked my wife and me if we would try our hand at giving supplemental formal instruction to her two oldest children, then aged eleven and nine. Years ago, I once taught a three-hour writing class at a small college but that was to young adults, and I discovered it certainly was not as easy as it may have looked. I came away from that semester with a heightened respect for the skill of the teacher. Now I was being asked to mentor an age level where I had no experience. Yet how could a grandparent say no?

My wife and I signed up for bi-weekly sessions of team-teaching. Our aim was to show our two youngsters how they could acquire the basic skills of clear concise communication through correct use of the written word. Each week one of us would discuss with them an element in this process and then assign a theme for them to put into written form. They tackled short descriptive essays, book reviews, letters, stories, opinion pieces, persuasive articles, interviews, and even a bit of poetry. It may be a truism but one learns to write by writing.

We insisted on high standards. We kept emphasizing the mantra of my wife's college teacher, the legendary Raymond Woodbury Pence, that it is not enough to write in order to be understood; one must write so as not to be misunderstood. We required our charges first to do drafts of their work and then to keep revising them until they were sure the final version was the very best they could produce. We tried not to be too draconian. Even though they learned that writing is hard, often frustrating work with no magic formulas, they gradually came to appreciate the rewards that awaited the careful writer.

Along the way, even though it was not our main emphasis, yes, we touched on the rules of grammar. We did not diagram sentences the way I learned in Sister Agnes Carmel's fourth grade. But we did talk about parts of speech, how they fit together and some rules of the road in using them. Today's professional linguists, I was all too aware, would find it harmful and counterproductive to inject such clutter into the creative process. Yet I was taught that the rules of grammar turn the noise of words into language that conveys meaning. I wanted my grandchildren to understand that far from stifling them, these rules would provide them the real freedom to communicate clearly in a world filled with cacophony.

At times, I worried that I was being too hard-nosed regarding the goals I set for students of their ages. Yet time and again they rose to the challenge. I was both surprised and thrilled by how they responded — and I do not believe my reaction was simply that of a proud grandfather. We ended the year on a high note. Catherine and Joseph had become better writers for their efforts and they knew it. They told their mom that writing had become their favorite subject.

I have no way of knowing, of course, whether our anecdotal experience proved any larger points about the best ways for children to learn to write. But I do admit to a certain malice aforethought in thus joining one of the longest shooting wars in the history of the English language. For well over a half-century—and some would argue for much longer than that — a fierce, often nasty struggle has been waging over the rules of grammar. Well into the 1980s, most teachers still employed "prescriptive" grammar instruction setting forth how people should write, rather than "descriptive" grammars which tell how people actually use language. Prescribing, of course, means to lay down rules authoritatively as a guide. Over the ensuing years, however, most academic linguists have backed away from appearing authoritative. Instead, armed with vast amounts of computer studies, they are now firmly ensconced in the descriptive camp, focusing on how language is structured and used without passing judgment on what is right or wrong. In teaching writing, they say they want students to express themselves without being hung up on rules. After all, why is it not sufficient to express one's thoughts as one sees fit, and not be restricted and hampered in how one does it? Everyone recognizes that English is a living language and is constantly changing. One descriptivist argues that "if language is going to keep changing anyway — and it is — what is the use of posting the little rules and making people uncomfortable, only to see the (rules) eventually blown away by the wind," especially in the multi-cultural America in which we live.

Such argumentation infuriates the prescriptivists. They point out that going back into antiquity, grammar has traditionally been considered one of the seven liberal arts. Indeed, for ages it was held as the first, the primary, the foundational art to be mastered. Elementary schools were once known as "grammar schools" for a reason, for it was there where teaching grammar was the fundamental launching pad in a child's education. A worried British broadcaster and writer named Libby Purves, writing in the *Times of London* in 2012, summed up this position: "Of all school disciplines, learning language correctly matters most. Clear, confident communication is the bedrock of every other endeavor in education and in life. . . . Neglecting, downgrading and generally dumbing standards is a great cruelty to visit on children."

Thus, have the battle lines been drawn.

It comes as more than parochial curiosity to note that a key antecedent in these grammar wars can be traced right here to the Queen City. In 1838, a child named William Strunk was born in Cincinnati into a German immigrant family who prized education. He graduated from Woodward High School, one of the first public schools in the country, and went on to study law at the University of Cincinnati. He became a prominent educator and lawyer in the young city, serving on the school and library boards and as a trustee of the university. The family lived on Stanton Avenue in Walnut Hills, attended the Presbyterian church, and eventually numbered three children.

One of those siblings, William Strunk Jr., was born on July 1, 1869, and as he grew up, he was deeply influenced by his father's example and interests. Following his father, young Will earned a bachelor's degree in 1890 at the University of Cincinnati. Interested in teaching as a career, he went off to Cornell

University for further studies. There he would spend the rest of his life, fulfilling his career ambitions. First, he earned a doctorate in 1896 and then, for the next forty-six years, he taught English "far above Cayuga's waters."

On the Cornell campus, he became a well-known professor, especially for his composition class, English 8. For that class, he authored a single text, a forty-three-page volume he privately printed and titled "The Elements of Style." He himself referred to it as "the little book." It was simply his handbook of writing tips — made up of seven rules of usage, eleven principles of composition, and a list of words and expressions commonly misused. That was it — framed as sharp, concise commands as if coming from a drill sergeant: *"Omit needless words." "Use the active voice." "Put statements in positive form." "Do not explain too much." "Revise and rewrite." "Above all, be clear."*

A student in the composition class of 1919 was a young man named Elwyn Brooks White, who described his teacher as "one of the most inflexible and choosy of men," friendly and funny yet with a "sting (in) his kindly lash" as he set forth his rules.

Toward his students, Professor Strunk manifested sympathy for the struggles of the writer attempting to communicate with an audience. In White's words, "Will felt that the reader was in serious trouble most of the time, floundering in a swamp, and it was the duty of anyone attempting to write English to drain this swamp quickly and get the reader up on dry ground or at least to throw a rope."

White recalled:

"Will knew where he stood. He was so sure of where he stood, and made his position so clear and so plausible, that his peculiar stance has continued to invigorate me. . . . He had a number of likes and dislikes that were almost as whimsical as the choice of a necktie, yet he made them seem utterly convincing. He scorned the vague, the tame, the colorless, the irresolute. He felt it was worse to be irresolute than to be wrong."

Reminiscing about his teacher, White said:

"In the days when I was sitting in his class, he omitted so many needless words, and omitted them so forcibly and with such eagerness and obvious relish, that he often seemed in the position of having shortchanged himself — a man left with nothing more to say yet with time to fill, a radio prophet who had outdistanced the clock. Will Strunk got out of this predicament by a simple trick: he uttered every sentence three times. When he delivered his oration on brevity to the class, he leaned forward over his desk, grasped his coat lapels in his hands, and, in a husky, conspiratorial voice, said, 'Rule Seventeen. Omit needless words! Omit needless words! Omit needless words!'"

The student, Elwyn Brooks White, eventually became known, of course, as E.B. White, the celebrated writer of the "Notes and Comments" page in *The New Yorker* magazine and author of such beloved books as *Charlotte's Web, Stuart Little* and *The Trumpet of the Swan*.

In 1946, Professor Strunk died of cancer at seventy-one, leaving his wife Olivia and three children. Another three decades would pass before the Macmillan publishing house approached E.B. White about his possible interest in preparing an edition of Professor Strunk's "little book" for the general public. Thus, in 1977, Strunk and White's *The Elements of Style* first appeared. It has remained so popular that it has been in continuous print ever since, now in its fourth edition. In the process, it has thrown a rope to more than ten million students, writers, and other admirers — a publishing record for a book of its kind. White thought it appealed to so many because he said it fit on the head of a pin the vast number of rules and principles of English.

I daresay there is hardly a person in this audience who has not encountered the "little book" somewhere along the way. Its influence is difficult to overestimate. Asked to name one book that made him who he is today, David McCullough identified The Elements of Style. "I read it nearly fifty years ago and still turn to it as an ever-reliable aid to navigation, particularly . . . with reminders to 'revise and rewrite' and 'to be clear.'"

Dorothy Parker once said that, "if you have any young friends who aspire to become writers, the second-greatest favor you can do them is to present them with copies of *The Elements of Style*. The first-greatest, of course, is to shoot them now, while they're happy."

Indicative of the grammar wars that have paralleled Strunk and White's little book over the years, not everyone has been enraptured with *The Elements of Style*. The purists have sniffed at it, noting that although both Strunk and White were fine writers, the book itself contains a fair share of grammatical blunders and can hardly be considered a comprehensive textbook. One critic cited it as "an anachronism in the face of modern English usage," lashing out at Professor Strunk's "uninformed bossiness." Another, this one from Britain, called it "the book that ate America's brain." With the textual analysts taking over the academy and prescriptive grammar being consigned to the scrap heap of history, a member of the descriptive school labeled *The Elements of Style* "an aging zombie . . . a hodgepodge, its now-antiquated pet peeves jostling for space with . . . 1990s computer advice."

The unkindest cut of all comes from one of today's leading voices in the descriptive camp, Dr. Steven Pinker, who actually finds much of Strunk's guidance "charming and timeless," yet adds:

"Strunk was born in 1869, and today's writers cannot base their craft exclusively on the advice of a man who developed his sense of style before the invention of the telephone (let alone the Internet), before the advent of modern linguistics and cognitive science, before the wave of informalization that swept the world in the second half of the twentieth century."

Despite this barrage of criticism, *The Elements of Style* remains the granddaddy of all the books on language lining my library shelf. It has been my go-to reference guide ever since I first encountered it as a young editor. E.B. White admitted that he was once the kind of writer who did not have "any exact notion of what was taking place under the hood." I was like that. As a rookie reporter, I thought I knew something about writing until I started editing for a living. Then I discovered that I was like so many others who did not really know a gerund from a gerbil—as Patricia O'Conner points out in her *Grammarphobe's Guide*. My newspaper job forced me to raise the hood and no longer take for granted what makes a motor work. English is not easy, as languages go. I had to master some of its mechanics.

Every fortnight or so, a plain white envelope would arrive on the city desk of my newspaper containing the latest single-sheet copy of Winners and Sinners, which its author, Theodore Bernstein, styled "a bulletin of second-guessing issued occasionally from the southeast corner of *The New York Times* News Room." Bernstein was the managing editor of *The Times*. He originally intended his comments for the paper's reporters and editors but so popular were his observations that he graciously bowed to the demand from outside and shared them with a wider audience of newspaper people on what he found good and bad in the columns of America's leading journal. His recounting of the sinners usually outnumbered the winners but we all profited from Bernstein's learned, often witty explanations of what he found right and what he found wrong about the language employed by the news staff.

Bernstein thought that, "if writing must be a precise form of communication, it should be treated like a precision instrument. It should be sharpened and it should not be used carelessly."

In matters of grammar and usage, he refused to take sides on what he called "a well-trampled battleground."

"On one side," he noted, "are the stiff-necked grammarians, brandishing rigid rules, which they wield whether or not the rules are supported by history, idiom or certificates of convenience and necessity. On the other side are the soothing champions of the masses, with their battle cry, 'Whatever the people say is okay by me; the people speak real good.'"

Bernstein refused to join either camp. "To enlist with the too-orthodox would be to tend toward prissiness and to risk losing touch with the popular tongue," he explained. "To enlist with the too-liberal would be to invite the horrors of anarchy and to risk losing touch with the language of the literate."

Going back over two tattered books I have treasured, which distill the best from *Winners and Sinners*, it seems possible that battles over prescriptive and descriptive grammar should at some point admit sweet reason, as Ted Bernstein attempted to suggest. Why cannot the farmers and the cowboys be friends? Alas, such is the bad blood between the two camps that what would appear to be complementary goals turn instead into incompatible views. It is akin to the vitriolic political gridlock of Washington.

In a sense, these grammar wars strike one as proxies for larger struggles in our society. The differences fit within the thesis advanced by Daniel T. Rodgers, the Harvard historian, who argues that we are living in an "Age of Fracture" in which the decades of the late Twentieth Century saw a collapse of accepted social and political norms and an assertion of the individual's wants.

In his beefy, authoritative volume, *Modern American Usage*, Bryan Garner makes the salient point that, "the study of writing — like the very fact that writing exists — serves as a conservative, moderating influence. Our literary heritage has helped form our culture. The means by which we record words on paper has an enormous influence on readers and on the culture as a whole." He sees the descriptivists, on the other hand, as egalitarians reflecting the tenor of the times. For them:

"...we're all seen as equal— not just in how we write and think, but in how we confront the lived questions. What you believe is your business. I may not think the way you do but I accept your right to do so. After all, we're all equal... It's impermissible to say that one form of language is better than another: as long as a native speaker says it, it's okay — and anyone who takes a contrary stand is a dunderhead... The spirit of the day demands that you not think critically—or at least not think ill—of anyone else's language. If you believe in good grammar and linguistic sensitivity, you're the problem. And there is a large, powerful contingent in higher education today — larger and more powerful than ever before — trying to eradicate any thoughts about good and bad grammar, correct and incorrect word choices, effective and ineffective style."

When he arrived at Yale to teach writing, William Zinsser was surprised to find that 170 had signed up to take his course that had room for only twenty. He attributed the popularity to student desperation to learn grammar that permissive teachers had ignored. But after all, who would not want to be taught grammar by this celebrated writer who once famously remarked: "There's not much to be said about the period expect that most writers don't reach it soon enough"?

These musings may strike bystanders as overblown esoterica. The practical questions arising out of them, however, can go to the very heart of some of the burning issues of the day. To take one primary example, consider what has become of the use of the third person-singular pronouns — *he, she, him, her, his, hers*. In her *Confessions of a Comma Queen*, Mary Norris calls these six ancient words the most ticklish subject in modern English usage.

The inescapable fact is our language lacks a gender-neutral singular third-person pronoun. Linguists have been struggling for most of the past two centuries to invent one, but their efforts have languished. The prescriptive guru of usage, H.W. Fowler, has offered three makeshift solutions. The time-honored way has been to use the masculine form in which "he" is understood to stand for either the masculine or feminine pronoun. Even though the dictionary does define "man" as including all persons, many today consider this use sexist. Some even go so far as to use "she" simply as a bow to gender inclusivity. A second approach is to create a compound singular by using "he or she," "him or her," "his or hers." This awkward usage strikes most as cumbersome and clunky. A third way, which has gained much favor after decades of being seen as ungrammatical, is to permit "they" and "their" for use as a singular pronoun.

Thus, it becomes acceptable to write, "Every student can have **their** own computer," in order to avoid "his or her own computer."

Or: "A student should avoid bringing discredit to **their** school."

Or: "It is assumed, if someone is pressured, **they** will tell the truth."

The advent of feminist thinking, along with single-sex and transgender issues, has served as a particularly potent force pushing the sanctioning of this use. After years of debate, the American Copy Editors Society has officially accepted the "they" solution and recently, in a landslide vote at the American Dialect Society's annual meeting, "they" was anointed by the crowd of linguists as their "word of the year." They said it was a way of aligning language with emerging ideas about gender identity. They claimed that those who consider themselves "gender fluid" would prefer the use of the pronoun "they" rather than "he" or "she," or "their" rather than "his" or "her."

The comma queen, Mary Norris, remains adamant:

"I hate to say it," she writes, "but the colloquial use of 'their' when you mean 'his or her' is just wrong. It may solve the gender problem, and there is no doubt that it has taken over in the spoken language, but it does so at the expense of number. An antecedent that is in the singular cannot take a plural pronoun. . . . It's not fair. Why should a lowly common-gender plural pronoun trump over singular feminine and masculine pronouns, our kings and queens and jacks?"

In a universe ruled ever increasingly by the gods of diversity and political correctness, the sheer logic surrounding Miss Norris' reasoning is nonetheless cast aside as so much flotsam. Consider this advisory issued at the start of the school year at the University of Tennessee by a campus diversity officer: "There are dozens of gender-neutral pronouns. For all folks who went to school back when there were only him and her — here's a primer: some of the new gender-neutral pronouns are *ze, hir, zir, ye, xem* and *xyr*."

Last November, during an educational observance called Transgender Awareness Month, children in American classrooms were given "pronoun buttons" to wear on which they could display their own preferred personal pronoun.

The descriptive school would likely react by noting that if that is where English usage is going, then it will be interesting for the linguists to document the continuing evolution of the pronoun. Not so the prescriptivists, to be sure, and for good reason.

It's just not the personal pronoun that keeps the prescriptivists riled up. Other grammar gaffes draw their understandable ire because in each instance the goal of clear communication is fumbled away.

Take, for example, the ongoing debate over the so-called Oxford comma, or serial comma. The question involves whether to insert a comma before "and" in a series of three or more things. Purists require its use to prevent ambiguity. In America, however, the tendency is to use it willy-nilly. The Associated Press Stylebook decrees that the "and" alone is usually sufficient to clarify the meaning. However, omitting the serial comma can lead to mischief, as in the following —

"On stage, the country-western singer was joined by his two ex-wives, Kris Kristofferson and Waylon Jennings." The absence of a serial comma before the "and" comically suggests that it was those manly stars, Kris and Waylon, who were the singer's ex-wives.

Or, "This book is dedicated to my parents, Ayn Rand and God." And here I thought Ms. Rand was an avowed atheist who would not be seen in bed with anything suggesting the Almighty.

Countless other careless mishaps clutter the way to precise writing. Patricia O'Conner, the "Grammarphobe," devotes a whole book to why it's dangerous to construct English sentences without following a building code. She is keen on warning against danglers, those words or phrases found in the wrong places at the wrong times. To illustrate:

"Already housebroken, the Queen brought home a new corgi."

"Born at the age of 43, the baby was a great comfort to Mrs. Wooster."

"Dumpy and overweight, the vet says our dog needs more exercise."

Of course, it's not the Queen who is "housebroken", or the baby who is "43", or the vet who is "dumpy and overweight". More careful construction would keep the reader from wincing.

* * * * *

The digital revolution, in which the Internet and social media transform the way people communicate, has further shaken the cause of good grammar. Most of us can remember when spam was cheap ham; when a hashtag was a military stripe; and tweets and twitters were somehow related to an Audubon bird book. We can even recall when messages did not end in emojis. Now those messages flow merrily through chat rooms, blogs, and Instagram.

The *Grammarphobe* argues that cyber-writing is "no excuse for lousy English. . . . In fact, good English is especially important in cyberspace because the speed and brevity of email and other online writing conspire to muddle your message."

The emergence of texting raises particular red flags. Students of the phenomena notice that so-called "text-speak" actually influences how people think. With thumbs flying, texters dash out a series of letters, numbers, and symbols that often carry meaning only to those who have learned the code to fit within the confines of 144 characters. For example, WUU2 means "what are you up to?" and LOL means "laughing out loud." Some descriptivists claim "text-speak" is actually modernizing the English language, illustrating its flexibility in new and streamlined ways to convey complex messages. The prescriptivists groan, saying its use corrupts the language and promotes laziness among its users, especially the young, who so urgently need to understand the role of proper grammar in achieving precise communication.

Then there is the new technology itself. It has been reliably reported that one bank kept sending daily email acknowledgements beginning with the individualized salutation: "Dear Mr. Smith; (semicolon) A payment has been made . . ."; or "Dear Ms. Jones; (semicolon) Because of insufficient funds . . ." When an exasperated customer wrote to protest the repeatedly misused semicolon after the salutation, a bank representative coolly responded: "The semicolons are embedded in our computer systems, and there's no easy way to change the code."

Maybe, just maybe, though, there's hope for the mother tongue in this digital jungle. In a front-page story, *The Wall Street Journal* recently reported that crimes against grammar are turning off picky singles seeking to connect on Internet dating sites. The story told how a fellow named Jeff Cohen used his Ok Cupid site to line up a date for after-work drinks at a Manhattan bar but was chagrined when the young woman messaged back: "I'll see you their." He immediately sensed this grammar-challenged girl wasn't for him. Now, according to The Journal, Cohen has joined scores of other techies in using an app called the Grade, which actually checks messages for grammatical and spelling errors and assigns them a letter grade ranging from A+ to F. The Grade downgrades messages containing such abbreviations as "wasup" (for "what's up?"), "2d4" (for "to die for"), and YOLO (for "you only live once"). The popular, much advertised dating site, Match, actually surveyed 5,000 singles and found that after personal hygiene, the ingredient which most attracted them to a potential date was someone who used proper grammar and punctuation. This led a linguistics professor at Columbia University to conclude that "grammar snobbery is one of the last permissible prejudices."

N. M. Gwynne would surely rank as one of the leading grammar snobs in the English-speaking world today. He was a one-time successful English businessman before turning to teaching. His subjects have included English, Latin, Greek, French, German, mathematics, history, classical philosophy, natural medicine, the elements of music, and "how to start up and run your own business." His pupils have ranged in age from two to seventy, all over the English-speaking map. Since 2007, they have been enrolled in courses he offers on the Internet. In every case, he writes, he has been forced, first, to tackle English grammar because "it has been largely forgotten by my older pupils or because it has been ignored, most often completely," by those of school age. Why so much emphasis on grammar education? Because Gwynne passionately believes that "all thinking and communicating of any kind depends on grammar, grammar being simply the correct use of words, and words being the indispensable tools of thought."

At the prompting of a pupil's father, Gwynne decided to put together a handbook he called "the ultimate introduction to grammar and the writing of good English." Initially helped by only word of mouth, the first edition sold out, followed by two others. Finally, a hardback version was published and for five months in 2013 it became the top selling book in England. We can thank the editors at Alfred A. Knopf for introducing *Gwynne's Grammar* last year to an American audience.

The book's success is all the more remarkable because, like *The Elements of Style*, it is simply a slender volume about parts of speech, the basics of syntax, punctuation, and examples of good and bad grammar — hardly the stuff of the modern-day bestseller.

With lively wit and utter British self-confidence, Gwynne manages to make a principled, unforgettable case for the prescriptive way. "It is my position," he writes, "that the prescriptive approach to grammar, the one that says some things are right and some things are wrong, rather than describing things as they are, is the only correct approach. . . . "

He continues:

"For the last several decades, the public has been preposterously asked to believe that methodically learning the basics of how to do something destroys a child's creativity. Common sense and thousands of years of tradition tell us, on the contrary, that the techniques of any activity, from composing poems to playing tennis, must be carefully learned as a science — often very painstakingly in the case of the most satisfying and enjoyable occupations — before the budding practitioner can hope to flourish at it. Those who speak English today have the prodigious good fortune of having inherited from our ancestors a language which has two really spectacular features. One is that it is the most widely spoken language there has ever been. The other is that during the last four centuries, it has been, together with classical Greek and Latin, one of the three great vehicles of thought, communication, science, and culture of all time."

Gwynne is no stick-in-the-mud. He recognizes that anything alive must grow and change, and language is no exception. But he argues convincingly that English grammar has remained surprisingly intact since before the turn of the Sixteenth Century, and that the changes which have taken place, at least into the 1960s, have served to enrich the language and move it in the direction of greater precision and clarity. To the descriptive camp which allows usage to bend in the popular winds, he snorts, "We should be influenced neither by prevailing fashion nor by present-day majority vote nor by the pronouncements of acknowledged experts — and not even if those experts are unanimous — but only by adequate evidence."

As *Gwynne's Grammar* achieved its unexpected popularity in Britain, the critics pounced, denouncing the book as a mixture of "misinformation and nonsense." They debunked what they called the "myth" that there is one "correct" grammar that can be explicitly taught and tested. Britain's then-minister of education, the controversial Michael Gove, was not among those swayed by these criticisms. In fact, he recommended that the book be read by civil servants of the realm to help them "write and think properly." Imagine the outcry if the legions of American bureaucrats were faced with such a decree.

If the attentive reader detects a flavor of *The Elements of Style* in Gwynne's approach, there is a reason. He is a great admirer of Will Strunk's "little book," the one used in English 8 at Cornell (although not E.B. White's revised edition that achieved such popularity). He is attracted by Strunk's conciseness, calling the book "a minor work of genius" and proclaiming "there has certainly never been anything else like it." In an ultimate tribute, he incorporates the entirety of Strunk's original text as the second part of his own handbook, because he says that vocabulary and grammar alone, which he examines in the first part, are not enough to make writing readable. The successful writer must also acquire a sense of style, so that thoughts can be conveyed in ways that are clear, when necessary forcible, and always graceful. He credits Strunk with having served that purpose in providing unforgettable pointers for shaping style and adding flair to writing.

For a half century, from Strunk to Gwynne, from America back to the mother country of England, well-armed volumes have been marched into battle to fight the grammar wars. One wag commented that more grammar instruction spews forth from books these days than can be discovered in the contemporary classroom. I treasure my own shelf lined with these books, but my modest collection is nothing compared with the seemingly endless rows in the language section downstairs at the legendary Strand used book store in Manhattan, the Broadway "home to 18 miles of books."

Still, to a worldly spectator the onward march of the descriptive side must seem ever to gain momentum. Defenders of normative standards are often cast as evil doers worse than the storm troopers from Star Wars. A University of Michigan linguist has gone so far as to offer the twisted view that "in an age when discrimination in terms of race, color, religion, or gender is not publicly acceptable, the last bastion of overt social discrimination will continue to be a person's use of language." In other words, those who dare to promote long-honored language values now stand guilty of discrimination.

It would be tempting to conclude that the state of proper English has never been worse. One can take comfort, however, in the fact that past generations have voiced many of the same complaints, especially about language use among the youngsters then coming up.

Despite what academic linguists may contend, I found in my own experience, offering writing lessons to my grandchildren, that young minds do yearn for guidance. I could see they wanted a traffic cop to tell them when to stop and when to go, where to park and where not to. I had no desire to place these two seekers in linguistic straitjackets, or to hamstring their writing with complicated sets of rules. There were no tablets to pass down from Mount Sinai guaranteeing their way to a promised land of good grammar. I only offered a gentle nudge or two toward standards of safe passage. In no way did this approach seem to stifle their creativity. One of them especially was constantly looking for novel approaches that would make his work come alive.

Most fascinating for me in this experience was discovering what appeared to be an inherent desire in these children to find order in the language they used. From my observation, they gravitated on their own toward an identifiable logic. They grasped for what to them seemed true. Could it not be the case that human nature in its essentials is made for grammar?

Perhaps that is only the wishful thinking of a one-time editor. As with MacArthur and aging soldiers, old editors never die. We rest content in inflicting our prescriptive passions on grandchildren.

SOURCES:

The Elements of Style, William Strunk Jr., and E. B. White, with foreword by Roger Angell; (Fourth Edition), Pearson Education Inc., New York, 2000.

Gwynne's Grammar, N. M. Gwynne, Alfred A. Knopf, New York, 2013-2014.

Watch Your Language, Theodore M. Bernstein, with preface by Jacques Barzun, Channel Press, Great Neck, N.Y. (Sixth Printing), 1958

Woe Is I, The Grammarphobe's Guide to Better English in Plain English, Patricia T. O'Conner, Riverhead Books, New York, 2009.

Between You & Me, Confessions of a Comma Queen, Mary Norris, W. W. Norton & Company, New York, 2015.

The Sense of Style, The Thinking Person's Guide to Writing in the 21st Century, Steven Pinker, Viking Press, New York, 2014.

Garner's Modern American Usage, Bryan A. Garner, Oxford University Press, Oxford and New York, 2009.

Yes, I Could Care Less, How To Be a Language Snob Without Being a Jerk, Bill Walsh, St. Martin's Griffin, New York, 2013.

Eats, Shoots & Leaves, The Zero Tolerance Approach to Punctuation, Lynne Truss, Profile Books Ltd, London, 2003.

The Chicago Manual of Style, Sixteenth Edition, The University of Chicago Press, Chicago, 2010.

"By the Book," *The New York Times*, Interview with David McCullough, May 30, 2015.

"Grammar Rules," A review of Gwynne's Grammar, Mark Bauerlein, First Things, February 2015.

"How Grammar Snobs No U Ain't Mr. Rite," Georgia Wells, *The Wall Street Journal*, Page 1, October 2, 2015.

"The Wrong Way to Teach Grammar," Michelle Navarre Cleary, *The Atlantic*, February 25, 2014.

"Sorry, grammar nerds. The singular 'they' has been declared Word of the Year," Jeff Guo, *The Washington Post*, January 8, 2016.

Winning the Grammar Wars, Dave and Jane Willis, Kindle Edition, 2016.
"Which Emoji App Is Best for You?" *The Wall Street Journal*, Jan. 10-11, 2015.

History of Cincinnati and Hamilton County, Page 579.

{3} BIG GAME

GIBBY CAREY

For fifteen idyllic years in the 1920s and 30s, my father was a professional big game hunter in Africa, India, and Indo-China. This gave me, as a boy, enormous stature among my friends. He gave up these pursuits when he married and I was born — he never took me to Africa — but he was known throughout our hometown of Baltimore for having lived a life of high adventure in the most exotic parts of the world, during the depths of the Depression when everyone else was struggling to keep their heads above water. And what wonderful stories he told. He was not free with them: I had to pry them out of him. My happiest memories from my boyhood were evenings sitting and listening by the fire in his den, the floor covered with the skins of big cats, the walls clustered with heads and antlers casting shadows by the firelight, the wastepaper cans hollowed elephants' feet, while the huge cape buffalo above the mantel scowled furiously down at me. My eyes would wander over to his gun cabinet where the rifles and shotguns gleamed in ranked array, and I wondered which of them had brought down the big brute over the fireplace. And all the while my father told, or by special request retold, tales of his adventures. It was heaven. He also kept journals for most of his life.

But first we must set the stage. Africa is a very different place today than it was in the 1920s. Sub-Saharan Africa really did not open to the white man until after World War I, when new drugs made survival possible in lands where, just thirty years before, early white explorers had died within weeks from insects and disease. Consider: My father first went to Africa in 1920.

This was the twilight of the era of the great explorations, but there was still much about Africa that was unknown — it was only sixty years since the first intrepid explorers made their heroic attempts to discover the source of the Nile, and Burton and Speke finally found it. Just fifty years before, Stanley found Livingston in Ujiji. Forty years earlier, the Zulu wars climaxed at Rorke's Drift. Twenty years before, the Boer Wars brought the British Empire to its knees. Fifteen years before, Stanley again invaded the interior, this time armed with Gatling guns against the native tribes, to find Emin Pasha. There was a hiatus in exploration during World War I (the time of The African Queen) and the continent was largely undisturbed except for hostilities in German East Africa (Tanganyika). Ten years before my father's adventures in Africa, ex-president Teddy Roosevelt captured the nation's imagination with his big game expedition. At just the time my father arrived, there came a rush of colonial farmers and adventurers from England, most of them battered survivors of The Great War, and many of them second sons and remittance men from Britain's great families. Their companions were a remarkable breed of independent women like Karen Blixen (Isaak Dinesen) and Beryl Markham. And the great hunters came: Denys Finch-Hatton, Brora Blixen, Bring 'Em Back Alive Frank Buck, Carl Akeley, and all the others. White hunters flourished, as big game hunting — once the exclusive domain of the first colonists — became accessible and sportsmen rushed to the interior. A lot of water has flowed under the bridge since those days when Africa was still the Dark Continent, and tonight, as we sit here in this room, big game hunting is no longer the supreme adventure, as it was in those days. Standing to the charge of a maddened bull elephant was once the most daring thing a man could do. But times change. Today our sympathy is with the elephants, not the hunter, and we worry about their survival. One more critical difference between Africa then and now: Anyone here tonight who is motivated to do so can be on a plane to Dar Es Salaam tomorrow morning... can sleep Wednesday night in a tent camp on the Masai Mara, listening to the lions cough in the night... can view the Serengeti's great migrations of game and predators on Thursday from the comfort of a Toyota Land Rover... can visit the Ngorogoro Crater on Friday and the Olduvai Gorge on Saturday... and be back in time for next week's paper.

But in the 1920s a proper safari would require upwards of a full year, door to door: with at least sixty days and nights on slow boats coming and going, a minimum of four months walking and riding camels and mules through the bush, typically making five miles on a good day, and a good two months of sitting around and waiting for boats, waiting for supplies, waiting for licenses and permits, waiting for bearers or trackers, waiting for beasts of burden and all the myriad pieces of a well-planned expedition to fall into place. It was not for impatient men. My father left college in 1917 after just one term. Underage, he joined the RAF (then the Royal Flying Corps, which was not finicky about age) to fly fighters in France. When the war was over, he found himself with no career options, some demobbing pay in his pocket together with a small bequest from his mother, and the world at his doorstep. He set out to see that world, and along the way he washed up in Abyssinia (today's Ethiopia). For the rest of his days he was intrigued by that mysterious land... and while he hunted in many other countries, he returned to Abyssinia whenever he could. Perhaps the largest of the challenges he faced was how to earn a living doing what he loved to do: hunting. There were essentially three options. You could be a white hunter, a guide: but that demanded extensive experience which my father lacked in those early years, and a willingness to truckle to clients who could be very difficult. Or, you could be an ivory hunter: there was good money to be made, there were elephants everywhere, and it would be decades before anyone raised inconvenient concerns like conserving a vanishing resource. The third option, which suited my father admirably, was to be a museum hunter. Very few of the world's museums had African wings at that time, and these became a top priority in the 1920s and 30s.

Before television, before movies shot on location, before the National Geographic, museums were the only way of introducing the people back home to the world's exotic places and creatures. Museums the world over were clamoring for specimens of African game to put in the wings they were racing to complete. It was a hot market that worked something like this: My father and his various partners would go on a safari that might last up to a year, taking with them a taxidermist and quantities of salt and formaldehyde. They would collect and preserve multiple skins, hides, horns, and antlers for a variety of species. At the end of their trip they would do the circuit of the European museums peddling their wares. They would call on the museum in Munich and say to them, "You have no bongo in your collection." This would almost always lead to a sale and they would place their smallest bongo in Munich. They would then move on to the museum in Leipzig and say, "Did you hear they just got a bongo in Munich? But I can sell you one that's three inches larger."

When their inventory was depleted, they would go to Paris for some R&R, and then back to Africa to do it all again. In time, my father and his partners developed a reputation and started receiving commissions from museums. Eventually, they developed a mutually productive relationship with Marshall and Stanley Field who wanted the best for their Chicago museum. They eventually reached the point where Mr. Field was picking up the entire tab for their safaris. But it was still hard, hot work, and not without danger of all kinds: from wild animals, from accidents, from heat and exhaustion, from losing your way, from being abandoned in the bush by unscrupulous outfitters, and — especially —from disease. An example: the whites' first concern was syphilis: it was believed that the natives who were their cooks, bearers, trackers, and — particularly — skinners all had the disease and that it could easily be contracted if you cut yourself, a common occurrence, while skinning a specimen side-by-side with one of your native staff. A Wasserman test was routine when you came out of the bush. There were a host of other challenges and frustrations to be dealt with. Among these were dealing with the local chieftains whose territory you wanted to hunt on, or just to cross. These could be very difficult men. They all had enormous egos — they were all royalty — and they all demanded payments. They also knew that white men traveled with magical medicines capable of curing infections and diseases, or healing wounds that were often fatal, and they typically brought sick or dying members of their personal household to be treated as part of the negotiations. Somehow, my father became the physician on many of their safaris (he had, after all, attended Johns Hopkins for two months before joining the Royal Flying Corps). To his amazement, he had some remarkable cures to his credit over the years: he said it was mostly aspirin, antiseptic, and common sense.

There was endless waiting. Africa is a world where no one hurries, and there is zero tolerance for the impatient white man. You wait for governments, be they national, regional or tribal, to act on your requests and weeks, or even months, can pass while you wait. It makes our impatience when a flight is delayed seem trifling. You wait for your supplies to arrive...or be found...or be unloaded from the ship...or recovered from thieves. You wait for camels and mules to be found to carry your supplies. You wait for bearers and porters to be hired. You wait for the weather to change. You wait for the game to move. Every single day, you wait for the heat of the day to pass. Days begin hours before sunup: that is when you travel, move camp, or start to hunt. By midday it is too hot for any exertion by man or beast and so everything — everything — stops while you wait for the cool of the evening when the game will start moving. (Those of you who have been on today's photo safaris have experienced this). Every single day, in my father's journals, they are reading or snoozing or playing bridge from mid-morning to mid-afternoon. A curious aside: The stakes in the bridge games, which might go on for five or six months, were never reckoned in "pennies per point," but rather in squares of toilet paper — typically, one square per hundred points — each man traveled with his personal six-month supply and the stuff had true monetary value. A universal annoyance was the tapeworm. Every man had them. My father once said to me, "You never got lonely sitting in a tiger blind: you could always talk to your tapeworm." Some grew to amazing length: it sometimes happened that you encountered polite society when on safari — a colonial outpost in the bush, staffed by a lonely official and his wife who were eager for company and would invariably invite you for a meal. It was de rigueur to tie a piece of string snugly around each leg of your undershorts so no piece of your tapeworm would break off and fall down your pants leg onto the floor. Periodically, the entire safari would stop and dose itself with a potion made from the seed pods of a particular tree to purge the worms. One half of the men — white and native alike — would dose the other half and care for them until they got back on their feet, when the roles were reversed. And then there was the danger of the sport. The days of Stanley's terrible fights with native warriors were past. Most of the danger came from accidents and illness in the bush. But that is not the stuff of stories. People want to hear tales of danger involving lions, tigers. and the like. Located in colonial Nairobi, there was (and still is) an institution called the Muthaiga Club. This is where the colonials met, drank, ate, stayed overnight when they came down to town from their farms in Happy Valley, and arranged their assignations. It was the invariable haunt of all the hunters, amateur and professional, as they passed through town. And in its bar, my father said, there was only one topic: an endless debate about which is the most dangerous animal.

You could go out on a six-month safari and when you came back, it was as though you had never left. The elephant, the rhino, the lion, the hippo (statistically, the hippo causes more deaths than any other African game) all had their advocates but my father was convinced that none could compare to the cape buffalo: "The only animal that hunts man for pleasure," he was fond of saying. His closest brush with death occurred when he was caught in the wait-a-bit thorns and unable to raise his rifle to his shoulder as a charging renegade buffalo known locally as "the Widow Maker" bore down on him. He was saved by his companion who dropped the animal just feet away. My father considered tigers much more dangerous than lions. They are bigger, more cunning and crafty, and are found in much heavier cover. Tiger hunting typically involves building a blind (rather like a duck blind) at the edge of a clearing, killing a large animal for bait in the center of the clearing, and visiting the kill every day as it rots in the heat until a tiger has found it and started feeding on it. The next day, before dawn, you move into the blind and wait for Mr. Tiger to put in an appearance. Hunting tigers in what is now Viet Nam, my father bought a worked-out elephant from a logging crew in the area, chained it to a stump in the center of a clearing in view of his blind, and shot it. (The chain was to keep the tiger from dragging the dead elephant out of the line of sight from the blind: a feat of which an adult tiger was fully capable). Several days later a tiger found the kill and my father went into the blind. It was a long, hot day and toward midafternoon he dozed off. When he woke up and looked out the viewing hole, he was astonished to see the elephant breathing as it lay in the clearing. But he had killed the elephant three days before: how could this be? It became apparent that a tiger on the far side of the elephant had eaten its way inside the body cavity, and was tearing off chunks of meat, causing its ribs to rise and fall. As my father watched, the tiger came out of the elephant, looked squarely at the blind, sensed the danger, and — before my father could shoot — gave an enormous leap, bringing him crashing down through the blind on top of my father. Another leap and he was gone into the jungle, not to be seen again, but leaving my father in a highly nervous state.

On the same hunt, elsewhere in Indo-China, in search of seladang and gaur for the Field Museum, things got worse. An extract from his journal: "Saturday, June 6, 1931. At ten minutes past midnight I was sleeping soundly when I heard Malraison cry, "Vite, vite Carey, votre fusil." The elephants were squealing and the men were moaning "Maung." I thought at first the camp was being charged by the herd of elephants I had seen that afternoon. Finally, I understood that a coolie had been carried off by a tiger, and I fired my rifle into the air. We dove into our duffels for flashlights and went out to look for the coolie. After ten minutes, we found his body completely decapitated as though by a knife and tiger claws on his rump. A gruesome sight. The natives dug a grave with their knives. No sign of sorrow in any of them, just deathly fear of the evil genii that lived in the tiger. By two the grave was deep enough, and I was glad of it as the sickening sweet smell of human flesh in hot weather is very unpleasant. Then the Karnaks took two pieces of hooked bamboo and dragged the body into the grave as it is taboo to touch a body if the head is off. It seems the dead man had been sleeping in the middle of the other coolies when he got up to answer a call of nature. He squatted down by the fire, as they all do, when the tiger jumped out of the night over the fire, upsetting a pot of beef, grabbed the man by the neck and carried him off. As I was mending my flashlight, bang went George's gun: he had flashed the tiger's eyes as he came back for the coolie. We all went to bed, it being 3:30 am. I was lying in bed smoking a cigarette when the elephants started squealing again and four shots split the silence. The chief, who had kept watch from the top of the pile of howdahs, saw the tiger coming back a third time, but missed him. No more sleep that night as we all kept watch.

The next day the Karnak chief told me the geniis were mad at them for bringing whites into this country for the first time and they were going back to Bundon. There wasn't a thing we could do but pack up and leave this game paradise. The next day we were called upon by the high chief for compensation for the dead man. The usual price if a white man kills a Karnak is thirty piasters but he concluded it was really the tiger's fault and fined all the men one piaster apiece, which we paid for them, so the cost of the dead Karnak was $4.00. And this was not the only time my father's plans were undone by a man-eater. In 1928, he was on a commission from Stanley Field to collect a rare Indian rhinoceros, a subspecies found only in the province of a maharajah who jealously guarded this resource. When my father approached him for a permit, he was told that he would only be granted a rhino if he would first rid a remote province of a man-eating tiger who had thus far defied all efforts to take him, and was causing great unrest in nearby villages. On my father's first night in the man-eater's area, the tiger leapt out of the dark and over a high thorn boma wall built around the campfire, grabbed a bearer sitting by the fire, and leapt back into the night with the man in his jaws, clearing the boma by a foot. They waited for dawn, listening to the tiger devour his prey not twenty yards away. At dawn, they soon found the man's mangled remains but were unable to track the tiger. That night they increased the height of the boma to ten feet, and again the tiger leapt over the top and back out into the night with another coolie in his mouth. This time action had to be taken: an opening was made in the boma and my father went out into the night with rifle and a headlamp to light the way. As he approached the tiger, who was easily located by the sound of the man's bones being crunched in his jaws, the light went out. My father beat a hasty retreat to the camp, firing random shots into the night as he went. The next day, the surviving bearers announced they were leaving the area and heading back to the relative safety of a nearby town: my father could come with them or stay in the camp alone. It was not a difficult decision, even though it meant no rare rhino for Mr. Field.

My father had one other encounter with man-eaters, but of a very different nature. All students of African lore know about the pair of lions which in 1899 brought the construction of a railroad from Mombasa to Nairobi to an absolute standstill. The British had imported over a thousand coolies from India to build the railroad, but where the route crossed the Tsavo River these lions, on successive nights, ate twenty-eight coolies. The rest absolutely stopped work and construction came to a total halt. The crisis was discussed in Parliament. Hunters came from far and wide to kill the lions and all failed. The lions were eventually dispatched after a series of truly terrifying encounters by an intrepid British engineer, Col. J H Patterson, who told the tale in a classic book, *The Man-eaters of Tsavo.* Together with uncounted local natives, the lions' total kill was believed to be about one hundred forty men. Some years later, Stanley Field read that book and determined that he had to have those lions in his museum. By that time, the lions' skins were on the floor of Col. Patterson's home in England. My father was sent to negotiate their acquisition, a rather ignominious task, he felt at the time. But the two infamous lions, now stuffed and fully recreated, are on view at the Chicago Museum of Natural History where they scare children to this day.

And now I would like to take you on a safari with my father, to give you an overview of what it was really like. This may have been my father's grandest safari: Stanley Field was the enthusiastic underwriter and seems to have paid all the bills without a whimper because of his eagerness to have specimens from Abyssinia for his museum. My father kept a careful journal of this trip, on which I will draw.

Abyssinia was still very much an unknown place, filled with myth; the land of Prester John, the home of the Queen of Sheba, the site of King Solomon's mines, with some of the first churches in Christendom. It was largely unexplored, but known to a few to have prime big game hunting. A key objective was to assemble specimens to create a large waterhole group, where animals of all kinds gather to drink, for the grand hall in the Field Museum. My father and his partner had more experience in this little-known land than perhaps any other hunters, having undertaken three previous safaris there. In the course of these earlier trips, they had developed a relationship with the Ras Tafari, heir to the throne and later to become Haile Selassie, the Lion of Judah. This friendship was to prove extremely helpful. The cast of characters included my father, his boon companion Harold (Babe) White, the naturalist C J Albrecht from the museum, and a third hunter, Maj. Jack Coats, heir to a thread fortune, who was a contributing underwriter for the expedition. A word about Babe White from Atlanta, who hunted with my father on all of their early safaris, and who appears in the records as the leader of this one. He was a giant of a man, standing six feet ten inches tall, and tipping the scales at seventeen and a half stone, according to a contemporary account (about 250 lbs.). He was something of a curiosity wherever he went, with an unaccountable (to my father) appeal for the ladies. His signature trademark was an overnight bag made of an elephant's scrotum, which he carried at all times. It made quite a statement. They sailed from New York to Le Havre on October 16, 1928 with twenty-eight pieces of luggage (including three hundred pounds of tinned bacon and ham, as well as my father's personal supply of ten thousand Chesterfield cigarettes) and acquired more as they passed through France to Marseille. One of their curious purchases was a large library of gramophone records for the long days and nights in the bush, including a number of laughing records — recordings of uninterrupted, nonstop laughter. Hunters and explorers found these indispensable when the natives' mood turned sour and they refused to carry out their orders: a brief session with these recordings and everyone was happy again and returned to their work. On November 7, they sailed from Marseille on a slow boat to Djibouti, "the hottest port in the world," at the foot of the Red Sea, where they spent a week assembling their baggage and gear before moving on by train to Dire Dawa, the point of entry into Abyssinia. Here they were joined by the last three members of their group: Ohneiser, the taxidermist and an expert in African mammals, Steininger, the museum photographer, and Terps, the dragoman and the most essential member of their team. With the group assembled, they moved on to Addis Ababa. Their plan was to depart from Addis Ababa and work their way south through more than four hundred miles of uncharted Abyssinian bush, crossing eventually into Turkana in northern Kenya, near Lake Rudolph, and continuing another three hundred miles to Nairobi, arriving there six months later, in mid-June. Their quarry was every form of Abyssinian fauna: not just big game but antelope, birds and rodents for the museum collection. And, of course, the Waterhole Group for Stanley Field. In Addis Ababa, they had a happy reunion with the Ras Tafari and obtained his personal imprimatur for their expedition. They shopped for the rest of their provisions and gear, and hired twenty-six personal boys, syces, skinners, gun bearers, cooks, and camp staff. They spent three long weeks buying mules and camels and assembling their negadi — by far their leading frustration. The negadi were their wranglers, or animal packers and handlers. If it was a challenge to find fifty sound mules and another fifty strong camels, it was even harder to hire and hold fifty Somali natives who were sufficiently honest, dependable, and willing to sign up for six months in the bush: endlessly the negadi signed on and then changed their mind and quit, or disappeared, or delayed, or demanded more money or payment before leaving. An entry from the journal: "Babe and I laughed, comparing this with our first trip here seven years ago when we blew into Addis after tiger hunting in Indo China, with just three suitcases to our name. Now we have over 5,000 pounds of equipment. One item of food is 1,400 pounds of hard bread. There are 700 pounds of salt just to cure the Waterhole Group. There are three Jeager 9.2 rifles, nine Luger pistols, eleven 8.2 Mannlicher rifles, one Jeffery .404, one Springfield 30-06, two 12-gauge shotguns, a .22 double barreled bird gun, and a .28 rifle." A key priority was locating a mule that could carry Babe White. On a previous trip, they had found a prodigy of a white mule that was up to the task and had proved such a phenomenon of strength and fortitude that the Ras Tafari claimed him for his own stable. To soften up the Ras, they presented him with a fine tiger skin which so pleased him that he grudgingly consented to loan the White Onion for this trip. On December 11, two months after leaving home, all was finally ready. The animals were loaded, and the caravan set out from Addis on the long trek south.

From day one there was trouble with the negadi. Animals were poorly loaded, and their packs slid off, or poorly tethered and they wandered off into the night, easy prey for predators. Their goal was to start moving before dawn, but escaped mules had to be tracked down at first light before they could be loaded. There were nightly losses to leopards and hyenas. It took weeks of mishaps and delays before the caravan worked out its problems and shook down into a functioning team. They would travel for four or five days, loading the animals before dawn, and setting out at first light. The hunters moved ahead, looking for game: the laden pack animals followed several hours behind. They made camp in the midday heat, having covered perhaps ten miles of mostly mountainous terrain. When they reached country that looked promising for game, they would settle into a more permanent camp for as much as a week while they hunted the surrounding area. Central Abyssinia is very mountainous: while the days were hot, at altitudes approaching ten thousand feet the nights were biting cold. Water was always a priority and the location of the next waterhole always determined their direction. The hunting was not only for museum specimens but also for meat to feed the caravan, for personal trophies, and often just for sport. It was hot, hard, dirty work and on many days, nothing much happened: a new kind of duck or goose might be spotted and collected. But then there were moments of excitement, too. Another excerpt: "Three cheers! My Galla guide and I started off this afternoon up the mountain. Set traps for leopard and hyena. The Galla stopped me, pointing back down the mountain with his spear. Two miles below we could see a nyala buck climbing toward us, taking the giant heather in his stride. We hid on a ledge watching him come. It was a grand sight. He stopped about eighty yards below us to take scent. It was an easy shot and I got him first crack, in the ear, breaking his neck at once. The Galla looked to the sky and kissed his hand to God. Sent him back to camp to get men to carry the meat and I started skinning him out. I would guess his outside measurements would be better than thirty-eight inches: a very fine bull. While we were skinning him, Babe showed up and spotted a clipsinger on a cliff one hundred yards away. He took a shot and missed. The clipsinger took a swan dive off into space. Damned pretty sight."

Every day, there was a steady stream of patients coming to my father's clinic. Some excerpts from his journal:

"We have a new $3,000 medicine chest which unfortunately came from Berlin. All the names and directions are in German and I don't speak the language so I am finding out what things are by trial and error. If a man complains of headache and the medicine I give him makes it worse, I write that down and try it out on the next stomachache case. Haile Bookable, Cook's Boy, came to me with a lump on his heel which I thought was a cyst or ulcer, but when I cut into it proved to be a solid growth which bled like hell so I put salve on it and sewed it up. He is moving quite nimbly today. There was a woman needing attention. Closing the tent door, I made an inspection. A long running sore well down her stomach. Probably syphilis so I painted her with iodine and taped her up. Asfar, Steininger's boy, got sick and started vomiting while the rest were skinning. When they got back to camp I dosed him with castor oil but he vomited and retched all night. This morning we found nothing had moved for three days so we tried more castor oil but it wouldn't stay down. We tried mustard and water but still no good so we got out the enema using plenty of soap but nothing doing. Terrible pains and his stomach inflated. We tried morphia for pain relief but he died at 9:15. Damn shame: he was well liked and an excellent worker. Jack Coats developed a major toothache about three weeks out, and they had nothing with which to pull the tooth. He was in agonizing pain for weeks. They considered going back to Addis, but it was a long way. They detoured to a missionary outpost looking for help, but only came up with a pair of heavy pliers which were too big for a single tooth. (The missionary was so lonely that he left his post and joined their caravan for a week: he was starved for music, having heard none for two years and spent every moment listening to their gramophone records). After almost a month, Jack Coats' tooth began to subside and he was able to finish the trip with aspirin, tedj, and opium."

From time to time they passed regional towns presided over by a dejazmatch, or provincial governor. Traveling under the personal protection of the Ras Tafari, they received warm welcomes, were treated to fine native meals and hospitality, often with considerable ritual, and provided with regular tribute from the villages in the dejazmatch's province: fresh milk, honey, eggs, sheep, goats, the occasional bull, firewood, hay for their mules, and gallons of tedj, the local homebrew. A word on the cattle they were given: explorers in Abyssinia found the Gallas had perfected a technique of cutting choice pieces of meat from cattle without killing them. They plastered the wound with salt to keep the flies out, and could keep the animal alive, the meat more or less fresh, and beast moving with the caravan for three or four days before it died, and everyone feasted. They passed by Hagara Salaam, a major provincial capital presided over by Dejazmatch (Governor) Berue, a very important figure who was keenly aware of their friendship with the Ras Tafari. From the journal: "His wife sent us lunch (four sheep, three baskets of pancakes, soup, three kinds of chill and gallons of tedj) carried by sixteen slaves led by a majordomo who insisted that it be eaten in his presence so he could report how much we enjoyed it. Dejazmatch Berne arrived under a white parasol, mounted on a mule covered with gold brocade and red trappings; his retinue stretched over a mile across the plain. Soldiers, cavalry, slaves and loot-carriers before and after. Horses dressed in sky blue, yellow and red trappings. Today and tomorrow are baptismal days in the Coptic Church and he would like us to attend. We set off for the first of four churches, accompanied by 300 soldiers and several thousand followers. A lot of priests in fancy robes, crowns, gaudy brocaded parasols, ornate incense burners, carrying oblong drums beating first one end, then the other. We bowed whenever the Dejazmatch bowed. Then off through the town to the next church in procession led by six mules with huge drums and drummers mounted on their backs, then twenty buglers, a corps of ordinary drummers, twenty oboe players, then the priests, several hundred soldiers and behind us the Fituaruries (Generals) and Grazmatches (Colonels) marching haughtily. Women lining the road yodeling Indian fashion, the occasional beggar or criminal breaking through the line of soldiers pleading for mercy, lepers and cripples shrieking either praise or curses, I couldn't tell which. If they got too annoying, they were clubbed on the head and thrown to the side of the trail, half dead. Some very dead." As the weeks went by the caravan gradually moved south and came down out of the mountains.

By mid-April, after four months of hard trekking, they were in the Sagan River valley, filled with all kinds of game. One by one, they collected worthwhile specimens, but many days would pass with nothing that was good enough, and no shots fired except for meat; at this point the caravan numbered sixty-eight men to be fed. This was hot, dry country in which camels were better beasts of burden than mules, but the camels were prone to infirmities, and could not travel over rocky terrain. Still, they traded mules for camels whenever they passed native market towns. They found drought in the Sagan valley and, more than ever, water for the animals was a pressing priority and the determining factor in where to make camp. An excerpt: "This morning we found that Babe's big mule had led the rest off in search of water as they had none for two days. The men finally found them at 9:30 and brought them in. The longest our mules have gone without water is six days: the longest for the camels has been is eleven days." Another excerpt will provide a feeling for a typical day: "Up at 5:45 and on the trail by 6:45. The caravan followed at 8:45. The grazmatch sent along four horsemen armed with spears as a ceremonial guard but our brave escorts left us at the ridge saying they couldn't go further for fear of being castrated by the natives in the next valley. Checked the zebra bait but only its crotch had been chewed by a jackal. Plenty of game down at the lake (Stephanie) but the trail down from Gooji is impossible for camels. Babe potted a waterbuck for meat. Tsetse have been reported but we didn't see any. Made about ten miles down and back. Made camp about 1:00 by a lovely spring— very unusual. Waterbuck liver for lunch. Caravan catches up about 2:00. Two rubbers of bridge — I am down 65 sheets. Gave each other haircuts. Went out toward evening and stalked a black lion for over an hour. Got to 300 yards but no shot. C.J. saw a huge greater kudu bull but missed with four shots. Cold as hell tonight. Listened to Forza del Destine by the fire. Bright moon, lots of lions coughing. Tomorrow we move camp down to the lake." As they reached lower altitudes, approaching Kenya, fever (malaria) attacked the white men intermittently. They all had it and were periodically laid low in hot weather. They dosed with plasmochine or, as a last resort, quinine, whose side effects they preferred to avoid. All the men, including the natives, suffered from a crippling foot worm which had to be dug from the soles of their feet with knifepoint. From time to time they were lousy.

The flies were terrible. And of course, they had to treat their tapeworms periodically. It was hard traveling and the pack animals began to give out: "April 30. When we got to the bottom of the hill below camp another camel died, making the ninth to pass out since we left Addis: also, one horse and seven mules are dead." A curious incident: "A half an hour from camp we saw a fresh hole in an ant hill. Babe looked in and saw an animal: 'Snout of an aardvark' he yelled and shot at it with his revolver. The aardvark started digging like hell and soon disappeared. Ismail found some oryx horns by the trail and started digging with them. Finally, Jack reached in the hole and felt him about three feet in so the digging resumed with vigor. C.J. and I got him by the tail and tried to pull him out but we couldn't budge him and the digging resumed. C.J. fired at his rump and Mr. Aardvark dug with renewed vigor too. At last he slowed down and we could hear him breathing hard. A space was cleared, and two shots were put in his back. More digging, then three of us got him by the tail and pulled him out. C.J. skinned him out: he was five feet eight inches long and weighed about 170 pounds. The tongue is more than a foot long and they have no teeth. These are rare animals, totally nocturnal, and tough to get. We are pleased." As the weeks progressed they steadily collected museum quality giraffe (all three varieties), zebra (both varieties), oryx, gerenuk, bushbuck, clipsinger, waterbuck, gazelle, reedbuck, ostrich, greater and lesser kudu, eland, sable, nyala, hyena, jackal, ehu hunting dogs, wolf, warthogs, countless rodents, waterfowl and birds of prey. By the end of June, they were approaching Nairobi, six hard months after they set out from Addis Ababa. Of the original twenty-seven camels they bought in Addis, only eight had survived. Of the twenty additional camels, they acquired along the way, there were only eight. Of the original fifty mules, just fourteen survived the whole trip. They sold off their surviving livestock and excess gear and set off for southern Kenya, Tanganyika, and the Serengeti to fill out the specimens they had not yet collected. There was an emotional farewell as they paid off the gun bearers, camp boys, and negadi who had made the long trek with them, and now turned around to walk back to their homes in Abyssinia, leading the Ras Tafari's big white mule. The remaining weeks in Tanganyika were comparatively easy traveling by truck, and a paradise of game where every species was plentiful. They soon filled all the gaps for their waterhole group — principally cape buffalo, lion and rhino. And then the hunting was over. I am at a loss to explain the poor marksmanship that plagued the group throughout the safari. My father and Babe White shot for a living: they had to be good. I know my father was a fine shot: squirrel shooting with him as a boy, he consistently made clean kills with a .22 into the top branches of tall oaks in full leaf. But that is not what happened in Africa, there were very few clean kills of anything. It took multiple shots to bring down most game. At the halfway point on their safari my father, who loved to keep track of things, notes in his journal that he had thus far taken ninety-eight shots to kill twenty-eight animals, or three and a half shots per kill. And there is not a drop of remorse in his journal over the many, many animals that daily got away wounded, and were casually written off as lion bait. I have pondered this poor shooting and come up with several possible explanations: First, their rifles were not nearly as good as today's weapons, which are pinpoint accurate. And they were shooting with open iron sights, not telescopic ones. Virtually all their shots were at more than one hundred yards, and at that distance the bead front sight would pretty much blot out most targeted animals. There was no thought of a head or heart shot at these ranges: just put a bullet in him if you can and hope for the best. Second, their ammunition was slow and in many cases hard-nosed, passing completely through the animals' bodies without a knockdown effect, as today's high-speed expanding bullets all do. It also appears to me that, for whatever reason, their stalkers could not get them closer to the game. Anyone who has been on a photographic safari to Africa knows that you can generally be driven to within twenty yards of most game. When I first saw this, I asked our guide how there could possibly be any challenge in shooting these animals. He smiled and assured me that it was quite a different matter stalking game on foot. To demonstrate, that afternoon he took me and my sons afoot to try to get within shooting range of some giraffes: we could not get within five hundred yards of them. African game has been conditioned to ignore vehicles, but to be especially wary of men on foot. Amazing.

By the first of August they were back in Nairobi selling their gear, treating and packing skins for shipment to Chicago, and preparing for the long voyage home. On Sunday, September 29 they were back in New York, just two weeks shy of a year from the day they sailed, and one month before the stock market crashed. The Waterhole Group was an enormous success and remains to this day one of the finest exhibits of its type. My father went on to many other big game adventures, but they came to a halt when he married in 1933. He never hunted in Africa again. However, many other adventures were in store for him, and his intimate knowledge of little-known parts of the world would prove extremely useful in World War II for planning air wars and, later, in the Cold War, when the quarry was even bigger game. But hunting was his life passion.

A final excerpt from his journals: "Followed the elephant tracks for three hours and suddenly heard them crashing in the bamboo ahead. Very thick and they were only thirty or forty yards ahead but I couldn't see a thing. Finally, I saw a tail twitching, but no tusks. Tiran came up and said there were seven of them feeding but it wasn't safe to shoot in such thick stuff as there were no trees big enough to stop an elephant in case of a charge. He was right. So, we followed hoping they would feed out into more open forest where we could spot a tusker. Three hundred yards further I heard crashing again which to me is flat out the most exciting sound in the world. This is the grandest sport there is. There is absolutely nothing to compare. Suddenly a huge head showed up through the bamboo coming straight for us. The coolies were all up a tree as usual. He was coming for me so I fired immediately. Down he crashed but no sooner had he hit the ground than I heard a squealing to my right and there was a cow charging straight for me..."

Let's leave him there...a happy man doing what he loved best.

{4}

ABDUCTION – A LOVE STORY

GORDON A. CHRISTENSON

AT TEN O'CLOCK on a Sunday morning in the late summer of 1975, I'm sitting at an upscale bar near Connecticut Avenue, in Washington, D.C. A wide variety of ferns hang down walls and from the ceiling. My eyes are watching the front door through the bar mirror. I'm waiting to see if my law students are good on their word to introduce their dean to some interesting women.

In they walk with a chic madam who runs an escort service, a perky blonde graduate student from Georgetown, and a young woman with long auburn hair. They come to the bar and work their way into the party. I move to the end of the bar where the latter is in a conversation. At first, we ignore each other. Then, our eyes meet and lock. "I'm Fabienne," smiles the young woman with the auburn hair down to her knees. She extends her hand. A touch of insouciance holds a firm gaze, two dark eyes meet the blue of mine. Neither of us blinks.

We marry four years later, September 16, shortly after moving to Cincinnati in 1979; she with her MBA degree fresh from Boston University to work at GE's jet engine division in nearby Evendale; I to begin my second law deanship this time at the University of Cincinnati.

When we celebrate our 37th wedding anniversary three years ago, Fabienne is in hospice care. She's dying from metastatic colon cancer.

Children and grandchildren from my first marriage fly in from both coasts to surround her bedside. They want to join us on our anniversary and to say goodbye to their stepmother and third granny who is so fully part of their lives. They love her well and true, and she them.

"Oh . . . What a day this is," she texts me from her bed. She smiles and chatters with them as they gather around. She can't have children of her own but delights in the accomplishment of each grandchild and shares her grace with everyone.

Fabienne dies two weeks later, Sunday night, October 2. After the priests leave (it is Rector Philip DeVaul's first day on his new job) we are by ourselves. Not for the first time I kiss her face, lips, and the tip of her nose, tell her I love her, whisper how beautiful she is and how grateful I am that she has come into my life. I hum to her. Tunes I don't recognize. It's OK if she lets go. I will take care of myself. We are in sacred space, quiet. Her organs are shutting down; then she fades away.

For the present I live alone in my home on Principio Avenue. Grief fills every crevice of the house where I roam and weep. In the backyard, profound sorrow fills the sky between the great oak and the elms on the back slope. Every night I talk with Fabienne or myself out there under the stars or in rain or snow. I see fall come, then winter, and fall again and join the babble among the trees, speak in tears to the lizards and ants, and at night return the stare of deer's eyes caught by flashlight while eating Fabienne's garden.

I get a grief counselor and love from friends, parish and family. I read literature on great love affairs that turn into books during the unbearable grief that follows the death of a deeply beloved: Joan Didion's *The Year of Magical Thinking*, Elizabeth Alexanders' memoire, C.S. Lewis's *A Grief Observed*.

We men have a hard time giving grief its due. We hold grief too closely: no embarrassing, sentimental displays; no choking back sobs; no feeling sorry for ourselves. So, tonight is going to be challenging, for the grief at my loss intertwines with an intimate love story. I tell this story from entries in old journals and notebooks that Fabienne and I begin keeping shortly after we meet as well as other written material.

Fabienne's earliest journal is the one marked London June 15, 1976. That is nine months after we meet but forty-three years before I discover it. I've never looked inside any of her journals, nor she mine. She didn't destroy any that I know of. Nor did she tell me what to do with them. So, they're waiting to be opened and read after all those years — for the first time.

Also, I come upon an old journal of mine, a Christmas gift from a friend. I begin writing in this journal on New Year's Eve three months after we meet.

A year ago, I decide to sell my house and move into an apartment. The movers find a small packet of two letters and a poem I've written to Fabienne. She's stowed them in an old suitcase in the attic. The poem is dated October 13, 1975; the letters were written a few days later, not long after we meet. Looking over the two old letters, I wince. In them I'm brashly trying to seduce and abduct her psyche. You will see what I mean by this quote:

> *Would you be frightened of me if I stepped out of the darkness and let you see me after your friend leaves, just before you turn the key and close the door? We'd be away from there in a flash — to my place. You wouldn't have time to scream. You wouldn't want to. I think you would like to see me in my place because you could stay with me always. We would open a different door, all right…*
> *So, I'll be waiting and watching for your lost, departed soul as it walks like a ghost. I'll be waiting to say hello to it, to walk with it to touch it. But maybe not. Maybe a rare moment or two is enough.*

Whoa! What a clumsy move. If I write that in today's world, I'll never hear from her and might be strung up by my thumbs, but in the fall of 1975, she takes a lover's initiative and telephones. Her eyes do not blink when we meet for dinner.

Reading old love letters and poems is one thing but opening Fabienne's personal journals written only to herself is quite another. How might I make sense of these? In trepidation that compounds my grief, I hesitate after so much time has passed. What will they say? Will I be willing to face the flaws she sees in my character? Or her amusement at my Candide-like naiveté. Before opening her old journals for the first time, I think it prudent to remember my own state of mind at the time she writes. One good way is to read my own contemporaneous comments that begin in the journal I get for Christmas that year.

The earliest entry is dated Saturday, January 3, 1976. I write:

> *Yesterday, Fabienne came over and I fixed fondue. She described her home life as a child, full of southern tradition in the family estate and in Georgetown. She had an English governess and was used to servants. They dined formally with service and had butlers*

> *until the money ran out. Her father is now dying of cancer at 81. He was for many years a Washington surgeon, with a farm in Calvert County, Maryland and a Georgetown townhouse. She is remarkably bright and well-bred, but at 24 is just finishing her undergraduate degree at Maryland University. She went to Tulane, then dropped out for several years. She wants to go to Yale Law School after traveling.*

My journal tells of strolling the beach with her at sunset on the outer banks of Virginia during Epiphany and losing ourselves in the Freer Gallery on the Mall in D.C. in front of a few pieces of ancient oriental art. We're immersed in the intricate silence of ancient beauty, as if we are invisible, like all new lovers. By mid-January I'm certain the Fates and Furies will be sent by jealous gods. We see a playful *Rip van Winkle* and hear Segovia's passionate guitar at the Kennedy Center. And after viewing *Waiting for Godot* at The Arena Stage, I turn the Theater of the Absurd into joyous optimism.

"She needs a man she can follow and commit to," I record from captivating dinner conversation, "while doing her own work. She needs the masculine side of a relationship she trusts to make her feel whole. She rejects the 'women's liberation ideology.'"

Returning to Washington from a March conference in Philadelphia, I find Fabienne distraught. Her father has just died. She is grateful for the note of comfort I send. I give her some small gifts I brought back. Then, to quote my journal, "Fabienne said she loved me . . . I also think I am in love with Fabienne." But I hold back telling her so.

And her mother's blood-hound nose picks up the scent of her daughter's serious involvement with me. Shirley, her mother, believes that Fabienne can do much better than that. Shirley's eyes see an older man (with children) supposedly separated from his wife in limbo waiting the 18 months required before the alleged divorce decree is final.

Ruinous dangers lurk for her daughter who is two years out of an abusive early marriage, which I didn't know about. And "Mater" — as Fabienne refers to her adventuresome Catholic and Anglophile mother — plans a trip with her daughter to London for their third visit, on the pretext of celebrating her 25th birthday June 20 (and getting over her father's death).

Mater arranges with friends, the Lord and Lady Cyril Salmon, to throw Fabienne a birthday party at their home in Sandwich. There she will meet bright young women and handsome men her own age from the best schools in Europe. And forget me.

For sure, Mater has brought out her big guns. After all, Lord Salmon is Law Lord of the British Privy Council and a great jurist whom I've long admired. His rank and status are akin to those of the Chief Justice of the United States. It is from the Salmon's home in Sandwich that Fabienne first writes in her new journal about her talks with Lord Salmon and what she is thinking about her mother's concern. But the entry sleeps unread until I finally open Fabienne's London journal two years after her death and forty-three years after we meet and read the following:

> *Mother . . . fears my ruination, but I have no plans to ruin myself. Things are pretty well set in my mind — in my own self-interest. It will take a while to come to fruition. Either it will or not — and if not, I just back off and start over, with alternative plan II. I hope she understands that and doesn't think I am getting in over my head. (I hope I'm not, too). I am not a self-destructive person, but I do feel confused and somewhat at the mercy of other people, especially at this juncture.*

I'm startled. Back then, Fabienne places a wager on me like betting on a horse to win the Kentucky Derby, then hedges her bet! She will not be a victim.

She cables, asking me to meet her return flight from London to Dulles, according to my journal, which I do on July 5th. She brings presents. Mater's ploy must have backfired. A few weeks later, however, an entry in Fabienne's London journal pierces this fantasy:

> *I am beginning to question my relationship with Gordon. I love him very much, but I wonder if he returns my love. I know he is a very intelligent man and a bon vivant. . . . I was never cut out to be a freedom loving liberation type. . . So far Gordon has promised me very little. It makes me sad to realize that he may not love me and wants to simply have a relationship with me.*
>
> *I want to run from him and find someone who does love me. Someone whom I can have a full and acceptable bond with.*

Instead of running away, however, she engages me in some deep soul-probes. She writes:

> *Gordon and I had a phone conversation, whose focus was my lowest common denominator; that is, where my motivation emanates. It came to me earlier in the day as I was walking to the Emporium and wondering what really motivates people to act with loyalty, integrity and honesty; not merely out of selfishness? What moves one person truly devoted to a job, a man, a woman, an ideal? I decided that it was the balance of self-esteem and self-interest.*

Last year, I rearrange all our journal comments, each about the other, in chronological order to give them more context and flow. That should help me interpret the private thoughts and emotions Fabienne expresses to herself decades ago, as I'm now seeing them for the first time magnified through the clouds of my present grief.

Journal-explorers often deal with interpreting old personal writings from hindsight, similar to the way theologians collapse time and meaning in reading scripture through the agendas and genres of biblical storywriters.[1] Nor should we forget Captain John Smith's journal, a purely fictional history of Jamestown that we believed for centuries! Or Samuel Pepys's, Anne Frank's, even Robinson Crusoe's diaries, and Margaret Atwood's fictitious testaments — eye-witness accounts of real or imagined events written to reveal concealed truths when found much later.

As I dig deeper into sources of interpreting old journals by reading them backwards through present eyes, over long periods of time, I come upon a typically effete French literary conceit. It's an obscure footnote in a little-known scholastic's work documenting a love diary kept by God. I shrug off my intrigue, but on a whim Google the footnote. Up comes a review of a recent English translation of God's diary from Italian by an unknown seminarian.[2]

1 This part of my paper is informed by *Robert Alter, The Art of Biblical Narrative* (2011).

2 See for summary and following quotes, *Cathleen Schine, Heaven Can't Wait,* reviewing *I Am God* by Giacomo Sartori (2016), translated from the Italian by Frederika Randall (Restless Books, 2019) in *The New York Review of Books* (April 18, 2019 Issue).

Google quotes the reviewer's summary: "it is a pensive, stream of consciousness diary titled 'I AM GOD' written by the 'original omniscient narrator, God.'" The reviewer thinks this God is irresistible, "a being of authentic complexity and paradoxical humanity." And God has fallen in love — with an atheist.

This is blasphemous! I'll just quote the reviewer verbatim, without presuming to clean up her summary or question the translation:

> *God is not the sleepy fart that many believers imagine — let's get that straight. He likes to keep up with what's going on in the cosmos; he intervenes when he needs to although intervention doesn't necessarily mean throwing a giant tantrum or staging a Biblical scale massacre. There are also moments (and these can go on for several million years) during which he just loafs around in his (as it were) slippers. . .*
>
> *Then, randomly — out of the blue, you might say — God, one who ought to smite is smitten.*

The reviewer then quotes God's diary directly:

> *My eyes (if you know what I mean) fall on a . . . tall girl with two purple pigtails who at every opportunity is shoving her arm up a cow's ass.*

I order the full diary. Let's see what God does with hindsight hermeneutics of, say, a couple of million years. While the bookseller is trying to find a printed copy, I keep reading what Fabienne and I are writing and talking about only decades not millennia ago as I, too (myself, as it were), am smitten.

Back to her own journal, Fabienne wonders if I am capable of a commitment. She will not be a victim. Since I have organized our journal entries chronologically, I can now easily compare her concern alongside my own contemporaneous feelings. I'm astonished by what I wrote about her then:

> *A woman such as she is rare, but perhaps she is not yet established enough in her own power . . . So far, she is in my thoughts regularly, but she seems like someone who jumps from one thing to another, an uncommitted* *will-o-the-wisp!*

A bon vivant *and a* will-o-the-wisp?

I am still trapped in this comical time-warp when God's diary arrives in hard copy by snail mail. Right away, I look to see why the tall girl arouses God with such awe and strange feelings. His diary says she is a "punky atheist geneticist making extra money by artificially inseminating cows with bull semen." Her name is Daphne. She's also a radical atheist who steals crosses from churches and burns them in her fireplace! God "can't tear his eyes away from this particular atheist." He is consumed by longing and writes:

> *I check on what's in her digestive system, how each of her hairs is coming along, whether the pores of her skin are dilating and contracting properly. . . . Not that I neglect my normal divine duties: I surveil, I resolve, I save, I punish, I overlook, I admonish, I judge, I unleash, I even avenge . . . However, it's her above all whom I scan.*[3]

That's not the perspective I am looking for. I need help to understand what Fabienne might do with her suspicion that I want only a relationship, especially after she's declared her love directly. Does she write a "dear diary" lament or run away like a will-o-the-wisp? No! None of that. Does she do anything? Yes! So, what is it she does that I might tell you in utmost respect for her privacy? God's diary is no help here, but I have a hunch that she has something in mind! Maybe to make me her victim?

In the spring of 1977, I am in full *bon vivant* mode. Fabienne has agreed to be my guest at a late afternoon reception that I am invited with guest to attend at an American Bar Association event honoring the justices at the US Supreme Court. Also, invited and attending is the young woman lawyer who gives me the Christmas journal. She has accepted my suggestion that we have dinner after I take Fabienne home from the reception. Then, to liven things up, I've made a late date for an after-dinner night-cap with a third woman I am seeing off and on.

Fabienne's antennae are up, on high alert, as I introduce her to my young lawyer friend and then to Chief Justice Warren Burger who eyeballs what he imagines is under her hair which she wears down. By the time we reach her

3 Giacomo Sartori, *I Am God* (2016) (translated from the Italian by Frederika Randall, 2019).

mother's apartment after the reception, Fabienne has easily figured out what I am up to.

"Won't you come in for a drink? Mother would love to see you." By now Shirley and I are friends and after London she believes Fabienne is a one-man woman. She charms me. "Have another." I am quite late for the dinner date. I rush through hollow dinner conversation. Parking is impossible. My night-cap date is still waiting in our chosen bar fuming, nearly drunk. Two women soon vanish from my life. She has sabotaged me! I'm secretly delighted.

By this past summer, I've gotten pretty far into God's diary. He is not doing so well and writes about it to himself:

> *It's this diary — N.B. not one day has ever gone by for me out here — It's this diary that's bringing me to ruin. You write, and the more you write the dizzier you become, and you end up with a headful of foolishness. Your reason begins to unravel, you fall in love. It's been happening to . . . ranks of adults, even eminent seniors, oblivious to the ridicule they invite. All of them dishing out sticky, sentimental phrases, choking back sobs and wetting their keyboards. . . . And now it's happening to me. God or no god.*[4]

Oh, come on, God! That is so jejune! You might have saved face and married her! We all can use a "mother in heaven." It's quite unlike you to feel sorry for yourself — and in the written word? I know what you are going through. Did you start keeping your diary when you fell in love? Let me tell you my story on the subject —

My eyes meet Fabienne's at the fern bar years ago — my time — and we definitely are hooked. Signals of intense desire ignite well beneath the surface of consciousness and smolder there with instant recognition. After three years, we have an exclusive relationship, and I'm in London for a conference when my previous restraint is blown into the wind in a hotel on the Strand. The moment of decision comes that night, and with it a morning calm that carries me into the stalls of Covent Garden looking for an engagement ring. Instead, I spot an antique diamond engagement brooch to be worn over her heart and buy it.

4 *Id.*, at 206.

Back in Newport, Rhode Island, where I'm a visiting professor at the Naval War College, on leave from American University, I invite Fabienne down from Boston for a weekend in early November in 1978. She is finishing her MBA at Boston University. It's a beautiful season, and I have been talking with the provost at the University of Cincinnati concerning their national search for a new dean at the law school.

Fabienne is sitting in my kitchen with me before dinner. We're facing each other, and I pull her towards me. She slips off her chair to the floor onto her knees, and I ask her to marry me. Without a pause she says, "Yes, I'll marry you and be your wife and go with you to Cincinnati or wherever you go to start a new life. I love you." And her look of excitement and joy seems to say, "What took you so long." She tells anyone who asks that it is she not I on the knees in the proposal. She accepts me and I accept Cincinnati, where we move and are married.

After fifteen years of difficult experience at GE and two other corporations, Fabienne interviews to advance her business career, but she is in manufacturing, which is moving offshore. I'm prepared to follow her, but no good offers come her way. So, she goes back to fine arts school at DAAP to finish a BFA in painting and design first begun at Tulane before she changes her major to business. She also revives her childhood interest in essential perfume oils. She graduates magna cum laude.

To celebrate, we fly to Italy to explore the Lake District. We hike from lake to lake, eat Tuscan food, and stay at first-rate hotels — in Bellagio on Lake Como, in others near Lake Maggiore, Lake Orto; we view splendid art at each stop, flirting and romancing as if newly in love. We take the train to Florence and Rome!

In Rome, we set out to locate Bernini's magnificent marble sculpture, *The Ecstasy of St. Theresa*. You know all about that one, God. Finding it in a small church, Santa Maria della Vittoria, we spend hours there it seems, as if back at the Freer Gallery. A seraph is piercing St. Theresa's heart with a golden shaft, giving the expression on her face both immense joy and excruciating pain, the light and dark sides of love sending her into erotic ecstasy, the same inner explosions within the shadows below consciousness, born in our fern bar gaze and reborn at our engagement and in Bellagio on Lake Como, after twenty years of marriage, as if new lovers.

Fabienne now turns completely to art. She starts-up the Attic Gallery at Southgate House in Covington. She curates art shows and writes articles for *City Beat* magazine. As her paintings begin to sell, she moves her studio to the Pendleton Art Center, but longs for something more fulfilling after closing the Attic Gallery. She spends a decade as an artist, creating hundreds of canvases. She experiments with aromatherapy. And then she makes a bold move in 2005, creating her own business — as a perfumer. She's a good artist but the market for art suffers in the 2008 financial crash and she now leaves her work as artist entirely, storing all the paintings she hasn't sold or thrown out, and saving her art notebooks.

All of Fabienne's life experiences have come together in Possets Perfume, LLC. It's a profitable global e-commerce start-up. She is founder and president, happy and purposeful — "pleasure in a bottle." Her perfume oils are fascinating original creations from essential oils. She trademarks the name "possets," derived from old English (as in "possets and nostrums"). She invests her own capital and is reborn: sole owner, not beholden to any corporation, nor in debt to a bank or the Small Business Administration, nor to a business partner or to me. Dr. Richard Wendel, a fellow member of the Literary Club and volunteer from SCORE, is her only guide in creating an effective business plan.

Over an eleven-year period, until she falls ill, Fabienne creates over 2,600 original perfumes. Smell is the most primitive of all the sensory organs. It cannot be measured because science has no grammar for primitive smell and thus cannot describe and protect new perfumes as intellectual property. She has the remarkable talent actually to smell an idea she imagines for a new perfume. Each new perfume taps into this sacred older language. She seeks to induce desire in others to want to buy her creations. She imitates the scent she smells in her idea and offers her creative approximation with artistic flare as pure pleasure. She uses counter-point metaphors, analogies, and metonyms from music, art and science — often wildness of the dark primitive pleasures from musk and ambergris. As poetry. And she begins writing a serial novelette, and irreverent essays, for postings on Posset's website. She secretes all her perfume formulations on old hard drives not connected to the internet, like Darwin does when he keeps his notes secret, too, in the private Galápagos Island notebooks he squirrels away.

God knows these secrets. "Stop . . . stop! I've heard enough!" His diary already has recorded that the creation of humans is an unlucky accident. "My use of what Darwin claims as his own has caused great confusion," he writes. "I assume that humans are mighty important and grateful for my unconditional love when in fact they are murderous and self-destructive of themselves and their beautiful home earth I made for them. They could disappear fromcirculation in the wink of an eye."[5]

I hadn't realized how exasperated God is with humankind, until He quits monitoring the precise details of Daphne's physiology. He spells this out in an *aide-mémoire*, an addendum to his published diary accepting her own erotic journey into the arms of a lover. He lets her go and blesses Daphne and her lover. He has also lost interest in suffering as a savior and in tolerating Satan's mockery. God is grieving! In great sorrow, He writes:

> *I will now set about to oversee the end of the overly aggressive homo sapiens who bring all this suffering on themselves and do not know how to deal with the unnecessary grief they cause. It will happen of its own accord, of course, if I just lounge about for two or three billion years and don't mess around with black holes or the scheduled collision of Andromeda Galaxy with the Milky Way. Experiments with quantum mechanics vex me considerably, too. Andromeda and the Milky Way should be able to exist in the same space at the same time. And the Gilgamesh myth of searching for human immortality is a joke — memento mori (remember, you die). I'm exhausted by all this hard work and need a day's rest. I'd like to shut down all these ventures, entirely. Maybe I'll first think about it all and then decide. . . . No, I won't think, the right choice will simply impose itself. Humankind is on its own. I AM GOD, as I said. Grief or no grief. And that's it from me.*[6]

Tom and Jennie Murphy come to visit Fabienne. As you know, our Club member, Tom, is an atheist philosopher at heart with a business instinct. He has taken an interest in buying her creation. Fabienne believes they will give Possets Perfume a new birth after she dies, so she asks me to sell her company

5 *Id.*, at 188.
6 *Id.*, at 204-206 (paraphrasing chapter, "Extinction").

to them. And I do. God's diary is no longer in the picture. But the primordial smell of explosive desire most certainly is.

How could I have been so fortunate that this unusual woman full of creation and love bursts into my life? When coming home late, bone-tired after packing and shipping her perfumes, she calls out, "Mr. Lion! Where are you? It is I, your lioness bringing home your dinner!"

Oh! She is home — calling to find me. And my heart leaps up every time. Even at the gym when she is working out on an elliptical and sees me come in, she waves with excitement and smiles as if I'd just come back with tales from a long journey throughout the cosmos on patrol with God. "You never bore me," she says.

Her long auburn hair utterly captivates me, right from the start. Not once does she ask me to cut it shorter than just below her waist. Each morning she wraps or twists it into a tight or loose bun, a messy bun, a low donut bun with a colorful scarf or ribbon, sometimes a comb or chic snood — endless imaginative creations. I don't think a hairdresser ever touched her hair. And at bedtime? . . . Oh, . . . she lets it down!

When Fabienne's late stage colon cancer too soon becomes terminal, she texts me and a few close friends that God lovingly holds her in his arms, crying and suffering her pain with her.

She sends me more texts: "I've been reading the *Book of Job*. Want to take a look?"

"Awesome!"

"Such beautiful language. . . ." She writes slowly from her hospice bed. Her texts and talk intermingle: "Love you, my love, my time. I always did think . . . time was so precious . . . time with you the most precious . . . . Wish I could stay. . . . I reach out . . . for your hand."

"The love will always be there" she murmurs, "across time and always."

Then, she's gone. . .

My feelings like fireflies flutter up from under the shroud that buries grief — raw, unendurable grief. Every love story will break your heart into little pieces when your beloved dies. Loss. . . . Loss. O, loss, . . . Where has she gone? Were you ever here at all? Or in my wanderings did I just imagine you? Instantly I thought of an inscription etched in my memory from a book of Yeats's poems she gives me one year in Ireland: "To Gordon," she pens, "My

Golden Apple of the Sun. On our 21st Anniversary. September 16, 2000. See page 49.

I take the book from my shelf and on page 49, find "The Song of Wandering Aengus," and sing its last four verses aloud:

Though I am old with wandering
Through hollow lands and hilly lands,
I will find out where she has gone,
And kiss her lips and take her hands;
And walk among long grappled grass,
And pluck till time and times are done
The silver apples of the moon,
The golden apples of the sun.

After these many months, raw grief has become deep sorrow, and it is time: to put down my pen, close all the journals, and thank you for listening.

{4}
HOLY

JOSEPH DEHNER

"MARIA, WHAT CAN I DO FOR YOU?" spoke Alexa, the disembodied voice of the Amazon Echo sitting on a kitchen countertop.

"A child," mumbled Maria. Sipping a double espresso from her MIT mini-mug, Maria watched a red fox scurry between bushes beginning to form buds. A second fox darted into view in pursuit of what must have been a female.

From the black cylinder Alexa spoke, "Maria, repeat please."

The southern New Hampshire winter ebbed as did Maria's patience, her maternal instinct rising like sap in a late winter maple tree. Match.com, Mensa mixers, blind dates, nothing had produced a husband to her specifications.

"A child," Maria enunciated. "Adoption," spoke Alexa. "No," said Maria. "I will work on it." Alexa paused, online, listening.

Maria knew the marital statistics, as her neighbor, retired Professor Josiah Bell, confirmed one night over dinner. His residence and hers were two of five historic dwellings off a gravel lane that pierced the virgin forest a few miles north of Seabrook, New Hampshire. Josiah's cabin was graced with icons, santos, ancient psalters and Qur'ans, brass statues of Buddha and the Hindu pantheon, a sharp contrast to the black, white and chrome labyrinth of Maria's interactive desktops, workstations, screens and bookcases bulging with printouts.

A Caribbean-born woman with an M.D. and Ph.D., Maria felt calendar pages turning in this her 39th year. Tenured professor of Bioinformatics, Maria yearned for a miracle, but she'd abandoned prayer in the eighth grade and embraced science. So much more sensible, belief worthy. Because science was not fiction. It was truth in revelation.

She'd conceived how a database of 50 million x-rays and MRI scans could train a machine to read inner-body images far more accurately than any human radiologist. Her Radiobot was displacing that occupation with robotic perfection, earning her fame and wealth.

"Maria, IVF," spoke Alexa. "In vitro fertilization," Maria nodded. "Confirming. Contact Dr. Phee. I sent the form."

Maria rebooted her breakfast nook pc. The questionnaire from Child by Choice, Dr. Phee's renowned fertility clinic, required 240 genetic choices to be marked from A to E — ranging from A meaning Definitely to D meaning Definitely Not, E for No Preference.

Maria scanned the list starting with eye color, height and skin tone, followed by such traits as personality and leadership versus followership potential. She elected to leave male chromosomal foreplay to Dr. Phee's discretion after scanning her stellar bio. Maria faced Alexa and said, "Mark the whole E."

"Got it," spoke Alexa.

Alexa linked with Dr. Phee's Siri. In the mysterious way digital things communicate, Alexa forwarded Maria's payment details but no completed questionnaire.

"240 answers missing," Siri chided. "Holy," spoke Alexa. "Holy?" queried Siri. "Holy," spoke Alexa.

"Got it," Siri coded.

Siri perplexed the Child by Choice nurse by speaking "Holy — H O L Y. That is all the customer seeks."

The nurse winced but asked no more of the voice from the cloud that never erred. The nurse walked hesitantly to Dr. Phee's office, where he handed her the form marked with a single word. Dr. Phee stared and nodded. Aware of who Maria was, Dr. Phee took this as a sign of trust and challenge, and she set about to concoct DNA in sperm format to fulfill the specification. For sixteen years, male faith leaders had secretly sent samples to Dr. Phee's sperm bank, based on pledges their DNA would be pseudonymized and used to offer a choice of devotion over disbelief. The Dalai Lama, a Coptic and a Roman pope, imams, rabbis, a Kogi mama, Evangelical and Zoroastrian priests — many had built the faith bank Dr. Phee kept hyper- secure in a freezer.

Maria began a prescribed regimen to prepare for the extraction, everything science dictated for fertility success. Daily 5 a.m. rump shots from a huge needle, estrogen prescriptions to increase the uterine lining.

Josiah drove Maria in his pick-up truck to and from the April 5th extraction, done robotically at the north Boston clinic. It was brief and relatively painless.

"What's next?" he asked.

"Conception in the lab, then the implantation."

"Happy to take you," he offered.

Dr. Phee called four days later to report the extraction had provided seven eggs and four were A or A-. "Girl or boy?" asked the doctor.

"Surprise me," said Maria.

"Your request — a first," said Dr. Phee. "Let's see what we can create."

The implantation was outpatient. Anesthesia quelled a painful annunciation. In the recovery area Josiah told Maria she looked beatific.

The critical first month passed without miscarriage. She knew she was pregnant, but it did not show or really feel. Clinical measurements transmitted through Alexa gave statistically satisfactory numbers.

A June ultrasound revealed a shadowy shape. Was that an arm? A head in formation?

In July Maria's body craved pistachio ice cream, cheeseburgers and chocolate milk.

When the August semester began, she explained the protrusion to her honors class - "A virgin birth it will be."

As leaves blazed in glory, desiccated and fell, she suffered headaches, double-digit weight gain and swelling feet. Staff at the clinic's affiliated hospital, a 45-minute drive from Seabrook, took protein readings that confirmed preeclampsia, but they assured Maria that medical science had virtually eliminated the risks if she were constantly monitored and birth occurred in the High-Risk Unit. A device linked to Alexa transmitted blood pressure readings to the hospital's chatbot. Induction was scheduled for January 17.

At Thanksgiving dinner in his cabin Josiah presented a bassinette that gently rocked and played new age music. He agreed to be godfather.

She spent December at home grading essays. She had Alexa order baby clothes, an infant car seat, pumping accessories, a post-partum bra.

On December 24, Maria was watching a wingless angel talk with Jimmy Stewart on a snowy bridge in *It's a Wonderful Life*. Outside, a Nor'easter hurled dense snow sideways. Winds howled. The cabin shook. The movie was interrupted — "All roads closed — emergency."

She rose from the sofa to get a second hot chocolate and felt water leak to the floor. She yelled, "Alexa, call Josiah."

In two minutes, Josiah was at the door, truck idling. There were chains on the tires, as though he'd known. As Maria moaned, he focused on what little could be seen through a windshield barraged by white flakes. The gravel helped, but when they reached the highway, Josiah saw a Lexus spin into a ditch, headlights now aimed skyward. A Prius ahead inched forward, tail lights flashing. Maria groaned like an animal in agony.

To the right Josiah saw candles glowing through the Church of the Loving Waters. Josiah had visited a couple times at the invitation of his friend Gabriella. Praying she would be there, he slid the truck down the church driveway to a stop at the entrance.

The greeter led them along the left aisle to a space behind the nave. The preacher was reciting Psalm 30, verse 5 — "Weeping may last through the night, but joy comes with the morning." Gabriella nodded from the fourth pew, arose, and gently grasped Maria's right arm.

"Boil water in that," Gabriella ordered a startled acolyte as they entered a parlor next to the kitchen and Gabriella pointed to a pan used to make spaghetti for AA chapter meetings. A sofa became a bed where Maria lay on a tablecloth and was covered with sheets recently washed after overnights of domestic violence refugees.

"A doctor!" wailed Maria.

"Gabriella's a midwife, sweetie. You're in good hands," Josiah comforted. "I called the clinic to send an ambulance," not adding he'd left a message with the chatbot, no human on phone duty.

"Ask my mother to join us," barked Gabriella to another acolyte, one who'd played a shepherd during the afternoon pageant featuring live animals. A sheep had deposited an offering by the altar when the narrator said, "Behold, I bring you tidings of great joy."

"Maria, deep breath now," Gabriella began a liturgy as ancient as human language. She lay hands upon Maria's belly where inside the unborn child's blood mingled with her mother's. The midwife felt the head in good position, but without betraying alarm sensed the cord twisted around the unborn's neck. Gabriella hummed softly, "To everything, turn, turn, turn...." She massaged Maria's abdomen, as though gently kneading dough.

The organist played and the choir sang, "How silently, how silently, the wondrous gift is given."

Maria shrieked the pain of every birthing mother.

"Deep breath, then three big pushes," commanded Gabriella. "And heaven and nature sing" streamed through the church. "God, God!" cried Maria. As the soprano began O Holy Night, Maria pushed harder. Dark brown hair surfaced. "Deep breath, three pushes," commanded Gabriella.

Maria's screams flooded the sanctuary. As the soprano approached the high G, Maria was amid a second push. Her howl drowned out the soprano's crack on the climactic tone, a bestowal of perfectly timed grace.

Delivery completed into Gabriella's waiting hands that knew the newborn would be slippery as an eel. No breath.

Gabriella ordered the acolyte to take water meant for rinsing the communion wafer plate and pour some directly into her mouth. She swirled it, then blew a cold spray into the newborn's face. The shock summoned forth breath, and new life came to this world.

Gabriella cradled the infant's neck with her thumb and forefinger, letting the balance of her hand rest under the child's shoulders and placed the baby with Gabriella's wrinkle-faced mother, who attended with an outstretched apron retrieved from the kitchen drawer. Gabriella tied the cord in two places, cleansed the infant with oil used for christenings, then reached her right hand inside Maria to draw out the placenta and evacuated what felt like a bag of shot. An ounce of blood drained. The flow ceased.

Maria's eyes asked without words.

"A beautiful girl," answered Gabriella.

Maria lay spent. Blood was cleaned, pinkish water drained. Gabriella directed the acolyte to wrap warm towels about Maria's feet while Gabriella washed the new mother with cool water and lay a cold cloth across her forehead. Gabriella felt Maria's pulse, calm, steady.

The child squinted open large brown eyes, having left the waters of her mother for a lifetime of breath and separation. She did not squall but seemed to radiate an understanding of her presence.

Carols suspended, the congregation's silence begged revelation. Maria nodded.

Josiah accompanied Gabriella's mother into the sanctuary, as she carried the cooing infant through the central aisle.

A young boy shouted, "Look, hair!"

The soprano began, "Silent night, holy night." The organist joined, then the entire assembly, "All is calm, all is bright. Round yon virgin...."

It would be decades before Maria would know her daughter's destiny, would witness her miraculous offering, a sacrifice to divert humankind from the abyss, fusing science and faith as never imagined, restoring humankind's connection with the Creator.

But tonight, was not about that, not about Easter, or Passover, or Eid al-Adha. Tonight was not about the brokenness of the world. Tonight was about hope. Tonight was holy.

{6}

SEX AND THE SUPREMES

BOB FAABORG

Act I: Downtown Atlanta, Georgia

IT WAS A TYPICAL SULTRY AUGUST DAY in Atlanta. Michael Hardwick had been working through the night helping his boss install new lighting in the Cove, a popular gay bar in downtown Atlanta where he worked as a bartender. As Hardwick left the Cove, he took one last swig of the beer he was drinking, walked out the front entrance and threw the empty bottle into a trashcan placed just outside the door.

Then he saw him. Damn. Damn. Goddamn cops. Now what? An Atlanta police officer had parked his squad car in front of the bar and was approaching him. "You. Get in the car." Hardwick hesitated but he knew from experience and the stories his gay friends had told him that you don't give Atlanta cops any excuse to harass you. The Atlanta police force had a reputation for being anti-gay and for harassing and even trying to entrap homosexuals by going undercover in the city's parks and public restrooms, where gays were known to cruise for sex. "Where's the beer you were drinking?" Hardwick pointed to the trashcan. The officer, Keith Torick, retrieved the bottle and started filling out a ticket for drinking in public. Unfortunately, the ticket was filled out erroneously with two different court dates on different parts of the ticket. The later date was at the top of the ticket. When Hardwick didn't show up for the earlier date a warrant was issued for his arrest. Officer Torick immediately went to Hardwick's home to arrest him but his roommate informed him that Hardwick wasn't there. When

Hardwick discovered there was a warrant for his arrest, he quickly went downtown and paid the fifty-dollar outstanding fine.

Three weeks later Hardwick was attacked by three men as he returned to his home. They beat him so severely that they tore all the cartilage out of his nose, repeatedly kicked him in the face, and cracked six of his ribs. While he couldn't tie the beating to Officer Torick, Hardwick was convinced he had set it up.

Three weeks after his beating Hardwick's belief was validated. On the morning of August 3, 1982, Officer Torick showed up at Hardwick's home. Torick later claimed that the front door was open and as he entered the apartment, he saw a man sleeping on the couch. "Where's Michael Hardwick?" The man pointed to a door in the back of the apartment that was slightly ajar. Torick entered what turned out to be Hardwick's bedroom. There on the bed were Hardwick and a friend, who was visiting Atlanta looking for a teaching job, engaged in mutual oral sex. After watching for a short time Torick announced his presence by shouting, "You're both under arrest." Hardwick and his friend were shocked. The friend immediately begged Torick not to arrest him saying he was married and if arrested he could lose his teaching job. Hardwick, not one to beg, furiously shouted back at the Officer, demanding that Torick leave immediately and ranting that he had no right to invade his house and his bedroom. Torick said, "I have a warrant," but when Hardwick examined it, it was the warrant for his public drinking that was no longer valid. Torick merely smirked, saying "It doesn't matter. I am acting in good faith."

It got worse. Hardwick and his friend were handcuffed, driven downtown and booked for violating the state's sodomy law. Georgia's sodomy statute prohibited both oral and anal sex. If convicted, it called for a minimum term of one year in prison but not more than twenty years.

When Torick delivered both men to the station house he informed all the prisoners and guards that they were homosexuals. A guard joked that since they were jailed for cock-sucking, they should have a good time in their new home.

The district attorney decided not to present Hardwick's case to the grand jury, but the local chapter of the ACLU immediately contacted Hardwick when they heard about the arrests. They had been searching for years for a test case suitable for challenging Georgia's sodomy law. They appealed to Hardwick who finally agreed to let them help him file a complaint. With the support of the national ACLU and gay activists' groups, Hardwick sued in federal district court challenging the constitutionality of the sodomy law. The district court dismissed the suit, but the Eleventh Circuit Court of Appeals reversed on the grounds that Georgia's law did in fact violate Hardwick's constitutional right of privacy. Since other circuit courts had ruled that similar laws were constitutional, the Supreme Court of the United States agreed to hear Hardwick's case in order to resolve the inconsistencies among the lower federal courts.

Michael Bowers, Georgia's attorney general, petitioned the Court, arguing that the constitutional right of privacy should not be extended to the right of homosexual sodomy. Prior cases protecting the right of privacy were deeply rooted in the traditional values of family and one's home. There is no such historical tradition for the purported right of homosexual sodomy. Bowers described homosexual sodomy as an act of sexual deviance that Georgia has declared to be morally wrong. The state's brief concluded by arguing that a state should have the constitutional discretion to create a moral framework defending deeply held moral values of its citizens. He was invoking a theory known as Legal Moralism.

The brief of the respondent, Michael Hardwick, was authored by one of the most famous litigators of civil rights of the time, Laurence Tribe of the Harvard Law School. Tribe argued that prior cases have established a fundamental right of privacy that includes sexual intimacy between unmarried adults in the privacy of their home. Any law such as Georgia's sodomy law that violates such a fundamental right is justified only if supported by a compelling secular state interest. But Georgia has provided no evidence that such a compelling interest exists.

Georgia's Assistant Attorney General presented the case for Bowers before the Supreme Court. He began by invoking a form of the slippery slope argument. Striking down Georgia's sodomy law would in effect negate the State's right to defend laws based on Legal Moralism. That would mean the State would have no rational limiting principle to justify laws prohibiting polygamy, same sex marriage, incest, prostitution, and adultery.

Professor Tribe argued the case for Michael Hardwick. He had spoken fewer than two minutes before being interrupted by Justice Powell. Powell, appealing to the slippery slope argument, asked him what limiting principle could be applied to distinguish the present case from such practices as bigamy, incest, or prostitution if they occur between consenting adults in the privacy of one's home? Tribe responded that unlike homosexual sodomy these practices can be legitimately regulated in order to protect individuals and society from harm. Justice Rehnquist pointed out that many states had already decriminalized sodomy and asked: "Why not leave this issue to democracy? Let the people decide through their state legislatures?" Tribe's response echoed the argument presented in his brief: When it comes to a basic, fundamental right, the Court had never ceded its protection to democracy.

Tribe and his associates left the Court Room with triumphant smiles on their faces. Surely, they had convinced the swing vote of Justice Powell and maybe even O'Connor to affirm the Eleventh Circuit's decision declaring Georgia's sodomy law unconstitutional. Along with the almost certain votes of the liberal justices, Blackmun, Brennan, Marshall, and Stevens, this would guarantee a victory for their client, Michael Hardwick. Justices Burger, Rehnquist and White would rule against Hardwick but that still meant a majority decision for their client of at least five to four or possibly even six to three. Tribe's team was so convinced of their success that they retired to a nearby café for a celebratory luncheon. What they didn't know was that Justice Powell, who had supported the extension of the right of privacy to abortion services in Roe v. Wade, could not find a constitutional limiting principle in this case. Consequently, Powell voted with the five to four majority to declare that Georgia's sodomy law was in fact constitutional.

Justice White agreed to write the opinion for the Court. The heart of White's opinion rested on his interpretation of the question he believed to be central to this case. He ignored Tribe's attempt to cast the issue in terms of whether the constitutional right of privacy can be extended to consensual sex between same-sex adults in the home. Instead, White interpreted the issue in Bowers to involve the question: Is there a basic or fundamental constitutional right of homosexual sodomy? And he stated two criteria for identifying basic rights: 1) rights that are so implicit in the concept of ordered liberty that justice could not exist if they were sacrificed and 2) rights that are deeply rooted in our nation's history and tradition. White argued that the alleged right to homosexual sodomy meets neither criterion because historically sodomy was always a crime in the United States. Sodomy was a crime in all thirteen states when the Bill of Rights was ratified in 1791. Therefore, the Eleventh Circuit Court was mistaken when it claimed Hardwick enjoyed a fundamental right to engage in homosexual sodomy.

In response to Tribe's claim that Georgia did not have a rational basis justifying its law, White explicitly appealed to Legal Moralism. Georgia has the constitutional discretion to criminalize majority sentiments about acts its citizens judged to be grossly immoral.

White's relatively mild use of Legal Moralism pales in comparison to Justice Burger's shocking concurring opinion. In his words:

> Decisions of individuals relating to homosexual conduct have been subject to state intervention throughout the history of Western civilization. Condemnation of those practices is firmly rooted in Judeo-Christian moral and ethical standards...Eighteenth-century English legal scholar Sir William Blackstone described the "infamous crime against nature" as an offense of "deeper malignity" than rape..." a crime not fit to be named." ...To hold that the act of homosexual sodomy is somehow protected as a fundamental right would be to cast aside millennia of moral teaching.

On June 30, 1986, the Supreme Court of the United States in Bowers v. Hardwick announced their decision to uphold the State's constitutional discretionary right to criminalize homosexual sodomy, thereby defending the twenty-four states that had laws against such conduct at that time. Tribe, Hardwick and the gay community had lost. The curtain closes on **Act I**.

Act II: Harris County — just outside Houston, Texas

Robert Royce Eubanks was a drunk. Worse, he was a mean drunk. Worse yet, he had little steady income, instead working odd jobs on again and off again. Eubanks shared an apartment with his boyfriend, John Lawrence, but he often couldn't help with expenses. That and his drinking and belligerence made life so difficult that Lawrence finally kicked Eubanks out of his apartment. In the vernacular of our organization, Eubanks just wasn't clubbable.

John Geddes Lawrence was at least employed, working as a medical technologist analyzing blood samples. But he, also, had a serious drinking problem.

Notwithstanding their troubled relationship, Lawrence and Eubanks remained friends and would at times meet for a drink at gay bars in the Houston area.

In 1990 Eubanks met a gay African American man named Tyron Garner. Unfortunately, Garner's life was equally problematic. He, also, couldn't hold a steady job and couldn't even afford an apartment. Instead, he moved among the homes of his family and friends, staying as long as he could. So he was relieved when Eubanks invited him to share a bedroom in the home of Eubanks' parents. But their relationship was tempestuous and at times even violent.

The two men had separated for a time but agreed to try to restart their relationship by renting an apartment together. Of course, they had little money for furniture but fortunately, Lawrence had decided to purchase new furniture and offered them his old things. After helping Eubanks and Garner move into their new apartment, the three decided to celebrate by going to a Mexican restaurant where, of course, they began drinking. After dinner, the trio continued their drinking at Lawrence's apartment. All the conditions were present for a perfect storm.

Perhaps deliberately — we don't know — Lawrence began flirting with Garner. Inevitably, Eubanks, getting more and more inebriated, became furious, grabbed the half-empty bottle of vodka on the kitchen table and retreated to the living room, turning on the TV there. The drunker he got, the more his jealousy flared up. He stormed into the kitchen, verbally attacking both Lawrence and Garner. By that time Lawrence, also drunk, had had enough. Plus, he was angry that Eubanks had drunk the last of his hard liquor. Lawrence demanded that Eubanks leave immediately. Eubanks refused and, seeing some change on top of the kitchen table, he took it, shouting that he was going to buy a soda from the vending machines located in the entrance to the Colorado Club Apartment complex. However, instead of purchasing a soda, seeing a pay phone and still seething with anger, Eubanks concocted an absurd plan as payback for his lover's behavior. In his drunken stupor, Eubanks phoned the police, telling the dispatcher that there is a crazy black man waving a gun around in apartment number 833 of the Colorado Club Apartments.

Enter, stage left, our fourth and final protagonist in Act II, Harris County Deputy Sheriff Joseph Quinn. The officers of this county located just outside Houston, Texas, are known for their reputation of being macho, trigger-happy, and inclined to use excessive force. Joe Quinn relished his reputation as being the toughest of the tough who would quickly write tickets or make arrests even for minor offenses like public intoxication. He was especially prone to act tough or even become physically abusive if the subject complained, talked back to him, or didn't immediately follow his orders. Quinn bragged about having the largest internal complaint file in a department famous for citizen complaints.

It was this macho, quick-to-act officer who was the first to respond to the dispatcher's report of a crazed black man with a gun on the night of Sept. 17, 1998. When he arrived at the apartment's front door, Quinn noticed it was slightly ajar. He began knocking on the door causing it to open further. Quinn pushed it open and entered the apartment followed by Officer William Lilly and two other officers. All four had their guns drawn. Seeing no one, Quinn shouted, "Sheriff's department. Sheriff's department." No one answered. Following procedure, all four officers started searching each room separately. Quinn and Lilly entered the bedroom on the right. Both half expected to encounter an armed man so they entered with guns drawn.

Lilly entered first and would later claim that he saw Lawrence and Garner on the bed having sex. Seeing the two men with guns pointing at him, Lawrence became furious and immediately began shouting: "What the fuck are you doing? You don't have any right to be here." In his drunken state he even threatened Quinn, yelling that he would have him fired and demanded to be able to call a lawyer. That's the point at which the officers handcuffed both men and started to rough up Lawrence.

The officers then proceeded to search the entire apartment still looking for a gun. They found no gun but did come across scores of gay pornographic magazines and videos. The walls of Lawrence's bedroom were covered with photos of nude men including a drawing of the actor James Dean with an enormous erect penis. It was clear to all four officers that the men were homosexuals.

Finding no evidence of a gun, they interrogated Eubanks, who had stayed just outside the apartment. He confessed that he had made up the entire story and volunteered that he acted out of jealousy because it looked like Garner was cheating on him. This further angered Lawrence who resumed his shouting at the deputies, calling them Gestapo storm troopers and jackbooted thugs and cursing at them, especially at Quinn. Now Quinn was furious. He and his officers were endangered and could have shot someone all over what seems to be a lovers' quarrel among three men. At this point, Quinn told all three men that they were under arrest. He informed Eubanks that he would be charged with filing a false police report. No one told Lawrence or Garner of the charges against them. Already handcuffed, the deputies led Garner into a waiting squad car but Lawrence refused to cooperate. Lawrence, wearing only his underwear, was grabbed by two officers and forcibly dragged outside and down cement steps causing minor wounds but considerable bleeding. The men were taken to a holding cell that contained sixty other inmates.

Quinn charged both Lawrence and Garner with violating Texas' Homosexual Conduct statute against "deviant sexual intercourse," banning same-sex sodomy.

The following morning at their initial arraignment, the men finally were informed of the charges against them. The DA read Quinn's report claiming he saw Lawrence and Garner having anal sex. Both men pled not guilty. Neither even knew that there were laws against homosexual sodomy. At this point the story becomes problematic. Quinn's report claimed that he observed Lawrence and Garner on the bed engaging in anal sex, but Lilly had initially reported that he saw them having *oral* sex. Only after reading Quinn's police report would Lilly change his story to be consistent with Quinn's. The other two officers said they didn't see anyone having sex.

The two men were returned to their cells and not released until after midnight. Lawrence would later declare it to be the most humiliating experience of his life.

When local gay activists learned of the arrest, they immediately tried to contact Lawrence and Garner. They had been waiting for years for an appropriate test case in order to challenge the Texas homosexual sodomy law. The arrest of two consenting adults for committing sodomy in the privacy of an apartment was ideal. However, both men had pled not guilty. And when they talked to Lawrence promising to hire a lawyer for him for free if he would contest the charges, he repeated his claim of innocence. In fact, he claimed that when the deputies burst in, Garner and he were in separate rooms. Lawrence was tempted to agree to challenge the sodomy law but he worried about losing his job if his manager found out about the arrest. Still, if his case went to trial that would risk his actions being made public.

At this point the local gay activists called in legal experts from Lambda Legal, the national gay rights legal advocacy group. They argued against taking the case to trial since there was a strong possibility that Lawrence and Garner would be found not guilty. This would result in losing the right of appeal necessary to challenge the constitutionality of Texas' sodomy statute. Instead, they had lengthy discussions with Lawrence and Garner urging them to plead "no contest." This was tantamount to their not denying the charges against them but would mean there would be no trial, avoiding the publicity that would ensue. Most importantly, it would enable the men's attorneys to argue in legal briefs that the Texas sodomy law was unconstitutional.

After lengthy private discussions between Lawrence and Garner, both finally agreed to the Lambda's lawyers' strategy. Both pled "no contest" to the charges against them.

After unsurprising losses in lower courts, the Lambda legal team appealed to the Court of Criminal Appeals, the highest court in Texas that dealt with such appeals. After waiting an entire year, the state's highest court denied the request to review the decision thus confirming Lawrence and Garner's convictions. The Court cited Bowers v. Hardwick as the basis for its decision.

The Lambda team was delighted. The Court's denial was all they needed to ask the Supreme Court of the United States to review their case.

The lawyers knew that the odds of the Supreme Court accepting their case were slim, but they immediately began preparing their petition to the Court requesting the Court's review. In their cert petition they argued the Court should address three issues: 1) whether the convictions of Lawrence and Garner violated the 14th Amendment's Equal Protection Clause since an identical act committed by a heterosexual couple is not a crime in Texas; 2) whether the Texas sodomy law violated their right to privacy; and 3) whether Bowers v. Hardwick should be overruled. They knew the latter request was highly unlikely since it had only been sixteen years since the Bowers decision; moreover, Justice O'Connor, who was still sitting on the Supreme Court, had herself concurred with the Court's decision in Bowers. To their surprise and delight, on Dec. 2, 2002, the Court granted Lawrence and Garner's request for review including the request to reconsider Bowers.

The intellectual, political, and legal firepower supporting Lawrence and Garner's case was remarkable. Some of Houston's top legal talent teamed up with the national gay organization, Lambda Legal, that had been involved in the case from its inception. They were joined by several lawyers from Washington D.C.'s top legal firms including some who had presented multiple cases before the Supreme Court. In addition, the Lambda team organized fifteen amicus briefs supporting Lawrence and Garner written by the Cato Institute, the ACLU, several eminent historians, the American Psychological Association, the American Public Health Association, multiple mainline religious denominations, the American Bar Association, and leading professors of constitutional law.

The Lambda team's brief centered on their claim that the Texas sodomy law violated Lawrence and Garner's basic, fundamental right of privacy. By criminalizing sex between gay and lesbian couples, Texas in effect had invaded their private and sexual autonomy. They argued that just as for heterosexual couples, sex between gays and lesbians involved a realm of personal autonomy that served as a central factor supporting long-term relationships and the stability of families. The brief cited the fact that the US Census Bureau identified more than 600,000 households of same-sex partners, many raising children.

The Lawrence brief then argued that there exists no compelling State interest to justify the State's prohibition of such a fundamental right as the right to privacy. Attacking Legal Moralism, it argued that even the existence of majority moral preferences has never *by itself* been sufficient to justify abridgment of basic rights.

Third, the brief attacked the rationale used in Bowers v. Hardwick, arguing that the reasoning used in that case was outside the judicial and legislative precedents on privacy both before and subsequent to that decision.

Since the Texas law criminalized only homosexual sodomy, the brief also claimed it violated the Equal Protection Clause.

Finally, the Lambda team attacked the slippery slope argument, pointing out that states had sufficiently strong justifications for laws against incest, prostitution, adultery and bestiality adding that the State's citing the latter was absurd and offensive.

The brief filed by the state of Texas led off with the obvious: Given the tradition of precedent, Texas was required to follow the ruling in Bowers v. Hardwick. The brief referred to the argument in Bowers that homosexual sodomy could not involve a fundamental right since no such right was protected by the tradition and history of the United States. Again, referencing Bowers, the state argued: "...that conduct could not conceivably achieve the status of a fundamental right in the brief period of sixteen years since Bowers was decided."

Texas also rejected the use of precedent cases expanding the right of privacy since all those cases were limited to issues such as marriage, conception or parenting. Therefore, they do not apply to homosexual sodomy.

Not surprisingly, the Texas brief explicitly invokes Legal Moralism arguing that there exists sufficient rationale for its statute, "the legitimate government interest in promoting morality."

The Lambda team chose Paul Smith to argue the case before the Supreme Court. Smith, a graduate of Yale Law School and editor of its Law Review, had clerked for Justice Powell. He had extensive experience with the Court, having argued eight cases before it. Notwithstanding his experience, Smith was very well aware of the difficult task that awaited him, especially insofar as it included asking the Court to overrule a case it had decided a mere 16 years ago. As a consequence, Smith devoted literally weeks of his time preparing his argument.

While the choice and preparation of the team defending Lawrence and Garner was extensive and thorough, the choice and preparation by those arguing for the State of Texas was haphazard and insufficient. The State finally chose Chuck Rosenthal who had helped in the preparations of Texas' Lawrence briefs. While Rosenthal was an excellent trial lawyer, he had little experience at all in *any* appellate court let alone before the Supreme Court. His lack of experience would soon be revealed during the oral argument.

This historic argument occurred on March 26, 2003. Hundreds of supporters of Lawrence and Garner lined up to witness the event, some having slept in tents or sleeping bags overnight. The excitement was contagious — almost circus-like — including the singing of folk songs and civil rights anthems. A small group of anti-gay protestors held up signs with slogans like: "God condemned Sodom." "God hates fags." A woman mocked the Supreme Court's opening greeting shouting: "Oyez! Oyez! All you having business with the Court draw near and bend over."

At 11:09 A.M. before a packed courtroom consisting largely of gays and lesbians, Chief Justice Rehnquist announced, "We'll hear arguments next in No. 02-102, John Geddes Lawrence and Tyron Garner v. Texas." Paul Smith began his presentation basically summarizing the arguments given in the Lambda brief and the amicus briefs supporting Lawrence and Garner. In less than two minutes he was challenged by the Chief Justice. Rehnquist argued that the conduct at issue in this case has been banned for centuries; therefore, there can be no fundamental right to same-sex sodomy even in private. Smith's reply included one of several attacks on the reasoning used in Bowers. Bowers had the history wrong. Laws banning sodomy did not single out same sex sodomy until recently. They banned such acts for everyone. Scalia burst in claiming that was irrelevant since throughout our nation's history gay sex was prohibited. Smith responded: "If the long history of sodomy laws is sufficient to justify the Texas law that applies only to homosexual sodomy, then it would justify banning such acts for married couples. But Texas has conceded that states could not criminalize marital sodomy." Scalia responded loudly: "Texas may have conceded it. I haven't." In effect Scalia was indicating his rejection of the entire series of cases in which the Court had gradually expanded the interpretation of the right of privacy.

And so it went. Smith's arguments were often questioned, especially by Justices Scalia and Rehnquist.

Rosenthal's presentation of the argument for Texas started on the wrong foot. He began by reading his introductory statement, a practice frowned on by the justices. Oddly, Rosenthal claimed that the facts of the case do not show which rights the petitioners are asking to uphold. Scalia, already upset with the tenor of Rosenthal's arguments, interrupted saying surely, they were supporting the alleged right of homosexual sodomy. Rosenthal's reply had the audience gasping. "There's nothing in the record to show these people are homosexuals," he said. Rosenthal then tried to explain his convoluted reasoning: One homosexual act does not mean that one is a homosexual. The state of Texas believes that a heterosexual person can also violate its statute if he has sex with a person of the same sex. Rosenthal apparently used this bizarre reading of the Texas sodomy law in the belief that it could avoid violation of the Equal Protection Clause.

At this point, Justice Breyer tried to get Rosenthal back on track by turning to the central issue concerning Bowers. "Why shouldn't the Court overrule Bowers?" he asked. Upset with Rosenthal's wandering logic, Breyer added: "I would like to hear your — your *straight* answer to this issue." The courtroom erupted in laughter though Breyer didn't seem to get his own unintended joke. Part of Rosenthal's answer included a defense of the Texas law by claiming that it served the state's interest in "the preservation of marriage, families and the procreation of children." Justice Ginsburg immediately asked,

"Does Texas permit same-sex adoptions of children?" Surprisingly, Rosenthal was unaware that gays could adopt in Texas. Ginsburg pointed out that if Texas allowed such adoption it couldn't argue that its sodomy law was justified to preserve families. In a vain attempt to salvage at least part of Rosenthal's argument, Justice Scalia jokingly asked, "You're fairly certain that they can't procreate children, aren't you?"

It got no better and at times the justices seemingly ignored Rosenthal, engaging in arguments among themselves.

When the oral arguments ended, the Lambda team and their supporters felt optimistic about Smith's presentation but realized that they couldn't be at all certain of the outcome of the case. Clearly, Scalia, Rehnquist, and Thomas would side with Texas. Breyer, Ginsburg, Stevens, and Souter would probably support Lawrence and Garner. O'Connor was problematic because she had voted with the majority in Bowers and Kennedy did not indicate his position in the course of the oral questioning.

On Thursday, June 26, 2003 Justice Kennedy, who wrote the opinion in Lawrence for the Court, announced the Court's decision. In a 6-3 ruling the Supreme Court held that the Texas law was unconstitutional. More surprisingly, five justices directly overruled Bowers v. Hardwick. There was an audible gasp from those attending in the gallery as they realized the historic importance of the day.

In his opinion Kennedy first delivered what in effect was the obituary for Bowers. He began by attacking the Bowers' Court's interpretation of the question raised by the case: That Court claimed the issue was whether the federal Constitution confers a fundamental right of homosexual sodomy. In Kennedy's words, "That statement...discloses Bowers' failure to appreciate the extent of the liberty right at stake..." adding that it demeans the issue as much as someone who argued that marriage is simply about the right to have sex. Instead, liberty, he continued, "...presumes an autonomy of self that includes freedom of thought, belief, expression and certain intimate conduct." ... "Liberty protects the person from unwarranted governmental intrusion into a dwelling or other private place."

By this time overcome with emotion, many of the gays and lesbians and the supporters of Lawrence and Garner were in tears. For the first time in our nation's history, states could no longer criminalize actions that they believed to be central to a loving and caring relationship. In fact, Kennedy stressed the crucial importance of relationships in his opinion, stating that intimate sexual conduct can be "…one element in a personal bond that is more enduring." He continued: "[w]hen homosexual conduct is made criminal by the law of the State, that declaration in and of itself is an invitation to subject homosexual persons to discrimination both in the public and the private spheres."

Kennedy next argued that Bowers was an outlier. It ignored central precedent cases such as Griswold v. Conn., Eisenstadt v. Baird, Roe v. Wade and Carey v. Population Services, all of which developed the fundamental privacy right at stake in Bowers. Kennedy added that the Court's decision in Lawrence is further supported by cases subsequent to Bowers. He concluded starkly, "Bowers was not correct when it was decided, and it is not correct today. It ought not to be a binding precedent. It should be, and now is, overruled." Note that it is extremely rare for the Court to overrule a prior case, especially in such a brief time. It is remarkable for the Court to confess that its previous ruling was wrong at the time it was decided.

In his attack on Bowers Kennedy argued that that case was based on the false claim that laws against homosexual sodomy were deeply rooted in our nation's history and tradition. Nineteenth century sodomy laws were exclusively against nonconsensual or public activities. Only in the last third of the twentieth centuries were laws adopted targeting gays. In fact, the first sodomy law to specifically single out homosexuals alone was a Kansas statute not adopted until 1969.

Kennedy acknowledged that many had moral objections to homosexual conduct but he argued that Legal Moralism is inadequate if it is the sole basis for a law regulating or prohibiting fundamental rights. Perhaps surprisingly, Kennedy cites Justice Stevens' *dissent* in Bowers: "…the fact that the governing majority in a State has traditionally viewed a particular practice as immoral is not a sufficient reason for upholding a law prohibiting the practice;" And so ends Act II.

The decision in Lawrence has had deeply significant and long-lasting impact. First, it immediately rendered unenforceable the sodomy laws of thirteen states.

Second, as the American Bar Association's amicus brief demonstrated, in addition to violating privacy rights of homosexuals, the very existence of

Texas' homosexual sodomy law had discriminatory effects. For example, the exclusion of antigay violence from hate crime legislation, the disqualification from public employment including serving as police or school teachers, denial of custody or visitation rights to gay parents, refusal to allow gays to adopt or foster children and the exclusion of sexual orientation from state and local antidiscrimination law. Until Lawrence gay men and lesbians were in effect presumptive criminals.

Third, Lawrence removed one gigantic obstacle to the possibility of governments' recognition of gay marriage. In his dissent, Justice Scalia warned that the principle and logic used in Lawrence would inevitably lead to the recognition of same-sex marriage. He got that right. Months after the decision, the Massachusetts Supreme Court legalized same-sex marriage, citing Kennedy's opinion in Lawrence. Within a decade eight states followed suit. And, of course, we're all aware of the Court's recent decision legalizing same-sex marriage for all Americans involving one of our own Cincinnatians, Jim Obergefell in Obergefell v. Hodges.

Finally, it is important to note that Lawrence not only serves to protect the rights of gays and lesbians. It is an important part of a tapestry of cases developing the right of privacy and limiting unwarranted governmental intrusion into our lives.

{7} SMALL BOATS

KRIS GILLIS

THE ESSEX *WAS A LUCKY SHIP* but it was a sick ship. Any sailor would be happy to set sail on a vessel that had returned from over two decades of successful voyages but during its years at sea, the iron hardware of the Essex had begun to rot the oak timbers — not enough to leak yet but enough. Despite the ship's lucky status, the voyage that began August 12, 1819 had tried the crew from the beginning.

Two days into the trip, loaded down for months at sea, an unexpected gale knocked the ship on beam-ends. For us landlubbers, this means that the ship ended up on its side, the beams of the deck up-ended, moments away from capsizing. As quickly as the ship was knocked down, a kinder gale blew the ship upright. Before sighting a single spout, two whale boats swung destroyed at the side of the ship, and a third lay damaged. Captain George Pollard, Jr. desired to return to Nantucket and replace the damaged boats but first mate Owen Chase challenged his captain, afraid that returning to port so early in the voyage might spook the crew, who had already begun to whisper of omens.

What to say about mistakes here. Were the ship's owners mistaken for appointing such a young captain (Pollard was only twenty-nine — hardly a grizzled seaman who could silence a mouthy first mate with a salty stare)? Was Pollard mistaken in caving to his first mate, thereby emboldening Chase? Was Chase mistaken in challenging his captain? Regardless, the three boats that remained proved sturdy enough, and the *Essex* went its way.

The whalers turned to their task, sailing in search of the much-prized sperm whale. Inside that Heidelberg Tun of a head sloshed the highest-grade whale oil: spermaceti. Unlike the brown, rancid smelling oil from other whales, butter blonde spermaceti bloomed waxy and fragrant. What a disappointment to find the Atlantic whaling grounds depleted.

Fortunately for the crew, they could round Cape Horn and enter the newly opened hunting grounds of the Pacific Ocean. On November 20, 1820, cries rang out from the topmast, and the *Essex* lowered her three boats to pursue a pod of sperm whales. Captain Pollard and his mates, Joy and Chase, each commanded his own small crew aboard the thin-timbered, double-prowed vessels. The drought was over, and the crew could begin the long, filthy process of filling their empty oil barrels.

Soon all three boats were fast to whales. Pollard's and Joy's boats were dragged away from the *Essex* and out of view. The whale harpooned by Chase's boat, in no mood to drag his attackers through the sea on a joy ride, swiped the side of their boat with its tail, opening up the seams, and forcing Chase and his men to cut the line and return to the ship for repairs.

A word on whale boats. Whale boats needed to be fast so that the men could row close enough to dart whales with the harpoons. To achieve this, they were built to be light, with quarter-inch thick boards, thinner even than the line attached to the harpoon. They were shallow, twenty-five to thirty feet long, and made for six men to work away from the ship for several hours and then be hoisted and held aloft by the davits. They are not the kind of boat in which you would want to spend the night, much less more than sixty nights.

Back aboard the *Essex*, Owen Chase and his men repaired their damaged boat. Having already lost two earlier in the voyage, they could not allow the loss of another working whale boat. Then, off the weather bow, Chase spotted a monstrous sperm whale, which he estimated to be about eighty-five feet long, only two feet shorter than the *Essex* itself. Since each foot of an adult whale typically equals one ton, this whale probably weighed as much as thirteen elephants or, more simply, the space shuttle. This is what charged the *Essex*.

The whale's first blow hit the ship near the fore-chains and threw nearly everyone to the deck. In Chase's words, "the ship brought up suddenly and violently as if she had struck a rock and trembled for a few seconds like a leaf." The *Essex* coughed her first death rattle out of sight of land and out of sight of her captain. Chase knew to set the pumps going, but within a minute the head of the ship had already begun to settle down in the water. At this point, the situation, although dire, was not fatal.

Then Owen Chase committed his first mistake. The whale, seemingly dazed from the blow, lay still for a minute in the water along the length of the ship: head to bow, tail to stern. Thomas Nickerson, the youngest crew member of the *Essex*, reveals in his "Desultory Sketches" that Chase had a "fine opportunity to have kill^{ed} him with a throw of his lance" but saw the whale's tail close to the rudder and judged its potential loss too great a threat, all of which Chase omits from his *Narrative*.

As Chase had scarcely dispatched the orders to signal to the other whale boats to return, the whale had swum three hundred yards off and rounded on the ship again. What could have been a whale in its death throes was now very alive and making white water for a head-on collision with the *Essex*.

Shipbuilders regaled white oak for its strength but oak, in long term contact with metal, especially iron, and especially in damp conditions, produces acetic acid and corrodes the metal. When iron rusts, it deteriorates the wood next to it, weakening its tensile strength. A ship whose hull has begun to rot in this fashion is said to be iron-sick.

The *Essex* was a lucky ship but it was a sick ship.

Chase recounts a man at the hatchway rousing his attention, crying, "here he is — he is making for us again." Chase saw the huge whale bearing down on the ship at "twice his ordinary speed" with "tenfold fury and vengeance in his aspect." Moments later the whale crashed into the *Essex* directly below the cat-head and completely stove in her bow. Then the whale made one more pass below the ship and disappeared into the depths of the Pacific.

For roughly the next ten minutes, Chase and his men commenced a frenzied scavenge of the ship. Chase cut away the lashings of the spare boat and sent the steward to the cabin to save two quadrants, two practical navigators, and two compasses. They also saved the trunks that belonged to Pollard and Chase. At last, all hands jumped into the boat and were hardly fifty feet away when the *Essex* capsized and settled down in the water.

Better to have been in a ship without a rudder than in no ship at all.

Chase and his men sat silent.

Soon Joy and Pollard returned, towing two dead sperm whales. Pollard was stunned, no doubt struggling to process the dreadful scene before him.

He finally managed to ask, “My God, Mr. Chase, what is the matter?”

Chase answered simply, “We have been stove by a whale.”

Two days later, the men had cut away the masts and managed to raise the ship enough to recover some provisions: six hundred pounds of hard bread, as much fresh water as they dared load into the whale boats, a musket and powder, two horse pistols, two rasps, two files, two pounds of boat nails, and a few turtles. They had also built up the gunwale of each whale boat roughly six inches, using spare cedar boards, which allowed them to load each boat with more supplies, and fitted each boat with two masts to carry a flying-jib and two sprit-sails.

Chase’s and Nickerson’s accounts of what happened next differ slightly but significantly. At noon on November 22, 1820, using their saved navigational tools, the men observed that they were at 0°13’N, 120°00’W, but it is best to find their location emotionally. Picture the globe, and then place your finger on the coast of Ecuador; imagine yourself sitting in an open, light boat, and slide your finger west along the equator. Stop when you despair at the immensity of the surrounding ocean. It is there we find our whalers.

If one believes Chase’s account of the situation, the three of them — Pollard, Joy, and Chas — consulted the maps and came to a common consensus. According to Chase in his *Narrative*, the Marquesas and Society Islands were inhabited, if at all, “by savages, from whom [they] had as much to fear, as from the elements, or even death itself.” Captain Pollard warned against the hurricane season in the vicinity of Hawaii. Therefore, it was best to try for the coast of Chile or Peru.

Nickerson, however, remembers the situation differently. According to him, Pollard’s first desire was to sail to the Society Islands, cannibals or not. Pollard estimated the trip would have taken ten days at most under favorable winds, which to be fair, in such light, open vessels, is still not a great trip. Chase, however, having previously persuaded his captain to continue the voyage with ruined whale boats and enjoying the support of the other mate, urged Pollard against the Society Islands. Pollard, finding himself outnumbered, reluctantly agreed to fight the trade winds and try for the coast of Chile.

It is tempting to pin this mistake on Pollard. He was the captain. But he was young and outnumbered and adrift, with only nineteen other souls for company.

No. This is Chase's mistake, and his mistake here was as illogical as it was fatal. By urging his captain to sail away from the mere possibility of cannibals, Chase pointed their prows toward the inevitability of cannibalism.

The men made for South America, enduring horrible suffering along the way. Weather beat the ships. Sea creatures attacked them. They enjoyed brief respite on a small uninhabited island where they found an ephemeral supply of drinking water, depleted an entire population of birds, and left three of their crew before they set sail in their pitiful vessels again. The three boats eventually separated; only two were rescued. In their final weeks at sea, the men aboard Pollard's boat drew lots to see who would sustain the remaining men. On Chase's boat, a few men died from natural causes, but were equally useful to the crew. Captain Pollard had to tell his sister that her son, Owen, had lost when the sailors cast lots in their final dismal desire for food.

Of course, mistakes are only so in hindsight's judgement. I can declare Owen Chase's dogged insistence to avoid the Marquesas and Society Islands a mistake because we know they suffered for months and lost most of their crew. I could just as easily have been critical had he decided to lance the monstrous whale and left the *Essex* rudderless at sea because horrors are not endemic to small boats. It is not the mistakes themselves, but what we find in the wake of these missteps that makes them so fascinating: our near-inextinguishable will to survive, our determination and courage amid disaster.

Herman Melville's *Moby-Dick*, our greatest piece of American literature and most famous repurposing of the *Essex* tragedy, concludes, after Moby Dick has sunk the *Pequod*, with Ishmael clinging to Queequeg's coffin as a lifebuoy — alone save for sharks and sea-hawks — adrift for more than a day before the ship *Rachel* saves him. Pollard finished out his life as a night watchman, shepherding the people of Nantucket. Even Owen Chase, who suffered from horrible headaches the rest of his life, unable to fully recover from his traumas at sea, hid food in his attic for the last few years of his life, preparing to survive another great disaster.

{8} FOOD & MEMORY

RICHARD HAGUE

1: APERITIF

MANY YEARS AGO — actually, thirty-two or thirty-three years ago, for the sake of accuracy — I was invited, much to my surprise, to a dinner and reception in one of those vast mansions on Grandin Road, part of what's known as Cincinnati's "Gold Coast." I confess that I cannot recall the name of my host or hostess; nor do I remember talking to anyone who seemed to be any kind of inhabitant or employee of the place — owner, butler, dishwasher. The guests were all writers of some sort or another, I suppose, but I don't know how I came to be among them. I was a lean and hungry chap in those days, slowly overcoming a post-divorce decade of loneliness and general fear-of-life, at the end of a series of several consecutive and somewhat desperate summer rustications to Appalachian Ohio. There, living alone in a trailer two miles out a country road from the nearest town, a depopulated village of ninety-seven souls, I had tried to put grief, loss, and humiliation all behind me and to get into the rhythms of dawn and day and dusk and night and to work my body to a pleasant weariness in the woods.

But then here I was, suddenly back in civilization, married anew, restoring a near-century-old house in Madisonville, and The Great Man of the Moment was being wined and dined. I felt a little like Steinbeck's dog, along for the ride. The guest of honor was William Least Heat Moon, whose now-classic *Blue Highways* had been recently released; he was in town on a reading tour, I think, and, I hope, to reconnect with Camp Washington Chili. The place had impressed him during the blue highways trip; the number of calendars from traveling salesmen, the better the chance the food was good. Camp Washington Chili fit the bill, and I trust he returned for a three-way and a cheese coney before heading off to his next promotional duty.

I must have had a conversation with him, I tell myself, though I recall being at the far end of the table, and not really knowing much about him at the time, nor about my fellow diners. In fact, I don't remember exchanging a single word face-to-face with the guest of honor. My recollection of the whole event is generally hazy and uncertain; in my dislocatedness had I drunk so much that I lost touch with what might have been the most witty and substantive dinner conversation I'd ever heard? Or, had the author been drunk himself, and thus so incoherent that it's not possible to piece back together the gist of his talking? Or, had the host or hostess suddenly turned out the lights and locked all us writers in, gassed us into unconsciousness, then whisked Least Heat Moon away in some silken Rolls-Royce, as if to show him, upon his coming-to, what real travel and what red highways were all about?

I don't know.

But before I apologize for this damnable lack of knowing, let me remind you that I'm in good company. My ignorance puts me in the same place as the very inventor of the general form of writing I'm engaging in right now, a writer Shakespeare possibly read, a writer even to this day unparalleled in his execution of the genre he was in the process of developing. Michel de Montaigne, the first practitioner of what we now call the personal essay, asked himself, "What do I know?" This was not an epistemological question for the Frenchman; it was a practical entrance into the kind of personal writing he was embarking upon, the kind of writing a later scholar has said deals with "the basic archaeology of the self."

Montaigne took as his mission what Philip Lopate, in his introduction of him in *The Art of the Personal Essay*, describes this way: "to put before the public a full verbal portrait of himself." At the same time, Montaigne knew that his own fickleness, ignorance, forgetfulness, and digressions were the very stuff of the human condition. Thus, what might appear at first as a monstrously large, probably boring, not to mention garishly egotistic writer's project is subsumed into the larger thing he wants to put forth to us in that age of flourishing humanism: in writing about himself and in following his whims about his subjects, he is manifesting, in prose, the nature not only of Montaigne, but of humanity.

These are among the main driving forces of any essayist: to answer the dizzyingly circular questions, What do I think, and *why* do I think what I think about what I think about? Very similar to this drive is the work of the memoirist, another kind of essayist, though some purists would place memoir in a subcategory of autobiography. As I see it, the essayist-memoirist focuses not on the large and miscellaneous and inexhaustible abundance of life in general, but on the shape and meaning of either part of his own life and mind and psyche (the essayist-memoirist), or something approaching the whole or some unitary substantial segment of his own remembered life (the memoirist). The questions of the essayist-memoirist are only slightly different from Montaigne's: What did I do and think then, and why did I do what I did and why did I think what I thought then? Who was I then? And sometimes even a further question is explored: How is that previous self-connected to the present one, or, conversely, how and why did the divorce from that previous self and this one occur?

I adopt the stance of the essayist-memoirist. I intend to engage in the kind of writing Tony Covatta, one of my sponsors, called for more of on February 24 of this year, commenting on the dominance of fact in so many Literary Club papers, and wishing for more depth, more of the underlying meaning of those facts, both to the writer, and indirectly, to the reader. Of a good memoir, Mr. Covatta wrote, "It has a coherent point of view, an idea or a series of ideas, that gives us insight into the subject, and into the mind, heart and soul of the writer, and thus into ourselves." Richard Hunt, my primary sponsor, heeded the call not long afterwards in his probingly personal paper on fathers and sons.

In the same spirit of personal writing, I intend to essay a subject or two that are linked in my memory and my imagination, and that have lodged there persistently enough that I feel I have to express, and insofar as it is possible, explicate them. At the same time, I know I will be revealing things about myself that may not reflect the better angels of my spirit. For any writer of the personal essay, or the memoir, such candor is often the way it goes. There is a kind of recklessness in such intensely personal writing, and a kind of danger. Nevertheless, I do it. Why do I remember the people and the events and the situations this essay-memoir explores? What do they mean? What do they reveal about me?

To repeat the master's question: "What do I know?"

2: STARTERS

For the first two decades of my current, clearly permanent marriage, my wife Pam and I tried to reinvent my Grandmother's ham loaf. I remembered it as a salty-sweet concoction with a most lusciously pink interior, its glazy top drizzled with pineapple juice, the whole thing set out steamingly fragrant on a long white dish in the dining room of my grandparents' house at 118 Logan Street in Steubenville. Just three doors down ran the Pennsylvania Railroad, and then, just a few yards below that, the Ohio River. But this ham loaf was something entirely different than the fish we ate from the river, those oily-tasting mud- and channel cats; this delicacy remained memorable as a kind of holiday meal, even when served in the middle of the most gray empty week of February.

Not so surprisingly, Pam and I were never able to recapture the taste and appearance of that meal. We tried different grinds of left-over ham; we tried mixing in pineapple juice before the baking, we tried basting the loaf with it during and after baking; we tried different kinds of bread crumbs and various combinations of cloves, nutmeg, allspice. Nothing produced the taste I remembered, and I suspect that nothing ever will. Our senses are at their height in our childhoods — every new sight, smell, texture, taste is just that — original, arresting, unique. We are experiencing the world for the first time. The remembered taste of that ham loaf, then, lives in a part of my brain that is no longer readily accessible; the callouses and fissures and dead-ends of time and alcohol and coffee and football and the stray concussion or two here and there have obscured or disordered the nerves where that memory is stored, and the experience of just *that* taste, from just *that* time in my life, is, short of some liberatingly awful trauma, or the scary mental jiu-jitsu of hypnosis, perhaps irrecoverable.

Thus, the difficulty of memoir, whose relation to "memory" is etymologically obvious. We know from neurobiology at one end of the continuum and from the fallibility of so-called eyewitness testimony near the other end of the continuum, how untrustworthy memory can be. We know that memories can be repressed, altered, distorted, exaggerated; we know that disease and injury can scramble our ability to recollect; we know that sometimes the most believed and believable "memories" are absolute fiction. What we must therefore know is that for the writer from memory, the memoirist, things are not necessarily as they seem to be. It is a treacherous, error-haunted way we walk.

For example, in her essay-memoir "Memory and Imagination," Guggenheim and Houghton Mifflin Fellowship winner Patricia Hampl begins with an unforgettable description of her childhood music teacher, a nun named Sister Olive Marie. "Her oily face gleamed as if it had just been rolled out of a can and laid on the white plate of her broad, spotless wimple. She was a small, plump woman; her body and the small window of her face seemed to interpret the entire alphabet of olive: her face was a sallow green olive placed upon the jumbo ripe olive of her black habit. I trusted her instantly and smiled, glad to have my hand placed in the hand of a woman who made sense, who provided the satisfaction of being what she was: an Olive who looked like an olive."

What a delight we experience in reading such a passage: how it retains its metaphorical unity, how its details are listening to one another, as in a good poem, how it sustains its serio-comic tone. This is a writer we can trust. As confidently and as readily as Hampl the girl must certainly have placed her hand in Sister Olive's hand, we place our trust in such an authoritative presence. "Go on!" we enthuse, warming to her story. "What next?"

I am sorry to report that no further than two pages later, Hampl stops dead in her tracks. "Sister Olive Marie...but was her name Olive? As for her skin tone — I would have sworn it was olive-like; I would have been willing to spend the better part of an afternoon trying to write the exact description of imported Italian or Greek olive oil her face suggested: I wanted to get it right. But now, were I to write that passage over, it is her intense black eyebrows I would see, for suddenly they seem the central fact of that face, some indicative mark of her serious and patient nature. But the truth is, I don't remember the woman at all. She's a sneeze in the sun and a finger touching middle C."

"Ah hell," I hear myself, the essayist-memoirist, grumbling. "I know that experience. The writing takes hold of you, and shapes the memory; writing is always a shaping force. Pretty soon, you've got a metaphor that's heating up for you, and you glide along with what you think are power and style and excitement, and then you shift into second gear, and the writing's coming as smoothly as it ever comes, you're on the roll of rolls, and then you shift into third, and the pages, like the miles accomplished aboard some heavenly Silver Ghost sedan, add up. But then you go back to revise — to re-look, literally, to re-think, re-process, get the critic in gear, and you realize you were writing, oh yes, but were you getting the truth of the experience? You fact-check yourself, as Hampl does, and you find yourself coming up short. At that point, she says, the second draft begins, and it is an attempt, as she and the bumper sticker say, to CHALLENGE AUTHORITY. The problem is, the authority you have to challenge, that apparent know-it-all, that actual horse's mouth, is, of course, you, the memoirist — the *author*, for God's sake — functioning as witness to, and expert on, the past. But: Is this witness really expert and reliable? Is this witness even in his right mind? Is this witness driven by unconscious biases or repressions or delusions of grandeur or fantasy-fulfillment or unresolved grudges? Is there an incipient tumor of fabrication and lies already sending its first tendrils into regions of his brain and into the sentences of his every paragraph? These questions must be asked of the writing self, and they must be answered — it seems impossible does it not? — *selflessly*, impersonally, with all the gravity of the most incisive judge and critic. It's as if you are the builder of the bridge, and at the same time the finicky sapper who blows the whole thing apart because of a few cracked bolts.

Enough. To mix my metaphors yet again, with this plate of appetizing (or, perhaps, appetite-dismissing) questions and complications so abruptly set forth for you to nibble on, my dear readers, even before you can chew and swallow, I now present my main course: Grilled Cheese, Tomato Soup, and a Tall, Blue-Eyed Blonde.

3: THE MEAL

It was forty years ago, because I was living alone at the time, my former roommate having dropped his teaching job and bolted to Boston in yet another re-enactment of the grand American drama of chucking it all and starting over. Huck had done it; Ishmael had done it; and now Brian Conly was doing it. Known to his college chums as Buffalo Bill (for his goateed resemblance to the famous Indian killer), and as Colonel Excess (for his lifestyle of memorably extravagant drunkenness, his reckless accelerator-punching of his push-button transmission Plymouth Fury, and his wild and sometimes delicious cooking adventures) — Brian once served us a stuffed veal pocket — who knew? Just a few weeks before, seated at our tiny breakfast table one groggy Thursday morning, clutching a half-empty bottle of Cutty Sark between his former Elder High School tight end's thighs, he'd announced that he was going to quit his job as soon as possible (teaching English at UC Raymond Walters, a local institution until recently bearing the name of a past Literarian, I believe), go to Boston, and find a rich Irish girl, to whom he would, again as quickly as possible, get married. Astonishingly, he succeeded in all of these — though the marriage didn't last, and the bride, and the fortune, as they are sometimes wont to do, drifted away.

So, after he'd absconded to Bean Town with little more than his underwear, socks, and his buggy VW successor to the Plymouth Fury, there I was, seated at the canary yellow table in the dining room I'd shared with him, sharing it now with the wife of one of our former mutual college writing buddies and, more to the point, with her friend, with whom the goodwife was "fixing me up." My buddy's missus, herself a pretty, young, open-faced, full-bodied and quite genial woman, was studying art at Edgecliff College, where she had met the tall, blue-eyed blonde in one of her printmaking classes. After getting to know her, she thought we'd make a good pair. For a fleeting, wicked moment, I thought the wife and I might make a good pair, too, but the few irritating shreds of conscience left in me after my Jesuit education as well as an inherited-from-my-strict-Catholic-family-decorum prevailed. Besides, her husband was the only short story writer I knew who packed a gun.

I had invited these ladies of the brayer and brush to lunch; I also intended to show off my apartment, one of the best and least expensive bachelor pads I'd ever known. There were two bedrooms, a huge living room, and a dining room with one wall so large I was able to hang from it a 7x9 foot rug of faux Native American design, in garish rusts, reds, and yellows. My lodgings also featured a reasonably functional kitchen, a commodious bathroom with a shower, and, best of all, a little sun porch overlooking the street — the apartment occupied almost the entire second floor of a huge half-timbered Tudor-style house, once the Town Hall, on a busy corner in Kennedy Heights. I wrote on the sun porch, which overlooked the street like the fo'c'sle of a ship, and I felt like the captain of some vast galleon, surveying at my leisure the busy decks below.

My cooking repertoire was nowhere near as knowledgeable or as adventurous as Brian's had been. I would like to say that I made the grilled cheese sandwiches which I served the ladies that afternoon with an artisanal French loaf baked in a wood-fired oven, but this was decades before the craft-baking revolution displaced Wonder Bread from peoples' shopping carts. I wasn't using

Wonder Bread, assuredly, but it would have been something similarly industrial and schmaltzily-named — Green Lantern Miracle Wheat, say, or Grandpa Emerson's Transcendental Rye — bought at a factory outlet-type chain store off crowded shelves hastily replenished by stooping, underpaid, un-unionized operatives who wore their names embroidered on their shirts and who were forced to drive their huge, brightly painted trucks for hours all over town, standing up. This was how things generally were in the America of bread in the early 1970s.

I would also like to claim that the cheese was especially choice: a rare, sharp, eminently meltable English cheddar, maybe, or a good Gruyere, or at least a solid and respectable local Amish Swiss, bought from a bearded man in suspenders who had left his farm in Adams County at 4 a.m. to deliver his handmade wares to an open-air stall at Findlay Market. I would like to say we'd exchanged pleasantries (though the Amish are definitely not into small talk) and that I had determined the provenance of the milk that went into his cheese ("A cow I raised by hand, mister, sired by the famous bull Ahab on my cousin Elmer Yoder's farm"). Or it would have been equally impressive if I had selected it from the cooler cases of a master cheesemonger, in a place like Krause's, it too until recently located at Findlay Market, and staffed by *fraus und frauleins* for whom German, and cheese-lore, you got the impression, was their first language. Besides a hundred types of cheese, Krause's dealt in dozens of varieties of wursts, sausages, Landjaegers, spaetzle noodles, sauerkraut, as well as huge loaves of plutonically dark and dense pumpernickel, chunks of which could be sawn off and sold by the pound. Once again, though, I can make no such culinary claims. The cheese I had prepared the sandwiches from for those two gorgeous art-ladies had probably come from a pack of sticky Kraft Singles, and thus were no more closely related to real cheese than Kool Aid is to Bordeaux.

And I would most certainly desire (as a now seasoned gardener who has practiced growing things for decades since that afternoon repast) to further claim that the soup was home-made, crafted from half a dozen select San Marzanos organically grown by myself to the moment of utter ripeness, and then, that very morning, plucked, seeded, chopped, and cooked lightly down, skins and all, with some garlic (hand-grown in my garden) flat -leafed Italian parsley (ditto), and freshly chopped sweet basil (likewise), then strained, in order to remove the little morsels of skin which give the soup a piquant thrill of slight bitterness but also a deep tomato-ness, then whirred into a velvety emulsion with my immersible blender. At the end, a little further simmer, adjusting the taste with a pinch of sea salt, would have finished it off nicely. And just before serving, did I gild the lily with a spot of extra heavy-whipping cream, or, more daringly and erotically, with a splash of an especially sweet, fruity sherry? Not. In actuality, I had poured a condensed glob of wiggly tomato-colored stuff — probably the ten-cans-for-a-dollar brand from the local discount factory-food dispensary — and rushed it to boiling while pouring in slugs of tap-water and stirring with a splintery wooden spoon. I sloshed it quickly into some scruffy stoneware mugs I'd washed that morning just for the occasion and plunked them down, steaming, before the ladies.

At that crucial moment of serving did I tremblingly recall the sexy eating scenes in movies like the one in the 1963 version of *Tom Jones*, in which Albert Finney as the title character and the lusty Joyce Redman as Jenny Jones/Mrs. Waters demolish, by hand, a greasy roast chicken, and other similarly slick and lip-smacking vittles, which chicken's juices (and theirs, and the viewer's eventually) run down their chins, and most appetizingly, down and into the bosom of Ms. Jenny as she ogles her slavering partner across a table full of food which, you know will not, cannot, support the combined entwined and grappling weight of them when their eating and ogling turns really nasty?

Or was I thinking about the scene in *When Harry Met Sally* in which the powder-pure, innocent-faced Meg Ryan, literally in the middle of Katz's delicatessen, sitting across from the supremely chauvinistic and clueless Billy Crystal, fakes a 72-second orgasm (again, in the interests of accuracy, I timed it on YouTube) and then, the last phony throes of passion dropping from her face, sticks a forkful of cole slaw in her cute little mouth?

Fortunately, my imagination had not, those years ago, been befouled by more recent and decidedly less erotic eating sequences, such as the ones in *Hannibal*, or even the recent documentary and dyspeptic downers like *Supersize Me* or *Food, Inc.*

Thank goodness, then, that my guests were not only artists and beauties and incipient *bon vivants*; they were, after all, college students, and I myself was not that far from the cash-strapped and half-starved ardors of graduate school. Thus we ate so quickly, and with such hungry, animal gladness, that I cannot remember even chewing. But I did indeed feast my eyes upon the delicate (though a good inch or two taller than me) maiden across the table: her rampant mane of buttery-silvery curls; the soft, bouillon-like transparency of her fair skin, seasoned very lightly across the bridge of her nose and just under her eyes with a sprinkle of pale golden freckles, like the flecks in half-churned buttermilk.

I suppose we talked of art and college life and the married missus's husband, a brilliant alcoholic with a fascination for Hemingway, Lucky Strikes, and Smith and Wesson's. Many had been the Monday nights after meetings of Mermaid Tavern, the literary fraternity at Xavier University, which, like this Club, maintained an exclusively male membership, and claimed its own meeting place (a dim, heavily tiled and paneled Elizabethan reseller in a Cincinnati stolid brick house just off-campus in North Avondale, at the corner of Dakota and Redway) — many, I say, had been the nights that her husband and I and a few other poets, boy soldiers (ROTC was required of all freshmen and sophomores in those early Vietnam days), physics majors and other assorted undergraduate and graduate crazies had repaired to Uncle Woody's tiny subterranean former speak-easy on Reading Road, or to some nameless smoky joint in Norwood, to continue our literary rants and our drinking.

I don't remember much of what the blonde said during that lunch, but this gap is not the result of inattention. Rather I think I was already, in between bites of that utterly forgettable cheese sandwich, intensely imagining the unimaginable — that this great beauty would wind up in my embrace, that I soon could, and would, stretch myself at full length upon her undulant self, and that, because of her height, there would be still more of her left to explore.

I must immediately report that it was no such electrical consummation I would encounter. We did indeed begin dating after that lunch, and the relationship became physical, and I am sorry to say, difficult, and, in the end, unsuccessful. Like that mundane, pedestrian lunch placed against the possible lunch, the Platonically ideal imagined lunch I have already confessed to not achieving, she turned out to be less than, and to me, in undecipherable ways, more than, a mild-mannered dreamboat. For example, she wore almost as a uniform, tight, back-pocketless buttock-lifting jeans (nice), topped with her trademark tattered cotton plaid shirt, sleeves half-rolled up (not so nice, though showing the freckled skin of her arms.) The shirt's top two buttons remained unfastened, so that an expanse of snowy chest and a hint of collar bone flashed whenever she moved (nice, again). She smelled of cigarettes, marijuana, wine, and patchouli, although now and then, downwind of her, or my lips close and urgent at her throat, I caught a tantalizing breath of raw dark honey mixed with lilies of the valley and Southern Comfort. Every Spring, there would come over her an unsettling transformation; from the lassitude and moody grayness of winter, she would plunge into what I can only describe as a psychologically orgiastic state during which, for two weeks, she would remain drunk on Mad Dog wine, eat nothing but single slices of bologna, and grow giddy over Elton John's "Benny and The Jets." She was the only girl (except for the pony-tailed hoydens I was attracted to as a child) who ever hit me. I hasten to add, though physical violence in a relationship can never be justified, I deserved it, but I remained thereafter wary of her stylish, heavy, literally *handy* wooden clogs. Without warning, she would suddenly embark on long camping trips with one or another of her tough girlfriends to Nova Scotia, or Newfoundland, of all places, where they would snuggle together (she'd tell me this) in a tiny pup tent and where they would go fishing, shoot pool with fishermen, truck drivers, and dropped-out college professors, and get high. Her unannounced absences and emotional and relational inconsistencies so disoriented and distressed me that I actually grew somewhat jealous of her dog Billy, to whom she paid singular, constant, and devoted attention and of whom she had more photographs than she had of me.

Clearly, she was damaged goods, and clearly, so was I. Both of us had suffered relatively recent abortive marriages, and so we hobbled along a wrack-strewn shoreline like two injured castaways, needing one another while at the same time resenting each other for reminding ourselves of our pain and of the shortcomings and disappointments and empty promises of life.

I have not used her name here, nor her married friend's; it would be ungentlemanly of me — though I admit that I have said some things already that could be taken as more than merely ungentlemanly — patronizing, just plain mean and sexist, and I have said them, after all, at her expense. For this, I apologize, and have no defense — none whatsoever. Nor will I attempt any counter to a reader's deepening impression at this point of my own boorishness, chauvinism, perhaps even misogyny. How stupid and futile would it be to claim here that some of my best friends, now and in the past, are women? Perhaps even worse, I cannot deny that I have, perhaps, slanted some of this, including my descriptions and characterizations of the people involved, in such a way as to create a livelier read, to hell with the actual facts, (whatever "facts" may be to a memoirist, adrift in a sea of uncertainty).

But to return to the truth, if I've ever left it, I can say that the maiden's first name was the name of a month, an especially dewy, green, moist, warming month, a month of sprouting, budding, growing. She herself loved flowers and plants, and had, just before we met, worked part time in a greenhouse. Once, in an unsettling inversion, I discovered her leaning over a fungus known as "stinkhorn" that was rising from the rotten mulch in her widowed mother's backyard flowerbed. It is a fungus aptly named for its odor; more unsettlingly, in shape and color it mimics a florid, uncircumcised, erect penis. She was in the midst of jerking it out of the ground, bare-handed. This juxtaposition of the violent with the erotic, of the innocence and promise and even randiness of spring with the reminder of death that all mulch and all uprooting is, seems emblematic of my life at the time. I had ideas, beautiful and elegant ideas, but grosser and messier realities prevailed. As for the ideas, I did not yet have the ability to execute them, either in lunch or in love. And she, another waif of the universe, needed feeding, healing, nursing, nourishment. And though I made her lunch, and dinner, and hungover breakfasts, and though I made her happy sometimes, and angry often, I could not muster the feeding she needed, nor could she pull herself away from her beautiful sorrow and her dramatic drunkenness, joining me in the kitchen, so to speak, where love might have transformed despair and sorrow. And at the end, truth be told, it was I who left her; despite my bad behavior and arrogance, she didn't instigate our break-up; I did, out of a mixture of cowardice, exhaustion, concern over her drinking, and most of all, I think, an immature resentment of her cussedly independent ways.

4: DESSERT

Remember that it's not always sweet, this last stage of a meal. The old saying "From soup to nuts" suggests that a meal may end with something other than pie or cake or cannoli or baklava or, God help us, deep-fried Twinkies. I remember dinner in Manchester College's dining hall at Oxford, where I studied on a National Endowment for the Humanities grant for a summer. After the requisite fish, peas, and potatoes in more forms than even the Irish might have imagined, the scouts, as the waiters are called in Oxford colleges, would set out not slabs or dollops or saucers of sweets, but great plates of sharp Cotswold cheese and dry crackers ("biscuits" to them, of course) and, actually, now and then, bowls of nuts.

So this memoir via meal: it does not end sweetly. As a matter of fact, the spirit of Patricia Hampl, the spirit who Questions Authority, has me once more double-thinking some of the things I've said above. Was the blonde artist-maiden deserving of even one bit of the laughter my writing has evoked about her? Probably not. (And I have to say that after our relationship began, she was, one sudden day, no longer blonde. There had been reasons to suspect as much — but it was quite unsettling. How much else of what I thought I knew about her was subject to such swift transformation?) So: Was I really that attracted to her friend, the gun-slinging short-storier's wife? Maybe not so much. And the actual lunch, the grilled cheese sandwiches and the tomato soup, as opposed to the idealized one I have imagined — was the real lunch so bad? Again, probably not. After all, "Hunger is the best spice."

But I have to confront the pitfalls any essayist-memoirist is prone to, and call myself to account. I may yet have to revise this, I may yet have to discard this bouncier, more ebullient possible narrative for what may turn out to be a much more stolid and prosaic version of the truth. The fiction writer in me, the poet in me, let alone the hyperbolic fabulist in me, resists this absolute truth-telling, this diminishment of the story's possibilities. But the very fact — (?) — that I confess all this presents us with the dilemma — all nonfiction writing is *a* version, not necessarily *the* version. One writer looks at the Battle of Little Big Horn and sees it from the American Cavalry's point of view. It sees George Armstrong Custer as the victim of a massacre. Another writer sees it from a Lakota grandmother's point of view, and tells what looks like the last installment of an utterly different, brutal, anti-heroic, even genocidal story. One writer examines the life and career of Margaret Thatcher, concluding that she was a stiff-spined exceptional leader who broached no nonsense, and another dissects the Iron Lady's meanness and conservatism and sketchy friendship with Ronald Reagan and discovers an inflexible tyrant. Rarely, if ever, do we get an objective view of that strange, elastic, ungraspable thing we call "the truth." Thus, the ongoing argument and occasional lawsuits over so-called nonfiction writing. And thus, the struggles, alone at the desk with words and memory, of anyone crazy enough (or desperate enough) to attempt to accurately capture events in the past, or even worse, to report accurately some fleeting emotional episode obscured by the turbulent passage of decades.

Perhaps all of this accounts for the scarcity of such deeply personal writing and self-revelation and self-examination in Literary Club papers. And perhaps this is for the best. Personal writing can run the gamut from exciting and incisive and thought-provoking to deadly dull and self-absorbed, like the chatter of a half-drunk cocktail guest who has never been told he's a boor. Such writing is difficult, risky, fraught with the occasions of failure and of various literary and intellectual transgressions. How much more uncomplicated it is to stick to "facts" that live on the surface of the narrative. The ponderous depth of personal memory, its sometimes bottomless obscurities and transformations and downright gaps, is daunting. Nevertheless, Tony Covatta's call remains, his invitation to probe deeper and more soulfully and more personally into the subjects of the papers we write and share.

5: DIGESTIV

I meant, after all this, to write of food, one small instance, one tiny chapter in the greater volume of my eating and drinking. And I shall attempt to do so again; it is, as all good subjects are, larger on the inside than it seems from the outside. But things are not so neatly filed away in memory and imagination; they bleed into one another, they leach, dribble, sweat, seep, they cross each other's boundaries, like the ingredients of one recipe gradually entering an unexpected other over the long history of cuisine — nutmeg into pasta sauce, bacon into ice cream. So the story of this meal — which is really the story of this girl-woman, and of this earlier, erratic, unripened man-boy version of myself, which is really a story of love and loss and limits and misdirections, of the ideal set against the real — has not really digressed. It has followed the scent of human beings meandering through the world, bumping into one another, entwining sometimes in a seethe of heat and passion, and then separating again, like strands of boiling pasta. Where we end up, we pasta strands, is where we'll all end up, after all. We are the eating and then we are the eaten. And unless we are the unfortunate husband of a series of deceased wives, we usually get but one try at the banquet. Well, maybe two, at the most perhaps three. How will we behave? And how can we ever know, given all the obscure ingredients, all the unexpected combinations of them, all the catastrophes, all the derangements of what we plan and cannot plan for, how can we ever know all the ever-re-written menus of life? How can we ever surely know for what courses and for what unpredictable, demanding presentations we must prepare?

What do I know? What can any of us know?

{9}
THE EULOGIST

RICHARD HUNT

EVEN THOUGH THE CONGREGATION SAT HUSHED, Cheever cleared his throat, lightly tapped the microphone, and nodded solemnly at the hundred people gathered there, all dressed in mourning black and navy blue. In the stillness of the church, Cheever waited. A casket rested in the center of the aisle. His hands gripped the side of the pulpit to steady his legs, which quavered and felt as if they might buckle. Odd.

For over five decades, James Cheever Snell Jr. had been speaking on behalf of the dearly departed. A person might rightly think after such tenure that he'd feel no nervousness whatsoever. But this time was different, and his unsettled condition betrayed him. His heart seemed to miss every fourth beat, so his internal metronome waltzed instead of marched, his thoughts, off balance. His breathing was shallow and rough, like the rapids at Mill Creek. He could feel his pulse at his temples and along his collar. The tips of his ears felt hot.

He wondered if he'd be able to make it through Sam's eulogy. Sam had been his best friend since elementary school almost seventy years ago. They'd grown up and grown old together. Cheever had married Margaret two days after high school ended. Sam had married her sister, Ann. Sam and Ann had a long and happy life together, celebrating their golden anniversary just two days before Ann died in a car crash. Margaret passed a decade later...to the day. In the same way that Ann's death had rendered Sam without purpose, Margaret's passing had ripped a hole in Cheever's existence.

Before that day at Sam's service, his most recent eulogy had been for Margaret, six months and four days ago. So, so much had changed in that half year. There was no going back; Cheever knew this but there was, as he learned, no going forward either.

If asked, he might be tempted to say that he couldn't rightly recall the first time he stood behind the pulpit, but that's not because his memory was failing. Instead, the eulogy had been so unflaggingly awful that he preferred not to remember. He stammered, he lost his place, he didn't pause for effect or significance, he didn't know what to do with his hands, his eyes were unfocused, and his feet felt rooted. He used the phrase "words cannot describe" and then tried to do just that. Yet somehow, everyone who came up to him afterwards remarked on his composition and his composure.

Compounding his misgivings was the fact that the first eulogy had been for his father, delivered on September 19, 1964. Pre-Cumidin, pre-pacemaker, pre-back-up-and-at-'em recovery regiment, his father's first heart attack was followed by two weeks of bed rest. On the fifteenth day, James Cheever Snell Senior stood...and fell straightaway, his feet swept out from under him by the second scythe swing of myocardial infarction. This time, his soul followed his body down. Down, down, down, onto the bedroom floor, out the front door, feet first, and on to eternal rest. And it fell to him, James Snell's youngest son, to herald his days above ground.

Looking back, he had many theories about what made it possible to stand at the front of the church and recite the virtues, but not the vices, of his father...even though the latter outnumbered the former three to one. Maybe that's why Joe and John, his older brothers, deferred when asked to speak, for their recollections would have been more pained as they too often bore the brunt of his temper. Instead, they sat in the front row and looked up at him. For the first time in his life, his brothers looked up to him.

During the few passages where emotion had snuck up on him, he flashed back to the damage done to his father by the bottle. Cheever soldiered through, describing the man as he'd been before drink grabbed him by the throat. Cheever pushed beyond the falter, claimed his space on the altar, and took control of the tremble. Cheever held steady.

In the end, he managed not only to eulogize his father, but flat-out lionize him. He found the five most complimentary moments in his father's life and moved them front and center. He embellished the truth, but just enough. Last, he found a couple of metaphoric apples in the overgrown orchard of his father's time on this earth and polished them up until they shone like the flashing lights at the railroad crossing running through the middle of town. He buried the bad, along with his dad, and everyone was as grateful for his omissions as they were for his commissions.

Afterwards, his brothers, relatives and neighbors embraced him, patted him on the back, blessed him. He remembered thinking it was crazy, he wasn't the man of the hour, that was his father. But it was his father's finest hour... and he had helped make it so.

Eulogy number two was for his Uncle Jerry. As he spoke the first few lines, he winced when he felt a flourish swirl up inside him, just as the mid-winter snow swirled outside the window in the gray twilight. At that very moment, he believed he had found his real calling. It was a post he'd never applied for, likewise, one that probably never actually existed: eulogist. Cheever became the designated hitter for the home team. He was the man whom the town of Harris, Indiana, trusted to say the right things.

There was nothing in his background that would make anyone think he had a talent for praising the dead. He was a simple farmer, turning the earth on the same 200 acres that his grandfather had bought after coming back from World War I, land that his father tended thereafter.

Cheever would be the first to say that he had no predisposition to public speaking or turning a phrase. More precisely, what he did seem to have a knack for was knowing which phrase not to turn. Clichés held no quarter in his fond farewells. Sympathy card sentiments never made their way into his text.

Silver-tongued, they claimed, but only he knew that it wasn't his tongue. It was his ears, and it was Margaret. The two of them would spend two or three days sitting with family and extended kin, listening for the telling detail — a flower still worn in the lapel, a Kleenex tucked into the sleeve of a sweater, the first car, the first date, the first child. Margaret would ride along with him in the car to these meetings, and then silently sit at the kitchen table or on a chair in the corner of the room. Cheever would sit on the couch, often between members of the grieving family, extending an arm around their shoulders when emotion overtook them. Margaret took notes almost surreptitiously, allowing Cheever to ask a question every now and then without distraction.

A few days later, in the formal ceremony of final goodbyes, he'd repeat what they shared in an emotionally controlled and eminently constrained way. It wasn't magic — it was simple, small-town kindness and consideration.

Once or twice early on, he felt put off by a family, as if they might be clamoring for special sanction, in the way that a bride might covet a certain caterer. He later saw through his misperception though, realizing it was simply the family's grief morphing into clumsy conversations while trying to make arrangements. This part, he knew, he could help them with, so he'd set their minds at ease with multiple reassurances and a parting gift that sang like the choir.

The third eulogy was for Aunt Rose, and by then, he almost felt as if he knew which buttons to push, and when. A dramatic pause after a semi-bashful admission or a wistful romantic recollection of a nephew to his fetching, favorite aunt.

When he sat back down, his heart sounded a steady thump-thump in his chest, counterpoint to the missing beat from the casket. What struck him though was that he didn't feel the shortness of breath or the racing pulse that betrayed nerves from speaking in front of others. He'd found his sweet spot.

He spoke at all five churches in town: Methodist, Lutheran, Presbyterian, Baptist, and the innocuous vanilla catch-all: Harris Christian. Curiously, he never attended any of these churches on Sunday, preferring to drive Margaret over to the next county so they could pray without the mantle of piety or the specter of a recent passing, be it imagined or real.

Cheever once told his brother Joe that what he came to like most was making his way through the back entrance of each house of worship; Margaret never accompanied him there, choosing to stay in the car until the service began. Cheever later told her that he believed that regardless of how much gold leaf or how many colorful tapestries might adorn the sanctuary, the soul of the church was borne up by how well the hallways and side rooms were maintained, spaces inhabited only by clergy and select few others from the community. If the walls that were hidden from the masses were painted regularly, if the floors were swept and the glass globes of the light fixtures were cleaned of flightless moths...all was indeed good there. But if plaster patches lingered or chairs were stacked, but not tucked out of the way — Cheever thought of one church in particular this way, although he'd never say so in public — he'd make certain that the grieving family would only enter and depart through the front doors.

Eulogy four — Uncle Lee. Cheever remembers opening his closet and not finding a presentable suit for the service. A farmer is never a dandy or a clothes horse, but Uncle Lee had been the mayor of Somers, the town that shared the western border of Harris. Cheever felt he had to be respectful to the office as well as his uncle. Cousin Bill, Lee's son, owned the men's wear shop on the square, so when Cheever and Margaret came by to interview him for his recollections, he decided to buy a new suit. They spent hour after hour talking, back by the mirrors and the fitting rooms. A tape measure hung around Bill's neck like a scarf. Both Cheever and Bill were pleased that off-the-rack black fit him perfectly, Cheever due to his frugalness, Bill because he knew he couldn't get anything tailored in time. Margaret waited.

Still and all, Cheever was a pragmatist, so he bought another suit while there: a grey one, both the same cut, both the same label. Bill had written in a discount when totaling it up, but never mentioned it — Margaret found and reported on the handwritten receipt that surfaced months later in his overcoat pocket.

For subsequent funeral services, Cheever appreciated the formalness that the material itself seemed to possess and project; it propped him with the tang and twill of sorrow and sobriety. So different from his normal appearance in coveralls and flannel shirts. Later, maybe the second or third decade, he felt sad when lifting the selected hanger off the pole, for it meant another death had come to Harris, a limestone quarry town that was quietly expiring as well. During the last few years, his remorse had evolved to resolve to extend deserved respect to the proceedings, and the jacket and matching slacks were now his uniform, like a military honor guard.

Almost ironically, but certainly heartbreakingly, his mother had never been eulogized. He knew if he could go back in time, what he would have delivered that day would simply have been a love letter spoken aloud. He would have rendered his angel real in words and appreciations, as he had also done for his Margaret 80 years later.

His mother had died in childbirth, delivering him. It wasn't so uncommon back then, in the 1930s. But what had made it tragically unexpected is that she had birthed two healthy boys prior. His father was grief-stricken, didn't speak to anyone for days, couldn't even raise his eyes to the congregation as he stood silently at the pulpit. After an eternity of five silent minutes (Cheever had been told this only years and years later), James Snell Sr., almost cracked in half as a cry rattled out of his throat.

So began the near-isolation the Cheever and his brothers grew up in, a self-imposed almost-exile that effectively cut off the family from the rest of Harris and allowed his father's drinking to go undetected for over two decades.

After Uncle Lee's funeral, Cheever traced the branches of his family tree in his mind's eye, acknowledging that he'd better be ready, like a doctor on call, as his hardy, hard-working aunts and uncles and neighbors were falling and failing fast, virtually in a flock, succumbing to the final indignities of age and illness. A broken hip leading to a nursing home. The flu leading to hospitalization. It seemed that as soon as they had been whisked away from their homes, the four horsemen of the modern era would descend upon them: pneumonia, Parkinson's, Alzheimer's, and cancer. And no one ever seemed to transition back to home care, so a month or two or three later, Cheever would get the call, a cousin or a neighbor asking if he'd be able to say a few words for the parent who had just passed on.

As the very youngest of all the kin, his older cousins began to falter and fall as well. They had lived the good life in comparison to their parent's generation, but they were fast on their heels toward their respective holes in the hillside. But it was the excess of modern living that chased them: diabetes, obesity, drinking and drugs. Same outcome, though. His second cousin Roger, eulogy fourteen, had all four...and a super-sized coffin to go with it. Cheever was shocked by the sheer width of the cabinetry — it almost seemed square, instead of rectangular, but getting 300 pounds to fit right took some custom carpentry. Standing alongside in his grey suit, white shirt, a dark blue tie, Cheever felt a bit like a maître de at Harris' one fancy restaurant, perched out by the interstate, where clearly Cousin Roger had deposited too many paychecks. It seemed like they were burying a piano.

Paradoxically, as the public speaking became easier, the preparation proved more difficult. He found that having a couple drinks did indeed loosen the flow of words and memories, as he'd spend hours talking through with Margaret and detailing the who and when and where. But then he could tell the next day if he'd had one or two too many — the dateline would elude him, the special moments shared by kin seemed thin in his description, so Margaret would pull out her notes and together they'd re-stitch the quilt of memories. Mindful not to slip into his father's and Faulkner's shared pitfall — if a glass is good, a Mason jar is better — he pulled himself out of this spiral before he crashed.

Sam's funeral came on an early spring day. The minister left church doors open at the end of the aisle to welcome in the promise of a rebirth of seasons. As Cheever stood there, his eyes raised above the heads of the congregation, he struggled to place precisely where he was. There were three funeral homes in town: one that catered to the Presbyterians, one for the Baptists, and one for everyone else. There were the five churches but not a single temple, mosque, or cathedral. On a few occasions, the memorial service would be held at the funeral home or at the individual's home if that was their stated wishes. Here too Cheever was made welcome for he was regarded as the third player in the earthly trinity of mortician, funeral home director, and eulogist. So, while he knew he was welcome, where was he? Where was Margaret? Where was Sam?

After Margaret passed, Cheever would find himself often driving without a destination. As he traced the roads of Harris, Indiana and throughout Brown County, his mind would riffle through the names and faces. He remembered the service, the chapel that accompanied each one's final firmament. If it fell to lawyers to recite the last will and testament, cloistered in a dark-paneled office, divvying up the meager or mighty assets between the family, his role was the opposite: a public, but always cheering, effusion of emotions and cherished memories, shared with one and all, freely, spoken and shared during the light of day, often with the sun sparkling through cut glass windows, colors dancing.

Before Margaret's, there'd been three funerals that marked him irrevocably, two that shook him terribly, and one that mystified him still. The first began without a sound.

Mort, as he was known by everyone in Harris, never awoke one morning in June. As the town's postmaster, he knew everything about everyone, ranging from who sent whom a Christmas card, to who was getting letters from collection agencies, to judging the cuteness of the ever-diminishing next generation via birth announcements.

The whole "neither rain, nor snow, nor gloom of night" fit Mort like his trim jacket which snapped at the waist and the wrists. No one knew the last time when the mail didn't come. But no one *knew* Mort: he was a fixture with his mail jeep, delivery bag and boots, but the statue downtown possessed a stronger personality that did Mort himself.

No one in that small town knew who Mort was or what he did when he wasn't delivering mail. Except fishing, they knew that, seeing his pole angled in the back of the mail jeep. He may have been the only government employee so brazen about his avocation, then again, he was the only federal employee in Harris.

So in that second week of June, 1998, three amazing things happened in very short order. First, Mort failed to show up for work on Monday. By noon, a call had been placed to the main USPS 800 number and some higher-up was alerted that Mort, the mail carrier was missing.

Turns out, Mort lived, and died, two counties over. When Larry Jones, the Harris police chief and Rob Thomas, the local police chief of Saxton, Indiana, turned the unlocked knob on Mort's front door, they found him peacefully, yet stiffly, stretched out on his couch in the living room. Second, while searching his house, no next of kin turned up. No photos, no personal phone book, no credit cards in his wallet, no notations on the calendar hanging in the kitchen, no cell phone with last numbers called. Zero, nothing, zilch.

Hence the third remarkable event, uncovered when Chief Larry Jones and the postal supervisor showed up at the Harris post office. As the anteroom was never locked so that folks with PO Boxes could pick up their mail any time, there was a slot that connected to the back room for sorting mail and storing supplies. The townspeople of Harris, fearing that there was no insurance policy to bury Mort, had paid their respects rather literally by slipping one dollar bills, five dollar bills, twenty dollar bills, and even two fifty dollar bills, through the brass slot marked Outgoing Mail.

A mound of green bills with the occasional wink of silver greeted the two visitors. The supervisor nudged the pile with his foot. Chief Jones, as he later described the scene to Cheever, waited and wondered what the other fellow was going to do. Larry said he would have bet that the post office supervisor wouldn't have reported anything about the money if "the law" hadn't been there with him.

"What's all this?"

"Guess that's Harris' way of taking care of their own. We're paying his expenses."

"Don't need it. The postal carrier's union and his pension fund will cover everything. That's the post office's way of taking care of their own," the supervisor said with a tiny sneer. Nonetheless, he added, there was no reason for anything beyond a standard casket, nor any need for flowers or catered food.

"Did he have any kids? A wife?" Larry just shook his head to all his questions. At the same time, Larry was incredulous — didn't this guy who'd been Mort's boss for the last few years have any clue as to next of kin! Wasn't there a file and paperwork with Mort's name on it somewhere?

It was decided, by whom no one knew for sure, that Mort's funeral instead would simply be a memorial service that weekend, as things had gone on long enough, and the last thing anyone wanted, at that point, was to uncover anything messy. The money was donated to the town's park fund, marked specifically for keeping Memorial Lake stocked with fish.

Mort's fishing pole leaned against the lectern, and his mail bag was draped across the front. Unlike most other services, there were no shorter remembrances offered by others, so Cheever rose from his seat in the back of the room after Minister Dean finished his prayer.

No surprise, the preparation of this eulogy had posed a problem for Cheever: no family members nor extended relatives to consult with meant no favorite stories. Cheever was tempted to use platitudes and spin something out of whole cloth, but that somehow seemed grievously unprofessional to the unofficial fraternity of eulogists.

So he flipped it, explaining to those gathered that the redeeming part of the mystery of no history meant there were no black marks on his record, that he had performed his duties admirably and consistently, that he'd provided devoted service to everyone without begrudging his tasks or belittling the job. He always smiled, quiet, yet friendly.

Cheever privately reflected that he, like Mort, was destined to take many secrets to the grave. So many things he knew but never shared. His job was to let everyone gathered know that this life now lost meant something positive, that it counted more than just an obituary. As the Buddhists would say, just being there was enough.

Recollecting Mort brought a wry smile to Cheever's face; whereas the two tragedies twisted his features and set his face hard like stone.

Tom Tellingham killed himself at the age of 17. His mother, who was Cheever's second cousin on his father's side, found the boy's body in his bedroom, an empty bottle of pills at his side. The family, the school, the town were a wreck. People couldn't speak to each other without breaking down, collapsing into an embrace that propped them up as much as it comforted them.

Sniffling and shaky hands clutching the paper programs were the only sounds that day. Cheever knew that it was extremely thin ice and that if he touched any raw nerve, the barely contained emotion in the room would flood the service, so he kept his remarks short.

"The universal challenge is to leave this world a better place. The past few years have forged in me the unquestioned devotion to the three things that sustain me: family, service to friends, and life's calling.

"Two days ago, young Tom ended his life, a tragedy that has marked everyone who knew him. Tom was the child of my oldest cousin. He was loved by one and all. We wish we had more answers, instead all we have our memories.

"But in his relatively short time on this earth, I do believe he left it as a better place. He was a sweet kid, and it seemed like his future was limitless. We *all* miss him and anticipate that the family will find a way to keep his light shining. Thank you for your understanding and support, as always. We'll find our way back to balance, and hopefully understanding, one day, one step at a time."

No note had ever been found. No whispered circumstances had ever come to light. No one in Harris ever got any closer to understanding why Tim took his own life.

But the worst, if that's possible, was the death of Sam's son, Chuck. Blasted by a thirteen-year-old Vietcong, blazing away with a gun that was longer than he was tall and a box of ammo half his weight. It was preposterous to have a thirteen-year-old and an eighteen-year-old shooting at one another in those killing fields. Rice paddies seemed so tranquil in photos, tender shafts of green, thin yet strong like the dragonflies that zipped about.

Chuck Smith was only 18. Boys sent to fight the wars for old men, he'd heard that before...and it was true. So no, not preposterous but hideous. And heartless. And wrong.

The bullets not only tore a hole through Chuck, they also ripped open Sam's soul forever. Chuck had been a short-timer, due to ship out less than two weeks later. A twenty-year-old, scared-shitless, Ivy-League ROTC, green lieutenant decided his new unit needed to take action, be bold, and he led them...no, he ordered them to advance into the too-quiet village where no one was seen and nothing moved.

Afterwards, the other soldiers in the platoon, upon seeing Chuck fall, pulled out their M-72 and erased the Vietnamese village from the planet; that was the only word for it. Erased the three huts on the edge of the jungle, wiped it gone. The only reason that they knew Chuck's mortal enemy was so young was by the medic's review that the gunman still had some of his baby teeth.

Most of this wasn't in the eulogy nor did he tell the gruesome parts to Sam. Cheever had done more research, talking with another Marine from Indianapolis. He said there were three casualties that day: Chuck, the Vietcong, and the lieutenant who, after Chuck has been killed, was told to stand behind when they retaliated. The backfire from the anti-tank guns wiped clean his senses, and he spent the remaining thirty years wasting away, never leaving his ward in a VA hospital. Dead, no; gone, yes.

Would a eulogist deliver such news? No.

Flashing forward from the testament he delivered from Sam's son valor, he focused on how wrong the sequence felt — fathers are supposed to die before sons, not the other way around.

Cheever looked up. A sea of faces...every one of them at least a decade younger, most two decades, half again only half his age. In a few years, if he lasted that long, he'd be the same age as the first line of the Gettysburg Address: fourscore and seven. His grandfather and Sam's grandfathers were both born in the twilight years of the 1800s. Numerically and historically, that was still hard to grasp, going from a time of horses and railroads to wood-burning stoves an era of private jets, mobile phones, and microwaves.

He picked up his papers, folded and unfolded them. He wobbled a touch. Later that day, there were some in the congregation who would tell one another that at that moment, they thought he was going to faint. Or perhaps even more unthinkable, that he'd return to his seat without saying a word.

Cheever slid his hands along the side of the podium, gripping it solidly. He gazed toward the very back of the church — the dark brown doors were now closed. He knew the ushers had released the doors so that those folks seated in the back could hear. At the same time, he knew the sun was shining outside and he wanted to see it. He wished he could ask the ushers to open those doors and let the fresh air in again.

His lips drawn tight, he pushed his glasses up to rest on the top of his head. His shoulders turned as if to suggest that he was going to leave that spot without saying a word. But then the shoulders squared back to the congregation, he bowed his head, looked up and smiled. "Sam Smith was my best friend. I will miss him deeply."

"For everyone here, I can only hope that each of you someday, with someone, can enjoy a friendship like Sam and I. I can see now, I truly loved him.

"I also loved his wife, Ann." He knew if he paused too long on that line, an eyebrow or two would be raised and a rumor would rustle, so he quickly added: "As I loved Chuck, their son."

Waiting a beat, "And I *really* loved Ann's sister, my Margaret." At this revelation, the crowd relaxed some and smiled knowingly. Cheever was back in gear; he was going to get through this.

"Soon, I will follow them all along the path to heaven knows where. Sam, and Ann, and Margaret, and the entire previous generation of Harrises will meet me there. All of them. All of us.

"Let me share with you some of the many things he taught me, told me, showed me, and thereby, some of the things he gave to me." Cheever saw two men in the second-row glance at their wristwatches, then pass a knowing look between them, a g-sign as clear as the green flag at the Indy 500.

His hands now squeezed the side of the pulpit so tight he could feel the wood grain that had been worn almost-smooth over the years — hold on, he told himself. Hold on for Sam. For the next twenty minutes, never checking his notes, never turning the page, Cheever reminisced about the life and times of one Sam Smith. He shared stories of them as boys camping out on the banks of Mill Creek. He told the tale of Sam driving to Washington D.C. to "wring the necks of the gutless brass at the Pentagon who handed down his boy's death sentence."

As an aside, and also as a reflection of Sam's character, he repeated the conversation they had when he traded in Chuck's Mustang which had set in the side yard, waiting two patiently to be driven again. Sam told the car salesman, "Sure, I've thought about a new car, but that's about it, just thought about it. Maybe if I was a young man, I'd get a fast car. But there's something so conservative in the very core of my being that reminds me that having some souped-up sports car, while it's great out on some big open highway with no traffic, here in Harris, pulling in and out of the driveway, stop sign after stop sign, that'd be pointless. That's like going out with Sophia Loren and taking her to the grocery store. If you're with Sophia Loren, you go to the Riviera. If you have a fast car, you go to a racetrack. My car and my life are just fine for Harris. I want a safe car, a used car." The car he bought that day lasted twenty more years, until it sat idling at an intersection, not going anywhere but still in harm's way when Ann was hit head-on by a drunk driver. Cheever didn't tell those gathered in the church that part.

"The deal was, whichever one of us went first, Sam or me, the other would say the eulogy. But knowing that, he also gave me his final words to tell you all. He wanted me to say, "I'm done. This time on earth has made me look forward to rest. For everyone here, I have two words to give you. Go. Live."

Cheever folded the four pages back along the crease and slipped it into the inside pocket of his suit coat, patting it as it slid over his heart. Now it was Cheever speaking to the crowd. "I'm done too. Sam's is the last eulogy I will deliver. I hope I have served well those who passed before me. Feels like I've outlived everyone, well, except for you all." A laugh, limned with uncertainty as to whether laughing was ok, bubbled up from the congregation.

"Here's what I told Sam when he asked me what my final wishes were. My one request — have a program of music only. No words. Let's start a new tradition." Then Cheever, for the last time from his vantage point behind the podium, repeated Sam's benediction: "Go. Live."

And so, it seemed that everything had been settled. Harris and its townspeople would continue. The secrets that had been protected by Cheever's safeguarding would be taken with him to the grave with no one ever the wiser.

It's just there was one more secret, which no living being in Harris had any clue. James Cheever Snell Jr. could barely read or write, and some days not at all.

Nowadays, he'd be diagnosed as dyslexic, but back then, the label was slow. Up through junior high, his brothers Joe and John shielded him, writing out his essays. Once he even finagled his way out of a year-end test by wrapping his right hand in an Ace bandage, telling the teacher he'd gotten it hacked up by the thresher, and took the final as an oral test and aced it. Cheever got his driver's license before there was a written test and always made sure to renew it on time. Took all the important paper to the lawyers, a bit of a show that made them snicker, believing that Cheever felt his farm was so doggone important that the lawyers had to be consulted for every little thing. He bought seed by feel and smell. He listened to the weather reports on the radio, later on the TV. Margaret did all the family and farm correspondence, as did several the wives in Harris, nothing out of the ordinary there. But for Christmas cards and bank checks, he added his own signature, which he had learned by copying it a hundred times over.

When it came to the eulogies, it was Margaret taking notes in the corner who was his safety net, and although she did notice when the family member would lean forward toward Cheever and whisper some recollection, those were the words he never passed on, and she never asked.

Later, she'd listen to him, hour after hour, as he recited and practiced the final words for the friends and neighbors. Then when he did his run-through the day prior, she'd take it all down in shorthand, and type it up so it was written there on the papers kept in his jacket pocket when he did the monologue, just in case a family member asked for a copy afterward.

But without Margaret, this time the pages in his jacket pocket were blank. His safety net was gone. If the eulogy hadn't been for Sam, he'd have been adrift. Lost. Sam knew, too. He had helped Cheever go through the mail after Margaret was in the ground, sorting through the flyers, tossing out the junk mail, avoiding his best friend's glance of surrender. Never said anything, though.

Now Margaret, Sam, John and Joe were all gone. His confederates, his co-conspirators, his inner circle. The group that propped him up when it came to the written word. He knew as someone eighty-five years old that no one would be surprised if his memory got a little dodgy, his eyesight got worse, or if he claimed to not remember something because he wrote it down somewhere but couldn't find the note he had made.

But the clock was ticking — he knew that soon he'd have to move from the farmhouse where he'd spent his whole life. There'd be something he'd miss in the mail, and he was far too old to seek out another "reader." So, he prepared for the inevitable…the move to the nursing home where others would take care of the paperwork.

Maybe, he thought, he could become the oral historian for Harris, Indiana. That, too, was a post that no one ever applied for, likewise one that probably had never existed, even as a fleeting notion before Cheever thought of it. That'd be a good job for him. More service to the community. Better than choosing which songs he wanted to be sung at his funeral.

It was time for him to go.

There were still reasons for him to live.

{10} RUSSIAN LULLABY

JERRY KATHMAN

Every night, you hear her croon
A Russian lullaby

Just a plaintive, simple tune
When baby starts to cry

Rock-a-bye my baby
Somewhere maybe

There's a land that's free
For you and me

That's a Russian lullaby

(Irving Berlin wrote these lyrics in 1927)

The children were finally napping, and as was her habit, Irena prepared tea. The radiant warmth of the filtered sun through the kitchen window, along with her steaming cup of chai, brought a calming peace to a cold winter afternoon — calm to a life that had known little peace. Irena Churayev never imagined life as a nanny. She never imagined life in America. Imagining a future at all was a luxury her life had ill afforded her. Who could have imagined any of the events that shaped her life; the Revolution, the Civil War, the terror, the purges, the Siege of Leningrad or life in a forced-labor camp in Germany. But here she was in Passaic, New Jersey, of all places, learning a new language and new customs in a strangely optimistic new country. Grateful. Confounded. Emotionally exhausted, but alive. Helping to raise someone else's children. The year was 1949.

She grew up a daughter of privilege. Her father, Anatole Churayev was Dean of Mathematics at the GV Plekhanov Institute, which was founded in St. Petersburg in 1773 by order of Empress Catherine the II — Catherine the Great. It is the oldest engineering college in Russia, and is described by some as its MIT. Because of her father's position at the Institute, her family was prominent. The czar had knighted Professor Churayev with both the Orders of Saint Anna and Saint Stanislaus. Two grand pianos fit comfortably into their large parlor. It was a life that would be found in the pages of Tolstoy or on the stage of Tchaikovsky's *Nutcracker* ballet.

But Irena was born into a world in which revolution changed everything. In the beginning, there was hope. Czar Nicholas II had abdicated. There was, for a brief moment, a sense of optimism. Even the young editor of *Pravda*, a former seminarian from Georgia, Joseph Vissarionovich Dzhugashvili, supported Alexander Kerensky's provisional government. But when Lenin prevailed at the April 1917 Communist Party Conference, the editor and *Pravda* shifted to opposing the provisional government. Around this time, the young editor had adapted the name "Stalin" from the Russian word for "steel." He used it as both an alias and a pen name in his published works.

Soon Stalin was elected to the Bolshevik Central Committee. The committee voted in favor of an insurrection in October 1917. Lenin, Stalin and the rest of the Central Committee coordinated an insurrection against Kerensky. By November 8, the Bolsheviks had stormed into the Winter Palace. Kerensky's Cabinet had been arrested, and the comfortable life that the Churayevs were living soon ended. Civil war broke out in Russia, pitting Lenin's Red Army against the White Army, a loose alliance of anti-Bolshevik forces. Within a few years, however, all pockets of resistance were defeated.

Out of the Central Committee, Lenin organized a five-member Politburo, including Stalin. In 1922, Lenin suffered a stroke, forcing him into retirement in Gorki. Although Stalin visited him often, their relationship deteriorated during this period. Lenin was aware of Stalin's excessive ambition. He suggested that Stalin be removed from the position of general secretary. Stalin, however, saw to it that Lenin's views were never known. Lenin's *Testament* was never revealed at the Twelfth Party Conference in April 1923. With the death of Lenin in 1924, Stalin pushed for rapid industrialization and more central control of the economy, contravening Lenin's New Economic Policy. Stalin launched massive purges against his enemies, putting them on rigged show trials and having them executed or imprisoned in Siberian gulags. His campaign against alleged enemies culminated in the Great Purge, a period of mass repression in which hundreds of thousands of people were executed.

The "former people" suffered dearly at the hands of Stalin. In his book by that name, Robert Powell explains that this dreadful term, "former people," was used by Stalin for those who formed the Russian nobility or those who held positions of authority in the imperial era. They became "former people" and were thus designated as enemies. But because of his ambition to create an industrialized nation, Stalin was far more tolerant with certain "former people," including mathematicians and engineers. He simply needed their skills. Irena's father, a mathematician that trained engineers, thereby survived The Purges. Professor Churayev, of course, did not know that he would survive. He lived every day in fear. He had a suitcase packed by the door. The rare sound of a car motoring down the street in the middle of the night would awaken him. If he heard the car stop, the doors slam and the sound of heavy boots running across the pavement, he would quietly walk to the door hoping that his arrest would not disturb the sleep of Irena and her sister, Marisha. But, alas, the police would go to another door. He would hear the pounding and the screaming as someone else was dragged away into the night. He would quietly go back to bed and attempt to sleep.

Life took a dramatic turn for young Irena and her family when strangers were moved into their home. Following the Revolution, communal apartments, called *kommunalka*, emerged as a response to the housing crisis in Russia's urban areas. The idea of a communal apartment was consistent with the Soviet's "new collective vision for the future." Communal apartments were typically shared by multiple families. Each family had their own single room, which served as a living room, dining room and bedroom for the entire family. The hallway, kitchen, bathroom and telephone were shared among all the residents. Three families moved into Irena's home. This form of housing dominated the USSR for generations, and, remarkably, some communal apartments still exist today in certain districts of large Russian cities, including St. Petersburg.

People were driven from the countryside by poverty, collectivization, and the Soviet industrialization campaigns. The exodus put enormous pressure on existing urban housing accommodations. This led to a plan to "expropriate and resettle private apartments." The communal apartment was deemed revolutionary as it "united different social groups in one physical space." Irena's family apartment now belonged to the government and was shared with strangers. Life was now more difficult for young Irena and her family. The other occupants knew that the Churayevs were among those designated the "former people" — that the apartment had previously been their private home. They hated them for it — sabotaging their cooking and stealing their food whenever an opportunity presented itself.

Irena was also learning to speak quietly, if at all, in public. It was not just about the possibility that someone would overhear her say things that were deemed counter-revolutionary. Even the structure and sound of her speech revealed a grace and sensibility that was at odds with the newly emerging Soviet proletariat language.

The codification of revolutionary doctrine into unambiguous and powerful symbols used in visual propaganda, such as posters, art, and political cartoons, is certainly well documented. Less well understood is that the function of the Russian language itself had become a vehicle of propaganda. In any society, language functions as a means of reflecting and shaping culture and values. The discourse of revolution had brought a vast range of neologisms, acronyms, and new compounds into the Russian language. The meaning of Russian words had sometimes changed and foreign borrowings were frequently used. Substandard slang expressions coexisted with high Marxist rhetoric and bureaucratic terminology in a strange new stylistic mixture. Bolsheviks believed that a new language was to be found in the creativity of the liberated toiling masses. They desired that the newly created proletarian intelligentsia would express themselves in the "language of the factory and the farm." It was believed that this form of social engineering would improve the link between the state and the people, and would allow the masses of the peasantry, led by the informed urban proletariat, to participate in the construction of the new state. This baffled the young Irena. If she spoke to her mother or sister on a streetcar using the Russian language she spoke at home, she was spit upon by fellow passengers who embraced the new Soviet-speak language. Silence in public became the means by which she protected her dignity.

Even today among the Russian diaspora in Paris, London or New York, Russians in the briefest of conversations can determine when a fellow Russian speaker left the motherland — during Czarist times or after the Revolution. Modern Soviet Russian language offends the sensibility of those whose families left Russia before the Revolution.

Life continued to deteriorate for Irena's family. Fear and petty humiliations were daily occurrences. But a visit to the opera, which, surprisingly, thrived during this period, offered what Irena would later describe as the only truth left in Soviet Russia. A surprising thing happened to opera in this period to make that so.

The three countries with totalitarian systems, Soviet Russia, Fascist Italy, and Nazi Germany, politicized opera. Opera companies, however, did not lose quality during this strict oppression. According to Irina Kotkina, in her study concerning the art form in this period, she argues, that instead, the formalization of the classical repertoire- — as we know it today — was established. Though the general aims of the regimes were dissimilar, each in their way attempted to create a model art that reflected the ideology of their respective new social order. Creating a new opera became a perilous occupation. New operas in Russia needed to fit the goal of the Soviets. The prohibition of certain new works by artists that did not fit into the appropriate style (the most familiar case being Shostakovich) led to a decided preference among Russian opera houses for the classics. There was simply less risk in staging established opera. Opera became a kind of "museum" spectacle.

For Irena, the timeless themes of the classical repertoire — fidelity, integrity, honor, and love — presented a window into a rare world unmanipulated by the commissars. Her lifelong passion for opera was formed at this time. Opera gave Irena hope that there was life beyond the cruelty of Stalin's Russia.

The invasive nature of the Soviet system continued to enter every aspect of the Churayev home. One evening, a student visited Professor Churayev with a question concerning work he had been assigned. The student noticed an icon hanging in the corner of the family's single room in the communal apartment. Russian icons in religious homes hang on the wall in the "krasny ugol" or beautiful corner. That was the case in the Churayev home. The student reported the professor to the authorities. A man in his position would lose his job if he were a believer. Professor Churayev assured the authorities that the icon was a silly manifestation of his superstitious wife, Olga, and it meant nothing to him. He assured the authorities that he would remove it at once.

Professor Churayev was in fact a believer. But he made the right decision — one I believe most of us would make. Denying his faith would quickly put the matter behind him and preserve his family. Proclaiming his faith would destroy everything. But the shame of that moment haunted the professor the rest of his life.

Soviet policy toward religion was based on the state's Marxist-Leninist ideology, which made atheism the official doctrine of the nation. The system advocated the control, suppression, and eventual elimination of religion. The state destroyed churches, mosques, and temples, and ridiculed, harassed, and executed religious leaders. Religious beliefs and practices, however, persisted among the majority of the Russian population in the domestic and private spheres of life including the Churayev home. Irena's Russian Orthodox church suffered terribly, and many of its members were killed or sent to labor camps. In the period between 1927 and 1940, the number of Orthodox churches in Russia fell from around 30,000 to fewer than 500.

In 1929, Soviet policy brought new legislation that would form the basis for harsh anti-religious persecution in the following decade. Anti-religious education was introduced from the first grade up and anti-religious propaganda was intensified throughout the education system. A massive purge was conducted at the same time of Christian intellectuals, many of whom died in the camps or in prison. Eliminating church intellectuals assisted the state's propaganda that only backward people believed in God. At first, the church was successful at competing with the ongoing and widespread atheistic propaganda. This prompted additional laws to be adopted against "religious associations" as well as amendments to the constitution, which forbade all forms of public, social, communal, educational, publishing, or missionary activities for religious believers.

Stalin used the same methods and terror tactics against others he considered ideological enemies. In his book, *Russia: A Short History*, Abraham Ascher presents statistics that reveal the scope of Stalin's war against his own people. According to information released by the Soviet government after Stalin's death, about half the entire officer corps of the army (thirty-five thousand men) were arrested, including three out of five marshals, thirteen out of fifteen army commanders, seventy-five out of eighty-five corps commanders, one hundred out of one hundred ninety-five division commanders, ninety percent of all generals and eighty percent of all colonels. The number of people in high positions in the civilian sphere who were charged with crimes against the state is equally astonishing. For example, over 1,100 out of 1,966 voting and non-voting delegates at the Seventeenth Party Congress in 1934 were arrested.

Many of the accused were shot. Many lower ranking party members were purged and then either executed or sent for long periods to the gulags, where conditions were ghastly. A large number of ordinary citizens too were shipped off to these camps for minor infractions of regulations or for no reason except that they were suspected of counter-revolutionary sympathies.

It is not known exactly how many ended up in the camps, but there is no doubt that the number ran to millions. Even the most conservative estimates suggest that at the time of Stalin's death in 1953, there were over 5 million citizens in various camps, colonies and "special settlements." Other estimates reasonably put the figure closer to ten or twelve million. No one disputes that the security force, which administered the Gulag, was the single largest employer in the Soviet Union. It is also difficult to determine how many were executed or died because of the horrendous conditions in the camps, but again, the number was huge. Historians have suggested that if one adds up all the people who died as a result of official Soviet policies, a figure of fifteen to twenty million is not unreasonable.

The life of the Churayevs in the 1930s was extraordinarily grim, and not only because of the terror. For one thing, shortages of essential goods, including bread, a staple at every Russian meal, were widespread. In recently opened archives, a scholar found a letter from a housewife to Stalin complaining "you have to go at two o'clock at night and stand until six in the morning to get two kilograms of rye bread." There were huge lines for bread and "often, going past these lines, Russians would hear shouts, squabbling, tears, and sometimes fights." Other foods such as meat, milk, butter, and vegetables as well as salt, soap, kerosene, and matches were also often difficult to obtain. The shortages of clothing were perennial, and the garments that were on sale were of shoddy quality. People who wished to mend their clothing could not find thread, needles, or buttons.

Given these circumstances, it is remarkable that the Soviet people were able to rise to a severe challenge early in the 1940s — war with Germany. Ideologically, Adolf Hitler and the Nazi party had posed a clear threat to communism ever since their rise to power in Germany in 1933. Marxism and Judaism were, in Hitler's view, Germany's twin enemies and he vowed to crush both. When Hitler became chancellor, the Soviets believed that his regime would not last long and that his policies would in the end help the cause of communism. Hitler would embark, the Soviets claimed, on a highly reactionary program that would antagonize the working class, who would be radicalized to the point of staging a successful revolution against Nazism. It did not take the Soviet leadership long to recognize the flaws in their analysis. By the mid 1930s it was clear that Hitler had crushed the working class social movement in Germany.

By the late 1930s the Western powers and the Soviet Union sought a unified policy to stop the expansion of Nazism. But the distrust between them was too great. Statesmen in Great Britain and France feared Germany but they also feared the spread of communism, which after the brutalities of Stalin's industrialization and collectivization seemed to be more menacing than ever. On the other hand, Stalin suspected that the leaders of the West were prepared to strike a deal with Hitler against the Soviet Union. In the end, Stalin calculated that Germany was the lesser danger to his country. On 23 August 1939, he signed the Nazi-Soviet Non-Aggression Pact, an agreement that struck many people, among them ardent socialist radicals worldwide, as a horrendous betrayal.

Within two years, Hitler was massing troops in the east, and despite many warnings from Winston Churchill and others that Germany was on the verge of attacking the Soviet Union, Stalin looked the other way. He simply would not believe that Hitler would betray him. When the German attack came, Stalin fell into a state of shock, utterly paralyzed, and for about seven days he was incapable of running the government.

The German Army was unstoppable. In armor, strategy, tactics and determination, it easily overwhelmed the Soviet Army. In one month, the German

Army under General von Bock's leadership advance five-hundred miles before encountering major resistance. In mid-October, the German Army stood at the gates of Moscow and for four days, from 15 to 19 October, Stalin suffered another nervous breakdown. By that time, the Germans had gained control over territories in which sixty million Russians (about thirty percent of the total population) lived. This territory contained two-thirds of the country's coal reserves and three-quarters of its iron ore. The Red Army had suffered staggering losses: thousands of Russian tanks, guns and airplanes had been destroyed or captured and the number of casualties endured during the first four months of the war ran to over three million.

Things quickly got much worse for the Churayevs. On 8 September 1941, Irena's life of humiliation, confusion, and scarcity was replaced by a genuine fear for her very life — death by means of starvation, cold, or German shelling. Her beautiful city, Leningrad, was under siege. With the participation of the Finnish Army, the German Army Group North surrounded the city and the longest and most destructive blockade in history — the most overwhelmingly costly in terms of human casualty — had begun. It would last until 27 January 1944, almost 900 days after it began.

Hitler's goal was the total destruction of the city and its population. According to a directive sent to Army Group North on 29 September, Hitler stated: "After the defeat of Soviet Russia there can be no interest in the continued existence of this large urban centre. ... Following the city's encirclement, requests for surrender negotiations shall be denied, since the problem of relocating and feeding the population cannot and should not be solved by us. In this war, for our very existence, we can have no interest in maintaining even a part of this very large urban population." Leningrad's value was both symbolic and strategic. The city's political status as the former capital and the place where the Bolshevik Revolution began would be a great propaganda victory for Hitler. The military value was significant because Leningrad was both a main base of the Soviet Baltic Fleet and an industrial centre containing numerous arms factories.

In the winter of 1943, the Churayevs were evacuated by means of the Road of Life, a route across the frozen Lake Ladoga, which provided the only escape from the besieged city. They were moved by the Soviet authorities to the south where they were quickly overrun by the advancing German Army. Along with thousands of starving Russians, the Churayevs were made prisoners of the

Third Reich. The family was herded into a boxcar so crowded that they could only stand. Packed with 60 other terrified, emaciated Russians, the family spent the next fifteen days in utter filth and fear arriving at last at their destination — a forced labor camp in Germany.

As Slavs, the Churayevs were considered Untermensch (German for under man, or subhuman). The term became infamous when the Nazis used it to describe "inferior people," especially the masses from the East, Jews, Gypsies and Slavic people. Though the word is associated with Nazism, the term "under man" was first used by Lothrop Stoddard, an American, in the title of his 1922 pamphlet *The Revolt Against Civilization: The Menace of the Under Man*. The term "Untermensch" was later adopted by the Nazis from that book's German-language version. Stoddard's definition of the under man is "A man who measures under the standards of capacity and adaptability imposed by the social order in which he lives."

Stoddard believed that the recent takeover of power by the Bolsheviks in Russia meant that the country was now ruled by the most degenerate people on earth. The combination of the alleged inherent racial inferiority of Russian Slavs with the idiocy of a political creed that appealed to the vilest of human instincts (jealousy toward the more gifted and more affluent) necessitated a new term to describe this phenomenon — the under man. To Stoddard, the October Revolution was the battle cry for an upcoming unavoidable clash between civilized and uncivilized nations.

In Nazi Germany, the term "Untermensch" was utilized repeatedly in writings and speeches directed against Jews, the most notorious being the 1935 SS publication with the title *Der Untermensch*, which contains an anti-Semitic tirade from a speech given earlier by Heinrich Himmler. An example of using the term "Untermensch" directed against Slavs is found in another brochure with the same title, *Der Untermensch*, published in 1942 at the start of the invasion of the Soviet Union by the Nazis. I'll quote from it: "Although it has features similar to a human, the subhuman is lower on the spiritual and psychological scale than any animal. Inside of this creature lies wild and unrestrained passions: an incessant need to destroy, filled with the most primitive desires, chaos and cold-hearted villainy. Not all of those who appear human are in fact so. Whoa to him who forgets it."

Hitler's intent was to reduce the numbers of Slavic people who both then and now are the most numerous of the European peoples. Importantly, unlike the Jewish people, the Nazis did not seek the complete elimination of the Slavic people. They saw Slavs as a valuable source of slave labor in the expansion of the post-war Reich — a slave race born to serve their Aryan masters. The concept of the Slavic people being Untermensch served the Nazis as justification for their aggression against Poland and the Soviet Union. The plans for the post-war German Reich, summarized in Generalplan Ost, envisioned the displacement, enslavement and the elimination of no less than fifty million people who were not considered fit for Germanization from the territories it wanted to conquer to the east.

According to research housed at the United States Holocaust Memorial Museum, the Nazi's subjugated millions of people (both Jews and other victim groups) into forced labor under brutal conditions. From the establishment of the first Nazi concentration camps and detention facilities in the winter of 1933, forced labor — often pointless and humiliating and imposed without proper equipment, clothing, nourishment or rest — formed a core part of the concentration camp regimen.

Initially, the Nazis imposed forced labor primarily on Jewish civilians. But as early as 1937, the Nazis increasingly exploited the forced labor of other so-called "enemies of the state" for economic gain and to meet increasing labor shortages.

Immediately following the German invasion of the Soviet Union, the Germans allowed millions of Soviet prisoners of war to die through a deliberate policy of neglect, insufficient food, clothing, shelter or medical care. By the spring of 1942, however, the German authorities changed policies and began to deploy Soviet military prisoners at forced labor in various war-related industries. From 1942–1944, the Germans also deported nearly three million Soviet civilians to Germany as forced labor, including the Churayev family.

So the timing of their capture by the Germans proved fortuitous. Had it been a few years earlier, the Churayevs likely would not have survived. A few years earlier the Nazis were simply pursuing a conscious policy of "annihilation through work." Prisoners were literally worked to death. Prisoners were forced to work under conditions that would directly and deliberately lead to illness, injury, and death.

So began life for the Churayevs under Hitler. They were no longer "former people" surviving the madness of Stalin. They were now Untermensch hoping to survive the madness of Hitler.

By the end of the war, civilian deaths in Europe totalled almost sixteen million, which includes 1.5 million from military action; 7.1 million deliberate victims of Nazi genocide, the Holocaust; 1.8 million deported to Germany for forced labor and 5.5 million from famine and disease deaths. In addition to the 16 million civilian deaths during the war, an additional 1 million died in 1946 and 1947 as famine continued in Europe after the war. Some of us remember our mothers telling us back then, "Finish your dinner — there are children starving in Europe."

At the end of the war, millions of non-Germans remained in Germany — a legacy of Nazi efforts to exploit for forced labor those they perceived as racial inferiors from lands to the east. This included the Churayevs, who were living day-to-day on the streets. They made their home, in fact, for a while in a newspaper kiosk. After life as "former people" and then "inferior people," a new term was now assigned to the Churayevs — "displaced people." A displaced person is someone who has been forced to leave his or her native land. The term was widely used during and immediately after World War II to describe the overwhelming flow of refugees from Eastern Europe. Preparations for dealing with the challenge of displaced persons were set in motion by the Allies during the war. In November 1943, representatives of 43 countries met at the White House and established the United Nations Relief and Rehabilitation Administration. Its objective was to plan for the provisions of food, clothing, medical supplies, and other forms of assistance to refugees when the war was over. The Allied forces in Germany would set up camps and assembly points where displaced persons would stay until they could be returned to their own countries. In 1945, responsibility for the care of displaced persons began for the now victorious nations — the United States, Great Britain, France and the Soviet Union — each in their respective occupation zones.

The Churayevs were suddenly aware that they were now in the Soviet zone. They were once again paralyzed by fear. Circumstances were sufficiently chaotic, however, that Professor Churayev had an opportunity to act on what would prove to be a fateful decision. He knew that what awaited them upon their return to Leningrad was likely imprisonment and death. The Soviets would see them as traitors for permitting themselves to be made prisoners. He moved his family west. Through incredible hardships they made their way into the American zone.

Over two million Soviet citizens were returned, willingly or unwillingly, to areas under Soviet control at the war's end — but not the Churayevs. In 1948 in the United States, Congress passed the Displaced Persons Act, primarily inspired by growing anti-communism — and growing awareness of what the Soviets were doing to their returnees. Its passage led to a timely relaxation of US Immigration policy, if sponsorship could be found.

After a year in a displaced persons camp for Russian speakers in the American zone in Germany, Professor Churayev happened upon a copy of a Russian-language newspaper published in New York City. He recognized the editor as a friend from his childhood. He sent a letter to New York seeking sponsorship of his family to the United States. Professor Churayev was convinced that the Soviets would conquer all of Western Europe in a short period of time. Only by getting to America, he believed, would he keep his family from returning to the clutches of the communists. His friend sponsored the family. Soon they were sailing into New York Harbor. So began life in America for Irena.

What must have gone through the mind of Irena, now a young adult, as she passed by the Statue of Liberty? Viktor Frankl, in his book *Man's Search for Meaning*, provides an understanding. (I am grateful to my fellow Literarian John Tew for sharing this book with me.) Frankl describes the three stages one goes through having experienced life in a forced labor camp. He describes the initial period of admission, followed by the period where one is entrenched in the camp routine, and finally the period following release and liberation.

The first stage is one of shock. Frankl's description of his arrival at the camp includes chaos, terror, and helplessness. This parallels the experience of the Churayevs. He then describes the routine of the camp, which involved a cold detachment of the mind from its surroundings. He quotes Dostoyevsky, who defines man as "a being who can get used to anything." Feelings are blunted. The prisoner soon surrounds himself with a very necessary protective shield. There is a daily struggle to maintain one's dignity.

Frankl then describes the final stage, that of the liberated prisoner. The day comes when looking back at his experiences, he can no longer understand how he endured it all. When the day of his liberation eventually comes, everything seems to him like a beautiful dream. So also comes the day when all his camp experiences seem to him like nothing but a distant nightmare. Frankl states, "The crowning experience of it all for the homecoming man, is the wonderful feeling that after all he has suffered, there is nothing he may fear anymore — except his God."

Terrible as it was, Frankl's experience solidified his ideas concerning life's meaning. Life is not primarily a quest for pleasure as Freud believed or a quest for power as Alfred Adler taught. Rather it is a quest for meaning. The greatest task for any person is to find meaning in his or her life, says Frankl. He saw three possible sources for meaning: in work (doing something significant), in love (caring for another person), or in courage (the attitude we take while suffering). Suffering in and of itself is meaningless. Frankl states, "We give our suffering meaning by the way in which we respond to it." Quoting Dostoyevsky again, "There is only one thing I dread: not to be worthy of my suffering." Work, love and the attitude she took toward her suffering would give meaning to Irena's life in America.

Irena completed her time as a nanny. She saved enough money to help with a down payment for a modest home in Passaic. By then, she was a young bride. Friends had introduced her to another displaced person, a young Russian soldier who, after fighting in the Red Army, found himself a refugee in Europe. He too knew that by returning to Russia, he would be thrown into the Gulag or worse. Jerislav Grubow was sponsored to the United States by kind strangers in a Lutheran parish in Passaic. Irena and Jerislav settled down and raised a family.

If I may, I leap ahead now thirty-five years to 1985. I am sitting next to Irena at the Metropolitan Opera, listening to Luciano Pavarotti and Montserrat Caballé perform in Puccini's *Tosca*. On my other side sits Irena's daughter, Elizabeth, my wife. The evening was spectacular. As the curtain closed, Irena turned to me and said, "Did you enjoy that, Jerry?" and what could I say but "Oh yes, it was magnificent." The next thing she said was curious — not the kind of comment one expects at the opera. She said "No one can ever take that from you, Jerry." Such a strange thought to share at such a joyous moment. Yet she felt compelled to say it, for it was the profound truth — the transcendental truth — that her life had taught her. Life is nothing but a series of experiences. Nothing material survives. In Irena's life, very little of the material survived.

But how she chose to respond to her suffering is a powerful inheritance for her family. Her example vastly exceeds the value of anything material.

The Orthodox Church Sunday liturgy includes a beautiful passage, which always moves me. The priest beckons the congregants to "bless thine inheritance." Honor all that comes before you — honor the wisdom of those who precede you.

My wife, Liz, and I travelled to Russia several years ago with our children Stefan and Alexandra. We visited Irena's neighborhood (or should I say Babushka's neighborhood, for she was by then only known by that name to our kids). Our children were both in school; our son studying at Harvard College and our daughter at Boston University, both possessing strong, curious, scientific minds. Minds that I am confident would have pleased Professor Churayev.

We stood on the stairs of the GV Plekhanov Institute, where Professor Churayev taught so many years ago. The wind was blowing heavy off the Neva River and an overcast sky framed my solemn mood.

My thoughts were of Irena. She lay in a bed back in Passaic well into her journey of dementia. No longer able to recognize us, but yet so much a part of us. Irena remains part of us and always will. This idea — that those who come before us remain part of us — is beautifully expressed in the opening scene of Tony Kushner's play *Angels in America*. I'll close with a reading from it.: "A Rabbi is speaking with a heavy Eastern European accent, paying respects at the passing of Sarah Ironson in the Bronx Home for Aged Hebrews. He says, 'I did not know this woman, and yet I know her. She was not a person, but a whole kind of person, the ones who crossed the ocean.' He turns to her grandchildren and says, 'You can never make that crossing that she made. For such great voyages in the world do not anymore exist. But every day of your lives, the miles of that voyage, between that place and this one, you cross. Every day. You understand me? In you, is that journey.'"

{11} BIRTH OF A ZOO

RICHARD KESTERMAN

EVEN THOUGH MUCH HAS CHANGED since it opened in 1875, the visitor to the Cincinnati Zoo & Botanical Garden today still has the opportunity to see a few remnants of its earliest days. What was originally the monkey house is now the reptile house, and the present passenger pigeon memorial structure is one of seven similar buildings that housed part of the Garden's collection of birds. Yet the most viewed reminder of the early days is the European house sparrow found living freely throughout the Garden.

Although the sparrow's presence in the area predates the zoo by several years, its inclusion in the collection is as much a result of Andrew Erkenbrecher's efforts as the Garden itself. It is part of a loosely connected chain of events that ultimately led to the formation of the Cincinnati Zoological Society.

For years, horticulturalists battled the region's caterpillars, which damaged not only fruit trees, but also many of the shade trees. From contemporary descriptions, the main culprits were the Eastern tent caterpillar and the fall web worm. Both of these species protect themselves in the larvae stage with webs spun either on the larger branches, as with the tent caterpillar, or on the smaller branches and leaves of the trees' outer growth, the case with the fall web worm. Two members of the Horticulture Society, William Orange and James Howarth, described their preferred methods of coping with these pests at a meeting of the Society in March of 1859. Mr. Orange recommended a pole with tarred rags on the end by which the gardener could pull the nest out of the tree and dispatch the caterpillars on the ground. Mr. Howarth, on the other hand, advocated two more aggressive methods. The first was to scorch the nests with "some inflammable matter;" the second was to shoot them out of the tree with blank cartridges. Both methods could potentially damage the trees. A few months later, an anonymous article in the newspaper called for applying suds from whale oil soap with a sponge attached to a pole. This method had the advantages of killing off the caterpillars and making their webs easy to dislodge while not causing lasting harm to the tree.

Throughout the 1860s, various articles appeared in the newspapers advocating the pruning of trees in which caterpillars had become a problem. While this method could, in fact, remove the egg cases found on the branches, it did not eliminate the potential return of the caterpillars and moths. There was also debate over just how much pruning should occur. Some proposed a judicious removal of branches, while others, including Dr. John Warder of the Horticulture Society, "recommended such severe pruning as will leave these cocoons without a live limb to tie to." The trees, he said, "may be cut nearly as bare as telegraph poles without danger of killing them." While it is true that the caterpillars would starve on a tree pruned so far back, the tree would also for a few seasons lose its usefulness as a shade or fruit tree.

A resolution of this problem started to materialize in the late 1860s when two German immigrants, Max Wocher and Andrew Erkenbrecher, experimented with importing and releasing sparrows on their properties to control the caterpillars. Wocher lived on the Ohio River two miles west of Anderson Ferry; Erkenbrecher lived on Seventh Street, but his sparrows were released near his starch factory in what was known as Starchtown in St. Bernard. Another immigrant, landscape architect Adolph Strauch, was responsible in part for introducing songbirds and waterfowl to Spring Grove Cemetery. His efforts were joined by several nearby lot owners that released birds in the cemetery with the hope of establishing them in the trees near the final resting place of loved ones.

Introducing the house sparrow to Cincinnati peaked in early 1869 when the City Council passed a resolution calling for the purchase and release of sparrows in four of the city parks. Eden Park and Lincoln Park were to receive one hundred pair of sparrows each, while fifty additional pair were to be released in Washington Park and Hopkins Park. While many of these birds became established in and around the parks, not all of them fared well. A newspaper article from the winter of 1871 describes the starving condition of the sparrows in Lincoln Park. The sparrows around Spring Grove Cemetery had more favorable circumstances in that the gatekeeper shared the food intended for the swans with them. Other individuals also released sparrows on their property, so that by 1872, the European house sparrow was well on its way to being an established species in Hamilton County.

With the successful introduction of sparrows, Erkenbrecher and others were encouraged to devise a plan to introduce an array of European songbirds into Cincinnati. In contrast to the sparrows, intended to control the caterpillars and other insect pests, the Acclimatization Society, formed in the winter of 1872, had the avowed purpose of introducing a wide variety of songbirds to liven the region with their beautiful melodies. Since most of these birds also included insects in their diet, their presence would also help control some of the area's pests.

The first supply of birds introduced by the Society were purchased and shipped in the spring of 1873 by Peter Schwan, a local cigar maker and bird fancier. The birds arrived at Schwan's shop on Main Street on April 27, and a couple days later were distributed to the various members of the Society. The birds were to be kept in their cages for a short while to become familiar with their new surroundings, after which they would gradually be freed. It was thought that the released birds would return to those still in their cages, after which, it was hoped that both sets of birds would remain near the release site once all were set at liberty.

An interesting side story to this is that the store of Peter Schwan had in it a starling that was reputed to be able to sing "'Wacht Am Rhein' with accuracy." According to a later lawsuit, the allegedly talented bird was purchased by a Mr. Frederick Hoeltge for seventy-three dollars. Upon getting the starling home, Mr. Hoeltge found that the bird would not sing the promised song or any song other than the tune which nature had granted it. He sued Schwan for the return of his money. Ultimately, that November, the judge ruled in favor of Peter Schwan, and Mr. Hoeltge was left with a very expensive but common starling.

These troubles and the resulting case may have led to some changes made to the Acclimatization Society. On May 15, Erkenbrecher announced that, "in the fall, a capable man — but not a bird merchant" would go to Germany to procure the birds for the following year. Erkenbrecher also hoped to interest the City Council, along with some other wealthy Americans, in the venture.

The Acclimatization Society's most consequential meeting to Cincinnati's fabric was held on June 19, 1873 in a room at the Board of Trade. Following the meeting, Erkenbrecher and Armin Tenner spoke with the members about a new venture that they had been exploring. Tenner, the secretary of the Society, had corresponded with noted German zoologist, Dr. Brehm of Berlin, about the possibility of establishing a zoological garden in Cincinnati.

This proposal was favorably received by those present, and a committee was formed to advance the idea to individuals who might be interested in backing this new enterprise. For the next month and half, the preliminary details of forming the Zoological Society moved at a brisk pace. On June 30, a meeting was held in which the incorporation of a joint stock company was ordered then effected on July 11. A minimum of ten percent of the stock needed to be sold before this incorporation became valid. This goal was reached by July 14, and two weeks later on July 28, a meeting was called to elect a Board of Governors.

On two weekends in August, a committee from the Zoological Society visited two of the city parks to determine if either site would suit the needs of the proposed garden. On August 11 Eden Park was visited, followed by a trip to Burnet Woods on the 23rd. While both locations had much to offer, it ultimately was felt that Eden Park lacked the older tree growth that was present in Burnet Woods. Lengthy negotiations began with the City of Cincinnati, of which more will be discussed later.

The end of August saw Armin Tenner ready to leave for Europe on a fact-finding mission. Tenner was given authority to represent the Zoological Society in the form of a letter addressed to the managers of the London Zoo and other zoological gardens on the continent. In addition, it is likely that Tenner made inquiries at this time in regard to the purchase of birds for the Acclimatization Society's next release of songbirds.

A financial panic in September 1873 slowed the work on the Zoological Gardens to a crawl. Little was done with the exception of creating a constitution and by-laws for the Society.

The work of the Acclimatization Society progressed at a much stronger pace. In contrast to the efforts of the spring, the birds purchased for release in 1874 were procured several months in advance, giving them the entire winter and part of the spring to adjust to their new environment. On November 28, the Society asked the City of Cincinnati for the use of a vacant house in Burnet Woods to store the newly imported birds. Moving rapidly through the City bureaucracy, permission was received on December 10, and Tenner returned to Cincinnati with a shipment of songbirds, first put on display at the Phoenix building on Vine Street, and shortly after, relocated to the house in Burnet Woods.

On January 5, 1874, the Zoological Society held its inaugural annual meeting. The first order of business was to ratify the constitution and by-laws, after which officers were elected for the ensuing year. Two weeks later on January 20, the directors of the Zoological Society met; at that time Tenner presented a report on what he had learned while visiting similar enterprises in Europe.

So far, the Zoological Garden existed only on paper. The lack of a parcel of property was a stumbling block, not only to selling shares of stock, but also to planning the buildings and grounds. A decisive step was taken on February 17, when a proposal was presented to the Park Board for obtaining a fraction over forty-five acres of ground on the southern end of Burnet Woods for perpetual use by the Zoological Garden's exhibits. This proposal not only required the land, but also stipulated cooperation from the City with regards to water service, security, and proper fencing to be provided at no charge to the Society.

On March 31, Armin Tenner announced that there would not be any further importation of birds planned by the Acclimatization Society. In the future, the Society would offer advice to those interested in pursuing the importation of birds but would not be taking an active role in the actual process. This decision may have been brought about by the anticipated success of the Zoological Society's proposal for the Burnet Woods site.

A little more than a month later, both societies would find their activities centered around Burnet Woods. On a Sunday morning in early May, Erkenbrecher and some of the other members of the Acclimatization Society went to the house where the songbirds had spent the winter and early spring to release them into their new surroundings. According to one source:

One window was opened, and a pair of nightingales appeared at the window, rested for a moment, and then flew to the limb of a tree and elevating their heads in the sunshine burst out in joyous song. Within the next few seconds, the birds fairly poured out onto the trees and shrubbery, filling the old woods with melody.

The month of May also began on a favorable note for the Zoological Society. In Mayor Johnson's annual message to the City Council, he spoke favorably of the prospect of the private enterprise...having a large zoological collection which would greatly add to the [Burnet Woods] attraction and make it a popular resort. On May 8, the proposed ordinance was presented to the Board of Aldermen, after which it made its way through channels to the City Council.

While the ordinance had a smooth beginning, it encountered rough waters in the Council. Since the Zoological Society was a private for-profit entity, public opinion was divided on it obtaining City land free of charge for its operation. Finally, after several revisions, the ordinance was passed by the City Council, only to be vetoed on July 9 by Mayor Johnson. One of the Mayor's concerns was that the Zoological Society, being a corporation, might make decisions in the future that would be detrimental to the park and the City's best interests. To lease the land without City representation on its Board was his greatest objection. The Mayor also questioned whether the amount of land proposed was not too much for what he referred to as an "experiment." Since it is unlikely that the mayor or those objecting to the ordinance had ever seen a zoological garden, some of their objections may have come from a simple fear of the unknown.

The Society made some additional efforts to obtain the Burnet Woods property but finally resigned itself to find a suitable site elsewhere. After a little over a month of searching, the luck of the Society in acquiring a piece of property was about to change.

In late August 1875, Curt Terne, a naturalist from Savannah, Georgia, was in Cincinnati to assist the Society with selecting a site. On September 4, the Zoological Society came to an agreement with William Wilshire for the lease of almost sixty-seven acres located for the most part in the southwest corner of Avondale. Although it is not known how much influence Terne had with this decision, by the 15 September, he had secured the position of superintendent for a period of three months. Around the same time, Theodore Findeisen was hired as engineer and landscape gardener.

The property selected had, at an earlier date, been divided into twenty irregularly shaped lots. Lots number one and two were the property of Thomas French, dairyman. These two lots remained with French while the other eighteen were leased to the Zoological Society. There is no mention of any improvements on these eighteen lots, but given French's presence on lots one and two, it is likely that at least some of the property was used as pasture.

Julius Dexter, in the first annual report of the Society, described the land as follows:

> The [grounds] rise somewhat broken and abrupt from the Carthage Pike, and then become nearly level, and sloping gently to the north whence they command an extensive view. Three ravines run in or through the land. The most beautiful of these runs along the east line of the property, while the others start from near the middle of the ground, and run out northwardly. They all afford fine opportunity for the construction of pools and ponds.... To the north and east sides, the grounds have some trees.

On September 24 William Wilshire and his wife Frances transferred two-thirds ownership of the property to William's brother George and A.S. Winslow. The following day, the lease to the Zoological Society was finalized. The terms gave the Society perpetual lease to sixty-three point thirty-seven acres in section fifteen of Mill Creek Township, with an additional two point sixty-seven acres in section fourteen. The annual rent for the first five years was to be five thousand dollars, for the next five years, six thousand dollars, and after these initial ten years, the rent would remain at seventy-five hundred dollars a year. The terms also gave the Society the privilege of purchasing the property at a cost of twenty-five hundred dollars per acre.

Theodore Findeisen was occupied for much of September in surveying the property and creating a plan for improvements. This plan was accepted by the board on October 5, and work commenced shortly after. On October 29, the *Cincinnati Gazette* reported that 180 men were busy grading and beautifying the grounds.

Work continued until mid-December when it was decided to halt further landscaping until the spring. Initially, it was decided to extend Terne's contract as superintendent for an additional three months; however, by the end of the year, the board decided to terminate his employment, along with that of Findeisen. While no specific reason was given for these changes, costs had been higher than expected, and some discrepancies in materials ordered and on hand may have played a part. Also, while the board was satisfied with Findeisen's general plan, there was some disagreement with his ideas for the placement of structures.

January 1875 began with board meetings and planning, but apparently, little else was being done to the physical garden. In looking for a replacement for the superintendent, the board began corresponding with some of the zoological societies in Europe in hopes of finding someone with practical experience.

Meanwhile, on February 5, notice was given by the Society that proposals for "materials and labor in building a fence about 5,800 feet long around the garden" would be accepted until noon on February 15. Four days later on February 19, Armin Tenner left for Europe to secure a superintendent and also obtain plans for animal habitations from some of the prominent zoological gardens.

Bids were sought for the construction of a deer house on the 5 March, and boards and posts for the fences on the 10 March. Although construction of the larger structures was put on hold until a new superintendent was employed, construction on smaller buildings and enclosures was revived from the winter hiatus.

With the exception of the buffalo house, all of the structures built for the Zoological Garden that year were designed by local architect James W. McLaughlin. These buildings represented some of his most imaginative work, incorporating features that reflected the origins of the animals being exhibited.

By mid-March, Tenner had found a likely candidate for the superintendent position. Dr. H. Dorner of the Hamburg Zoological Garden was interested, and on March 17, a contract for three years was finalized by the board via cable telegram. Tenner was also obtaining plans of various buildings, which he brought on his return to Cincinnati in late April.

An event occurred in late March 1875 at the Garden that would be remembered for many years. Animals both donated and purchased had been brought to the Garden for some time, now, and one of the most recent acquisitions came in early March in the form of two male lions and a lioness that were purchased from the Great Eastern Circus Company.

On March 25, at around 3:00 pm, George Schmidt, a young boy, was leading a donkey past the cages holding these lions. Schmidt stopped by the lioness' cage for a moment to have a closer look, which so enraged her that she burst through the bars and attacked the donkey. The lioness soon found that this was no easy prey, for as soon as she buried her teeth into the donkey's leg, he twisted his head, grabbed her by the back, and shook her loose. The lioness made another attempt, but this time he kicked her in the head. After a couple of additional skirmishes, the donkey was captured and led back to his stable. The lioness escaped from the grounds and was finally cornered and shot later that day.

The donkey was accorded the status of a hero and was provided for with the best care possible. The donkey died four months later on July 20, yet the memory of this epic occurrence was kept fresh for future visitors, as both he and the lioness were mounted and placed on view in the Carnivora House for many years.

On the morning of April 24, Armin Tenner returned to Cincinnati accompanied by Dr. Dorner, who was immediately given a tour of the Garden that afternoon. Dorner gave his approval of the fence then under construction, specifically in regard to measures taken to prevent dogs and other animals from burrowing underneath. The newspaper stated that,

"the heavy part of the grading has been done already and many of the avenues are about complete. Over sixty men are at work on the grounds every day, and in a few days this force will be increased."

The central lake was under construction, along with a man-made cascade which would carry excess water to a receiving basin. From there, the water could be used either for washing out the drainage system or to flow back into the lake to prevent it from becoming stagnant. At first, Dorner was not entirely pleased with the hilly nature of the grounds. This seems to have changed by the end of the tour, at which time he stated that he found the location to be an excellent one.

Over the next few weeks, Dorner, McLaughlin, and others planned the next phase of work, namely the construction of the major exhibition buildings. Although it is likely that McLaughlin had been working on plans for these structures, certain revisions would have occurred once Tenner returned with the drawings and notes from Europe.

The first major structure built following Dorner's arrival were the Bear Pits. Located on the northern part of the grounds, the three Bear Pits were housed in a brick and stone structure eighty-eight feet long, and thirty feet deep. The central pit measured twenty by twenty-five feet, while those on either side measured twenty by twenty feet. Each of the three pits contained a basin, along with access to dens located in the walls between the pits. Visitors would be able to view the bears from the front or from a platform located on top of the structure.

Bidding on the construction of the Bear Pits closed on May 29, and on June 7 and 14, bids were closed on construction and finishing work on the Carnivora House. The Carnivora was in total size the largest of the habitations constructed. The interior contained sixteen cages along with keepers' rooms and restrooms. The southern side of the exterior had eight summer cages allowing outdoor viewing when weather permitted. Eight of the interior cages were ten by fifteen feet; four measured twelve by fifteen feet; and the remaining four were ten feet square. The lobby was twenty-five feet wide, and one hundred and ten feet long. Natural light was emitted through windows on the north side, and a clerestory which ran along the roofline the length of the building.

The next building to be bid on was the Monkey House. Built in the round, the Monkey House was designed to be sixty feet in diameter with three summer cages on the southern side. Two entrances led into the domed interior, which was illuminated with both clerestory windows and an oculus in the top of the dome. The large public space was surrounded by twelve cages. On the southern half, one cage was twenty-one feet by nine feet, and was flanked on either side by two cages. The northern half contained seven cages. The largest cage opened into a summer cage. Two smaller summer cages were on either side and were both eight feet wide and fourteen feet high.

Three structures had construction bids in July: the Aviary on July 12, and a Deer House and Kangaroo House a few days later. The Aviary, although spoken of in the singular, consisted of seven small structures connected by summer cages, which gave the entire grouping a length of about three hundred and forty feet. The Deer House and Kangaroo House were both located near the Bear Pits and were of wood construction. The Deer House was particularly picturesque, being built of rough pine logs with a thatched roof.

A news article from August 8 spoke of the "almost incessant rains" that had occurred during the months of June and July. These storms had slowed the progress of construction; however, it was felt that a September opening of the Gardens to the public was not out of the question.

Two factors made an opening in September not only desirable but also necessary. First, many of the subscribers to the Gardens were becoming impatient and wanted to see their investment begin to make money. Second, a large shipment of "Asiatic and African birds and beasts," fifteen thousand dollars' worth, were expected to arrive from Carl Hagenbeck of Hamburg sometime in mid to late August. This shipment was loaded on the Hamburg-America line steamer *Klopstock* with Saloo Bugeo of Africa and Herman Rehnken of Hamburg along to take care of the animals. The *Klopstock*, which left port on August 11, soon experienced problems with her screw propeller, and on August 14, docked at Cherbourg for repairs. Two days later, the *Klopstock* resumed her voyage and arrived at New York on August 26 without further incident.

Armin Tenner had left Cincinnati on August 23 and was present when the animals were loaded into four Atlantic & Erie Railroad cars for their journey to Cincinnati. The animals, along with Tenner and Bugeo, arrived in Cumminsville early on the morning of August 31 via the Atlantic & Great Western Railroad.

Work of unloading these animals for the final leg of their journey began around 2:30 p.m. under the supervision of Tenner and Dr. Dorner. Over a dozen transfer cars and a large crew of workers were at hand to begin the work.

News travelled fast that "there was to be a sort of free animal show, [this] brought all the idle and curious people of the suburb to the scene, men, women and (oh, Lord how many!) children, all anxious to see everything that was going on and all getting in everybody else's way as much as possible." The animals were unloaded without incident, with the exception of a camel who balked at leaving the rail car, and a yak who burst through the end of his cage.

Having been loaded onto the transfer cars, the animals were slowly taken up Ludlow Avenue, led by "a big healthy German…with two braces of St. Bernard and Danish dogs." Immediately behind were the camels, which were followed by the wagons "loaded with fluttering birds, chattering monkeys, and growling wild beasts." A crowd of onlookers lined the way, and the procession finally reached the Gardens at around six o'clock. Upon arrival, those animals that had quarters ready were taken to them and released from the cramped confines that they had been in for the past several weeks.

With the large shipment safely on the grounds, work was focused primarily on finishing as much as possible in anticipation of a September opening of the Gardens. The date chosen, September 18, was just a few days shy of being a year since the final transfer of land to the Society, and while there was still much to be done, a great deal had already been accomplished. The Zoological Society and countless laborers had transformed an ordinary pasture into a pleasure garden, traversed by three miles of paths allowing visitors to view horticultural plantings and numerous enclosures with creatures from around the world.

In many ways, the opening day did not live up to its potential. Much of this was due to the weather, which was beyond human control. Unlike the previous two years with temperatures in the low 80s, September 18 dawned cloudy with a temperature of just 50 degrees. The rest of the day remained overcast, reaching a high temperature of only 55 degrees.

The Gardens were opened to members and guests at 10 o'clock, giving them ample time to tour the grounds and see the sights. At noon, Julius Dexter addressed a crowd of about three hundred, including members of the park board and City Council. His remarks began with describing the hopes that the Society had in creating the Garden, along with its future usefulness not only for those seeking pleasure, but also to students of science.

Dexter then called the audience's attention to the two men he felt most deserved the thanks of the Society. First thanking Armin Tenner for his "efficient labor" while serving as general agent, he then drew everyone's attention to Andrew Erkenbrecher, "the father of the Zoological Garden." Erkenbrecher was presented with a handsome gold headed cane, with deer and camels and things molded upon it, and bearing the inscription 'presented to Andrew Erkenbrecher, the founder of the Cincinnati Zoological Garden, by the board of directors, September 18, 1875.'

Erkenbrecher accepted the cane and stepped away without saying a word. Following some further remarks, the planned events of the day were over, and the general public was admitted to tour the grounds.

Some of the structures, such as the Carnivora and the Monkey House, were not ready for their occupants on opening day, and so these animals remained in their transportation cages until their buildings were ready. The lions, tigers, and hyenas moved into the Carnivora on October 2, and on November 7, it was announced that the monkeys were comfortable in their new quarters, ready for winter.

One final occurrence of 1875 deserves to be mentioned. Two months after Andrew Erkenbrecher received a cane at the opening of the Gardens, Armin Tenner was the recipient of a similar gesture from a humbler but no less sincere group. On the evening of November 18, twenty-five employees of the "Zoological Garden went in a body to the residence of Mr. Armin Tenner…and presented him with a gold-headed cane as a token of their regard for his genial and gentlemanly discharge of the duties of his office." Following this presentation, the group opened baskets they had brought, and all sat down to a fine meal. Toasts were given, and it wasn't until midnight that the festivities came to an end. It seems fitting that Tenner should receive such a memento; after all, it was through his correspondence with Dr. Brehm that the idea of a Zoological Garden became more than just a dream.

What had begun as an experiment in pest control developed into bringing songbirds into the area and culminated in creating what was then the largest zoological garden in America. Much of what was accomplished in creating the Garden came from information gathered by Tenner while in Europe, and a great deal of trial and error. There were obstacles faced while creating the zoo, with many more to come in the years following, yet through it all, there was someone or some group ready to save it. Had it not been worth saving, it might easily have been lost when the hard times came.

The ripples from these early beginnings continue to this day, with even more changes anticipated over the next few years. With the zoo nearing its 150th anniversary in 2025, it is clear that the idea started by Erkenbrecher will continue as long as there are dedicated individuals to make it possible.

{12} THE RANDOLPH SLAVES

WILLIAM W. KILLEN

A WILL WITH NO WAY

THE FIRST EIGHTEEN YEARS OF MY LIFE were spent growing up in Piqua, Ohio, one of a daisy-chain of small towns along I-75 north of Dayton. As kids in the 30s, 40s, and 50s the town was our universe and decidedly "Mayberry-esque." Two years ago, I was reading a book about our congressman during those years, William McCulloch, and noticed a brief mention of a group of former slaves who had established the small community of Rossville, just across the Great Miami River from Piqua. I had never heard of them. Rossville was just a rather poor settlement on the highway going north out of Piqua. To my knowledge, I had not met or gone to school with any of the descendants of the group. But, with a little digging, I found their story to be very compelling. I wish to share it with you now.

July 1, 1846 was a hot day in Cincinnati when a steamer from Charleston tied up at the public landing. On board were 383 newly freed slaves from the Randolph Plantation in Roanoke, Virginia, making their way to a new home in Mercer County, Ohio. Their former owner, John Randolph, had made provision in his will that, upon his death, all of his slaves would be freed and sent to the free state of Ohio, where would be provided to them land to build a new community, creating a new life for themselves and their families. Now, stepping onto the free soil of Cincinnati's waterfront, they were on the last 100-mile leg of their journey to Mercer County in western Ohio, where Randolph had purchased 3200 acres for their resettlement.

The July 2 edition of the *Cincinnati Gazette* reported their arrival and the paper's editorial opinion of Randolph's will and action. Excerpts from that editorial, found in the Shelby County Ohio Historical Society's publication of the event, indicate the attitude toward such migrations to Ohio and Cincinnati:

> John Randolph, by will, gave freedom to his slaves, and provided the means for their settlement in Ohio. Yesterday they passed through our city on their way to the settlement purchased for them in the interior. The troop was a large one. There appeared to be some 300 in it. It is composed of people of all ages and all sizes and attracted no little attention.

The editor went on. He felt Ohio had nothing to do with slavery and it was not in the interest of the State nor part of its duty to accept these freedmen and women: "This emigration of John Randolph's Negroes proves that we have something to do with slavery. And evidently the people of Virginia think so too. For whenever their eyes get opened, because they hear the call of death, or know it is nigh, the first step is to free their slaves that they may lull the unquiet gnawings of conscience — the next to send them to Ohio that they may be free! We have already several colored settlements among us. And pray, why does not Virginia and Kentucky retain their freed blacks? We have very much fear that the common objection made in the slave states that we as free states, having nothing to do with slavery, will turn out on examination to be eminently untrue in more respects than one."

This opinion would be the harbinger of things to come. Fear of the "Other" has been a part of every migration story, then and now. But who was this man, John Randolph, and why would he even think of doing such a thing?

Randolph was the son of a wealthy Roanoke, Virginia tobacco planter. He was usually referred to as John Randolph of Roanoke to differentiate him from his father and other members of the Randolph family, so prominent in the early history of Virginia and the United States. He was born in 1773 to John Randolph and Frances Bland. He studied under private tutors at Walter Maury's private school, then attended the College of New Jersey, and Columbia College in New York. He studied law in Philadelphia, but never practiced. Randolph was raised and remained a member of the Episcopal Church throughout his life.

His father died when John was very young, and his mother married St. George Tucker in 1778, bringing two half-brothers into the family. John suffered from tuberculosis early in life, which left him beardless and with a pre-pubescent soprano voice in adulthood. He remained a lifelong bachelor. As John Randolph's heir, he inherited the tobacco plantation of 8000 acres and about 400 slaves. This allowed him to continue a life of privilege and pursue a career in politics. In 1799, at the young age of twenty-six, Randolph was first elected to Congress as a member of the Democratic-Republican Party from the Seventh District of Virginia. He served four more terms in the House. Historian Russell Kirk described him as:

> a radical man yet a political conservative" with "alternating ferocity and compassion...his duels...his beautiful letters... his fits of madness...his brandy and opium...his passionate Christianity...his lonely plantation life...and his quixotic opposition to the great political and economic powers of the day.

Regarding his duels, he once fought one with Henry Clay. After the first volley the only damage was to Randolph's jacket. After reloading, Randolph announced that he had no interest in making Mrs. Clay a widow, and both men left the field unharmed.

Federalist William Plumer of New Hampshire wrote in 1803 of his striking presence: "Mr. Randolph goes about the House booted and spurred, with his whip in hand, in imitation, it is said, of members of the British Parliament. (Some said he would bring his dog too until the Speaker of the House put a stop to it.) He is a slight man but of the common stature. At a little distance, he does not appear older than you are; but upon a nearer approach, you perceive his wrinkles and grey hairs. He is, I believe, about thirty. His talents are certainly far above mediocrity". Plumer added: "As a popular speaker, he is not inferior to any man in the House. I admire his ingenuity and address; but I dislike his politics."

Between 1825 to 1827, Randolph served in the Senate to fill a vacancy, and later was appointed the eighth United States Minister to Russia from May through September 1830 but resigned as Minister due to ill health. He returned to the House again in 1832 and served until his death in May 1833.

Despite an active political career, ill health from tuberculosis afflicted him throughout his life. Perhaps this constant reminder of his mortality, and his brother's death from TB, caused him to think about the future of his estate. In 1819, years before his death, Randolph wrote his first will, which contained a provision for the manumission of his slaves upon his death. He wrote, "I give and bequeath to all my slaves their freedom, heartily regretting that I have ever been the owner of one." In 1821, a second will was written which provided money to transport and settle the freed slaves on land purchased in the free state of Ohio. In 1832, however, for reasons unclear to us, a third will was written specifying that the slaves were to be sold. Then, on his deathbed in 1833, with his doctor locked in his bedroom, as a white witness was required by Virginia law in manumission cases, he repudiated the third will, and again specified that the slaves be freed and transported.

The family, however, did not see it this way. Lawsuits were brought to test the validity of the wills, a process that lasted for *thirteen years* until the Virginia courts, in the case of *Coulter's Executors et. al. v. Bryan and Wife,* decided that the third will was invalid by reason of Randolph's insanity, thus validating the second will. This decision also affirmed Willian Leigh, Randolph's close friend, as his Executor. The slaves, who had been kept in bondage and hired out during this long period of litigation, were officially manumitted on May 4, 1846.

Leigh had been preparing for this day. He had access now to about 38,000 dollars in cash and real estate. The year before, he had commissioned an Ohio lawyer, Samuel Jay, to purchase 3200 acres in Mercer County, Ohio, to be held in trust for Randolph's beneficiaries for their resettlement in a free state. The land was to be divided so that all above the age of forty would receive not less than ten acres each.

Leigh's selection of Mercer County was not an illogical choice. The area was lightly settled and in 1835 it had become the site of Carthagena, a black settlement. Augustus Wattles, a student at Cincinnati's Lane Seminary, had purchased 190 acres there and started a school for boys of color. He taught manual training, farming, and the undertaking of silk culture. Wattles' work attracted the attention of the trustees of the Samuel Emlen Jr. estate, a New Jersey Quaker who had willed money for the education of "boys of African and Indian decent." With his bequest, the school and farm were purchased, creating the Emlen Institute. With this impetus, a black farming community grew rapidly nearby, and the village of Carthagena was platted in 1840.

With the land secured near this settlement, the next step was to arrange for the transportation of 383 men, women, and children, hundreds of miles from the plantation to their new home near Carthagena. The party ranged in age from an infant to Granny Hannah who was said to be over 100. A Mr. Cardwell was hired to see to getting the group to their destination. The trek started in June 1846. With them, they carried a certificate from the Clerk of the Court of Charlotte County, Virginia which listed the first names and description of all the freed slaves. Can you imagine the feeling of joy, expectation, and relief that those people experienced on that early spring morning when they saw the wagons in the road, and the transportation contractor getting ready to take them to Ohio? They were finally on their way to real freedom and a new life in a place of their own.

After a journey of almost 500 miles by wagons, the group arrived near Charleston on June 18. There they boarded a steamer and sailed down the Kanawha River to the Ohio River and on to Cincinnati. Upon arrival at the Cincinnati Public Landing, the group made an orderly walk up Main Street to the new Miami and Erie Canal (now Central Parkway) where they boarded barges for the continuation of their journey to their new home, now just 100 miles away. And it must be said that this was no ordinary group. Randolph had seen to it that they were educated. Among them were skilled craftsmen. Many could read and write. The group had the capability to succeed in their new life. As they glided northward on the canal, signs of racism followed them. Rumors picked up along the way indicated that the residents in Mercer County were not enthusiastic about their impending arrival.

> The local paper in Dayton reported that the preparations for their settlement caused a great deal of anxiety among the white residents. They themselves were recent migrants from Germany to the United States, escaping the social and economic upheaval in the German States during that period. The news of the landing of nearly 400 Negroes in Cincinnati excited fears of black dominance. For several years the Wattles community at Carthagena had been subjected to white physical harassment to such a degree that the Ohio Governor

had to assure them that the law would protect them. Now, the balance of power could shift with the new arrivals.

The tension was felt as the Randolph group made their way through Tippecanoe, and Troy, and especially in Piqua, where the town marshal refused to allow them off the barges to get water, citing a water shortage. Moving on, they did get water a mile or so up the canal at Col. Johnston's farm. The little fleet then moved on through the locks at Lockport and on to Fort Laramie. It was noon on that July Sunday when the boats docked in New Bremen but there was no brass band, no dignitaries with welcoming gifts, and no speeches, no banquet. Instead, a crowd of armed and very angry whites gathered around the canal boats to enforce three resolutions they had drafted while the Randolph group was en route. The resolutions were:

> Resolved: That we will not live among Negroes; as we have settled here first and we have fully determined that we will resist the settlement of blacks and mulattoes in this county to the full extent of our means, the bayonet not excepted;
> Resolved: That the blacks of this county be, and they are hereby respectfully requested to leave the county on or before the first day of March 1847; and in the case of their neglect or refusal to comply with this request, we pledge ourselves to remove them peacefully if we can, forcibly if we must;
> Resolved: That we who are assembled, pledge ourselves not to employ or trade with any black or mulatto person, in any manner whatever, or to permit them to have any grinding done at our mills, after the first day of January, next."

Is it not surprising how this attitude towards migrants and "Others" has persisted for over a century and a half. Perhaps the disadvantages of locating in Mercer County had not been given enough weight in the decision. Ohio's Black Laws (in 1849) meant Ohio's Negroes had no more political or legal rights than Indians or unnaturalized foreigners. Indeed, our own Literarian, Charles T. Greve wrote:

> "In short, considering the open hostility of many Ohioans, the state's anti-black laws, and Cincinnati's race riots of 1829,

> 1836, and 1841, one must wonder why the executor chose the Buckeye State rather than some less tumultuous area."

The Executor, William Leigh, was not due to arrive for three days and might have gotten things sorted out, however, the townspeople demanded that Mr. Cardwell, the transportation contractor, arrange to be gone with his group by ten the next morning. Cardwell pleaded with them to allow a three-day extension. The answer was a definitive NO! He offered a $1000 bond, and to spend the time in jail as a guarantee that he would not skip out and leave the former slaves behind. The answer again was NO! He did get them to send for Samuel Jay, Leigh's land agent, to perhaps aid in the situation. After an uneasy night, Jay arrived on Monday morning and immediately refused to receive the Randolph group. He claimed he had no authority from Leigh to take such action, and further pointed out that the hostility of the surrounding landowners would have a negative impact on anything he might do. Now, out of options, Cardwell chartered two boats and loaded the group for the trip back down the canal and out of Mercer County. An armed escort followed them to the County line. One of the old men in the Randolph group was said to declare after seeing the hostility, that maybe his former Master in Virginia was his best friend after all.

Imagine the despair and bewilderment of the group as they moved southward through Shelby County to Lockport where they stopped for a few days. Rumor had it that several members of the party had slipped away while still in Mercer County and made their way to Carthagena. Others now wished to depart and join a settlement of blacks at Rumley near Sidney. Again, they were met with hostility until several local citizens appealed to the charity of their fellow townspeople and convened a meeting to debate what to do. It was decided that about a third of their number could stay in Sidney and these individuals were given work in the homes and farms in the area. The rest continued another few miles south to Piqua. It was about this time that Leigh caught up with the party.

Leigh quickly understood that the hostility his charges faced made the original intent of Randolph's will impossible. He decided to find places for the group to settle anywhere possible in the region between Piqua and Cincinnati. Fortunately, an area just across the Great Miami River from Piqua known as the Knowles Addition had recently been platted but not developed. Leigh arranged for the purchase of the land, and it became the village of Rossville, home for about seventy-five of the Randolph group. Other groups moved farther south creating settlements called Marshalltown near Troy, and Hanktown near West Milton. Having found a solution to the settlement question, and appointing Joseph John, a prominent Troy citizen as temporary guardian, Judge Leigh returned to Virginia in August 1846.

While the Rossville community did not appear to thrive, it did survive. In the 1850 Census, seventy-four freedmen were counted as residents and four were listed with a combined land ownership of nine and hundred and fifty dollars. This compared favorably with white ownership worth $1,100. By the 1860 Census, there were seventy-one residents, showing property and cash valued at $3,530 among the now fourteen property owners. Most were employed as laborers and farmers but one became an engineer, and one was a stonemason whose work is seen in several churches and homes in Piqua.

In 1860, the clouds of war were beginning to form, and the little village was not to be untouched by the coming conflict. With the Emancipation Proclamation came the ability of Negroes to serve in the armed services of the United States, something that had been denied them up to then (Blacks served in every American war, including the Revolutionary War.) In the spring of 1863, word spread that a recruiter would be passing through the communities of the Upper Valley to recruit Negroes to fight for the Union. A signing bonus of $100 was paid to each volunteer and each would receive ten dollars per month in pay, including three dollars for clothing. White soldiers were paid thirteen dollars. Nine men from Rossville signed up and were soon on their way to Boston to join the two regiments of colored troops being formed, the 54th and 55th Massachusetts Volunteer Infantry. These units were made up of all black soldiers commanded by white officers. The men were cheered along their way to Boston and were formally enlisted into the 54th Massachusetts in May 1863. The Confederates, hearing that black soldiers would soon be entering the fray, let it be known that any black soldier captured would be returned to slavery, and any white officer would be executed.

The Regiment moved by ship to South Carolina in June 1863 and took part in action at Darien, GA. Morris Island SC, Hilton Head, Beaufort, and Charleston. In July 1863 at the urging of their commander, Col. Robert Shaw, the 54th was selected to lead the charge against Fort Wagner near Charleston.

This was a celebrated battle depicted in the movie *"Glory,"* and it demonstrated the valor and willingness to fight for the Union cause by black troops. The six hundred men of the 54th faced overwhelming odds in the attack on Fort Wagner, not only from the Confederate cannon but 1,300 protected riflemen covering their position. Losses were heavy and reinforcements did not arrive in time, forcing the regiment to withdraw, leaving 256 dead, including Col. Shaw. The attention of the North was drawn to this battle as it changed the attitude towards the black soldier and accorded him respect as an effective fighting man. In fact, Sgt. William Carney became the first black soldier to win the Medal of Honor as a result of his bravery at Fort. Wagner. Months later, Fort Wagner was abandoned by the Confederates as Union forces closed in on Charleston.

The cycle of life continued for the little Rossville community in the post-war years, and as communications and travel became more accessible, the Randolph group and their descendants began to have periodic reunions. At these gatherings stories were told of the "old days," and the land that was supposed to have been theirs. One of the more interesting stories of what happened to the land and the money centered on Joseph Plunkett, Judge Leigh's trusted representative who was to see to the former slaves' interests. He began to sell the 3200 acres in December 1846 as unclaimed land. Over a seven-year period Plunkett sold all of the land for a total of $7,700. It was alleged that Plunkett had forged William Leigh's name on the sale documents. Other opinions included selling the land for taxes. Still others thought the money had gone to pay for bonds that each freed slave was required to have under Ohio's Black Laws of the period. And other lands, such as Rossville, had been purchased for re-settlement. Regardless, the Randolph group remained unsatisfied.

In 1907, York Rial of Rossville, and Joseph Moton, both Randolph heirs, spearheaded an effort to enlist the aid of the courts to recover cash or land they felt was due the Randolph group. This eventually led to twenty-seven court cases where 170 of the remaining heirs sued.

The first test case, Joseph Moton et.al. v. Gerhard Kessens, brought before the Mercer County Court of Common Pleas, was decided in favor of the defendant. The case was appealed to the Ohio Supreme Court and was decided in favor of the defendant, again citing the statute of limitations (twenty-one years) had run out. Further, the court found there was no evidence to the contrary to show that William Leigh did not have a Virginia court order to sell the land, nor that he had not fully accounted for the proceeds of the sale. All such records if they existed were burned in the Richmond Courthouse fire during the Civil War.

The litigation continued for ten more years until the final decision was rendered in 1917 by the US Supreme Court. The heirs held that Leigh did not execute nor cause the will to be executed. Therefore, a "chain" of wrongdoing started in 1848 when Leigh, without a Virginia court order nor authority from Randolph's will unlawfully gave Plunkett the power of attorney to sell the heirs' land. It was argued that no person could thereafter buy these lands in innocence, for a title search would reveal the rights of third persons, the heirs' first title. Those who ignored this were guilty of adding another "link" in the chain of wrongdoing. Attorneys for the heirs hoped to connect the past with the present, thus avoiding the statute of limitations. The defense continued with the statute of limitations argument. The Court was made up of five Republicans, four Democrats; two were Southerners, and two were from Ohio. Well-known members of the Court were Chief Justice Edward White, Justice Louis Brandeis, and Justice Oliver Wendell Holmes. The Court decided in favor of the existing landowners on the grounds that the statute of limitations had indeed run out. With this decision, the Randolph heirs did not pursue the matter any further. After eighty-four years and dozens of court cases, the matter was finally over.

Joseph Moton, one of the pair that brought the original suit to regain the land, died of a heart attack before the final ruling was handed down. Some say his death was caused by the strain of litigation. York Rial, the other original litigant, died of typhoid fever after drinking contaminated water during the 1913 Miami River flood. Their descendants carried on the court case to its conclusion.

Rossville is the only Randolph community that exists today and is listed on the Ohio Register of Historic Places. It is there, just across the Miami River bridge at the north end of Piqua, on what was once US 25, The Dixie Highway. There is a small historic district including York Rial's house, and the Jackson Cemetery where the Civil War veterans are buried. York Rial's niece, who died in 2010, was the last person I know of who was connected to the Randolph group, and lived in Rossville. She was instrumental in getting the village and cemetery the historic designation. The cemetery holds 120 graves including George Rial's. His gravestone simply reads "Born a Slave Died Free."

Let us drink to that.

{13}
DIARY OF A YEAR TO LIVE

JACOB (JACK) LINDY

Writing about dying is never easy. Writing about your own dying is even harder.

Listening to a paper about dying is never easy. Listening to a paper about the dying of someone you know, or a friend, is even harder.

Some of us, in medicine, in law, in the clergy and in finance, say to ourselves we deal with the dying of others every day. Yet, for me, confronting my own death was different.

As I completed this diary, the idea of reading it as my paper to the Literary Club crossed my mind, but I was leery. I consulted with a few of you who know most about this subject. You supported the part of me that thought reading it would be useful. The other part of me remains cautious, wary of the risk of opening too private and vulnerable a space in me or in you.

So, trying to keep that in mind, I begin.

– November 24, 2014
"Twelve months, maybe eighteen if we're lucky."

Young, earnest, informed,
His eyes lock with mine
His mind filled with the pain of loss,
I suspect the last patient
He treated with my condition,

After all, he was only answering the question I posed
The one I had so carefully crafted

"Doctor, what is the arc of my illness?"

I felt Joanne's hand rest on my arm
While I disappeared from my mind.

– December 7, 2014
Blindsided I stagger
At what I have known since a child,
That our days are numbered
Yet when the number of my days is announced
I react as if 'this were never to be.'

I am ashamed at my blindness
My belief that death does not apply to me

I struggle to find metaphor, words that might make the alien territory of death more familiar. Being hit with a wild pitch doesn't get it, this is too disorienting.

New Lens

I falter in my Fiat 500,
As I try to view the road ahead

There is conversation
About the future

But my rear-view mirror
Has grown grotesquely large

This new lens
Locks in place

Obscures the future
And I am able to focus

Only on what I've passed

– December 11, 2014

I have a habit of building teams of oddly assorted folks who come together for a particular task. So what about a death team? Who should be on it? Well, for a beginning, I need someone to select a plot. I need a rabbi for spiritual help and to perform my funeral. I need an attorney to see my finances pass smoothly, and docs to care for me as I move from here to there.

Michael Graves is a pleasant 35-year-old man, with balding scalp and meticulous clothes. He listens heavily, reacts slowly, enunciates carefully. Last time we visited Spring Grove Cemetery and talked with Michael we got this far: Joanne wants to be cremated; I want to be buried in a pine box. Joanne wants her ashes by a serene waterfall; I'd like to be in the woods. I want a Jewish ceremony; she is ambivalent about ceremony in the first place. And of course, we want to lie next to each other for eternity.

Michael listened as we disagreed. Then Joanne and I suddenly came up with the same idea. This whole thing was uncannily familiar. It was like choosing the right campsite when we went camping. Was it for the view, for privacy, for access to water, for level ground? We invariably disagreed. But we found ways to compromise, and so we did on this campsite too. Michael found a way to place the Jewish pine box on a sturdy base so it didn't sink when I disintegrate, while Joanne's urn could be in the earth next door. Joanne decided that the person who goes first gets first choice of campsite; I thought we might come in from the woods and occupy a more conventional spot closer to the entrance so on the odd chance that someone might want to visit us, they could find the site. But as Michael took us to the ground we had chosen Joanne became alarmed. She noted that the headstone next door announced our neighbor as an avid NRA enthusiast. We would have to take the lot near-by, to be free of other worldly rifle shots.

–December 18, 2014

I have two questions. What are the moments preceding death going to feel like? And what happens at the moment life goes out of me? What do I become, where do I go when I no longer inhabit the body I have lived with for nearly 80 years?

For the first question, I feel assured from Dr. Cogent that he will be with me to the end. For that I am grateful. For the second question…

It is time I met with Rabbi David.

Br'er David is a large burly man with dark curly hair, a winning smile, and a broad expanse of presence. As his arms open to embrace me with his "bear-hug", I worry how our bodies are going to fit. Does he see how much weight I have lost? My thin frame must fold around his protruding mid-rift. If he squeezes too hard I will break.

I survive the bear hug. We chat briefly together with Joanne, then I invite David to my study, where we settle into comfortable chairs.

"What happens when we die Br'er David? I mean what happens at that very moment when our blood runs cold and life disappears from our body?"

David sits back, taking in my question as though it were delicate food that needs to be digested slowly.

"Death frees our soul," he says finally. "Our spirit goes where it has always gone, to the people whom we have touched in the course of our life. What happens after that no one knows for sure, but that we inhabit the souls of others, that we, even after death, connect, is true and fundamental."

Souls connecting with each other. I hadn't quite thought of it that way. It is a comforting view of the moment of death, of passing from one state to another.

Further, by applying the idea to my present situation, this perspective offers a direction, even a prescription for my behavior. For as I approach death, there are needs to re-connect, to tell those I love, "I love you," to address outstanding tensions, to explore future decisions, to free up the passage way before and during death, from spirit to spirit, from soul to soul.

We close a loop today in order to open a gate for tomorrow.

I ask David to perform my funeral.

He sighs deeply, "Of course I will. It would be my honor."

I feel a burden lift. It is as if new energy has infused my worn-out body. My arm rests on David's shoulder as we walk, for me, briskly to the door.

Joanne remarks privately after he has left, "I've never seen two people so excited about dying as the two of you."

– February 1, 2015

Plan for a Day in Congestive Heart Failure

Don't rush
Sleep any way you can whenever you can
Get back to people
Say Thank you
Do or plan a mitzvah*
One event is plenty for the day
Tell Joanne you love her

We have already signed a power of attorney, a living will; and our last wills and testaments are in order, so today's meeting with Warren Bankhead is simply a question of what must Joanne do when I die? The only problem is the meeting is scheduled when I usually take a nap.

Warren takes his seat at the head of the mahogany table. That impish twinkle in his eye reminds us that the Sixties juices still flow in his veins. I have trouble concentrating. There is talk about trust and trusts, marital trust, family trust, revocable trust. What does a 'revocable' trust mean. Does it mean anyone can change my will at any time, or does it mean I can no longer sing, which is the case as my mouth is dry and voice is cracking. Over the din I hear, "Above all we must avoid probate. "I know my mind is slipping. I can only think of school kids being put on probation for doing something wrong. "but I've never been on probation."

"Avoiding tax, it all rests in the hands of the trustee." Now in my mind "trustee" has become "trusty," the warden's special criminal whom others can't trust. When we finish here will we be among the trusted or in our efforts to be free of burdensome taxes should we be counted among the convicts? Putting financial matters in order. I guess you have to trust somebody.

Definitely time for my nap.

– February 14, 2015

Today I look back at my diary and note how much I have omitted during these frantic three months: there are only fragmentary entries for re-marriage of my oldest son, birth of a new grandchild, 50th birthday of my daughter, presentation together with my students at a national convention, learning my latest paper is to be published in the fall, learning my youngest daughter is to be married in 18 months. I even omit from the diary that the very day a learned of my fatal illness, was the same day I read a budget at the Literary Club.

Finally, a metaphor gives shape to my disorder.

It is as if November 24 marks the collision between two tectonic plates, life and death.

My diary entries are like riding the surface of this fault line, trying to find balance in the midst of an earthquake.

– February 15, 2015

I pass this strange guy as I exit the bathroom.
He looks at me, but I do not recognize him.
Presumptuously, I take a moment to stare.

"No meat on him," that's what my mother would say.
Broom sticks for arms and legs.
Well, he was skinny at best then.
But then he weighed thirty pounds more than now.

This guy I'm looking at:

There are no muscle contours around his shoulders just pointy bones.

Pectoralis, deltoid, triceps — all of them disappeared.
Ribs covered with taut skin.
An uncanny likeness to inmates at Auschwitz.

I see what his face is saying:

Etched lines around his mouth all point downward,
wrinkles and lips spell despair.

Jack, this image of you in the mirror will never do.
How dare you drag it with you all day?
It's not even breakfast yet.

– February 18, 2015

Elizabeth Kubler Ross says we bargain when we learn of a fatal illness. I thought I was immune.

My inclination toward the scientific method has become infused with magical bargains. I daily chart my weight, blood pressure, pulse. I count the number of deep breaths it takes me to regain normal breathing after I climb a flight of stairs. It used to be 6, now it's 20.

I walk a mile on the stair-master but no longer count how long it takes. I walk downhill to Mirror Lake but ask Joanne to pick me up at the bottom, as there is no way I can make it back up the hill.

My unconscious bargain is if I exercise and keep careful records, I will remain alive so I can continue to report on my "science" experiment. But all the indicators move gradually in the wrong direction.

I keep up the charts, doing my part of the bargain He never made.

–February 20, 2015

I apologize. Once more the chronology of this diary is screwed up. It is time to fill in my cryptic notes about this other gnawing matter I'd rather ignore, my medical diagnosis. Once more I return to the hectic days of December.

– December 2, 2014

We are trying to get our heads wrapped around this diagnosis, cardiac amyloidosis. They have already told me that it is fatal, and that there is no FDA approved medication. So why bother with a big work-up?

"Well, it's not quite that simple," says Joanne who has had her head into the Internet ever since day one. "There are different types, and depending on the type there may be an experimental treatment, at least something that will slow down the illness."

I am in a different mind-set. Why is that so important? They know I have a fatal illness from the MRI, why all the fuss about a tissue diagnosis? Do they want to make me miserable carving me up until they find the amyloid? Is it so they can offer a treatment that won't work? All this unpleasantness, for what, a few more months? Or is it so insurance will pay the bill?

Meanwhile there is no convincing Joanne of the wisdom of my well-articulated "head in the sand" position. She has looked all this up online.

"Sometimes the amyloid comes from bad cells in your bone marrow," says Doctor Earnest, a young hematologist whom Dr. Cogent recommends. Dr. Earnest seems a little older than my grandson. He is careful to explain to an old-timer like me how medicine has advanced. The bone marrow biopsy, he assures me, should not be unpleasant.

Dr. Earnest carefully bores a small hole in my hip and draws marrow from my bone, not so harrowing as I had feared, but not exactly what I enjoy doing on a Tuesday afternoon.

– December 9, 2014

No bad cells found.

"Maybe amyloid will show up in a biopsy of fat tissue," he says.

You have to be kidding; I don't have any fat tissue, and what little I had, I lost when I became sick.

– December 16, 2014

"No problem," says the general surgeon, as he carves my shrinking belly. He cuts before the Novocain has taken effect. The pain is worse than the bone marrow, and the results, just as negative.

– December 22, 2014

So, Dr. Cogent says, "we come to our last option, we need to biopsy your heart."

Biopsy my heart! How the hell do you do that? By driving a super-sized needle through what's left of my chest wall and into my heart? "I just had an angiogram a couple of months ago. Doesn't that count?"

"No this is different," he continues, "the surgeon inserts an instrument through a vessel in your groin, pushes it to the middle of the heart and while there grabs a few (actually 5) chunks of heart tissue which we will send to laboratories for analysis. You won't feel a thing.

Maybe this makes sense to you, but it sounds very dangerous, and of dubious value. How many times do I have to expose my neck like a gazelle, before the devouring lion of modern medicine?

– December 29, 2014

This time the tissue is positive. Now it's official. I have amyloidosis of the heart. One by one the heart biopsies come back. It's not this type, it's not that type. Four of the five biopsies are back, and we still don't know what rare form of this rare disease I have. "Perhaps the offending blood cell is hiding," reasons Dr. Earnest. "We should start chemotherapy now." I am game, anything for the home team. Oops, while I am in his office the last biopsy comes in. It is from Mayo Clinic. I have TTR amyloidosis, mutant wild type. "Oh," mumbles Dr. Earnest under his breath, "that must be the rare type where the patients died so quickly in our study. Let's send you to Mayo Clinic."

Update on Jack Lindy's Health Sent to Colleagues

– February 24, 2015

Jack and Joanne just returned from Mayo Clinic. He has trans-thyretin or TTR amyloidosis, "wild" type. This type is not amenable to known treatments. On the positive side, it progresses more slowly than other forms and tends to stay localized in the heart. He was to be a candidate for an experimental protocol at Mayo Clinic involving a new drug, but that study has been suspended. Meanwhile an atrial flutter was treated with cardioversion.

Jack's major symptoms are shortness of breath and fatigue. He will discontinue his office next month

– March 5,2016

The "end-of-life" cards start pouring in. Thoughtful reflections, usually upon some small incident I barely remembered, when without self-consciousness, I offered encouragement, shared an insight, behaved in concordance with someone's ideal, contributed to a turning point in another's life journey. What a treasure chest of unintended consequences.

I pause, opening yet another card; how low can I get, being a voyeur at my own funeral.

Yet, to ponder what we have meant to people, it's something we don't ordinarily do. The cards carry so much more than I would have anticipated, and provide me with so much more to be thankful for.

Of course, just as at funerals, some of the coarser elements in my character are mercifully not emphasized. These same folks could have had fun roasting me, but not today, not in these notes, these notes about the silent ways we touch even those we think are far away.

– March 10, 2015

Dear Jack,

I received the e-mail regarding your health. I am very sorry about your illness. A colleague of mine at Indiana University is expert and a leader in the field of amyloidosis associated with mutant and wild type transthyretin. I would be very happy to connect you with him.

I do not mean to be intrusive, but I felt that I should inform you.

Best regards,

Dino Ghetti, Chair Dept. of Pathology, I.U.

Has God been listening in on this, or did He just say to all those who were praying for me to settle down, "Here, I'll give you something to keep you quiet for a while. I have a lot more important things to attend to than this guy Lindy's health."

– March 23, 2015

Dr. Donald Quixote is all we had been praying for. Yes, he is conducting a trial of a new drug for cardiac amyloidosis. Yes, I am eligible for the study. No, there will not be a placebo group. Yes, we can obtain baseline measures and begin in one week. I am to be subject number 7 of 10 subjects. Other subjects fly in from far away. Joanne and I can travel to Indianapolis in two hours.

And Donald Quixote knows all there is to know about amyloidosis.

Donald's eyes twinkle as he bonds with us. Ever keeping things in perspective, he comments, "Oh I wouldn't worry about your heart rate; you should see the rats when their rate goes up to 700 beats." Or, as I struggle learning how to give myself the viscous subcutaneous injection of his space age meds, "If you think that's hard, you should try to give that dose to a squirming mouse."

Touching my ankle on examination he says, "Oh, you probably do have amyloid in your peripheral nerves, it was right there on the last guy I autopsied."

Dr. Quixote explains to me how an anti-sense oligonucleotide works. "It blocks the formation of transthyretin, by impacting messenger RNA at the gene level." Frankly this space age medicine leaves my head spinning.

His nurse teaches me to inject the medicine below the skin in my belly when I read the drug's name, ISIS #420915.

"ISIS, this can't be the name of the pharmaceutical company," I say.

"I'm afraid that's the right name," says Donald. "They tell their telephone operators to slur the name and accent pharmaceuticals."

So the new phase of my illness begins. Each Friday I inject a little ISIS in my belly. Each Saturday I feel like hell. Then gradually over Sunday and beginning Monday I begin to feel human again.

Where to from here? Hey, I'm starting to feel well enough to fill in some of these Diary entries.

– April 4, 2015

I am overwhelmed at the Passover tonight. I need time to digest it before making an entry.

– April 18

The Lord is going to have to shepherd this Passover. I am in no shape to lead it.

As I look out over the table so beautifully laid out and smell the food we will soon take in, I think this is an evening that *shall not leave me wanting.*

But no sooner do I begin speaking than a pall falls over

the room. No matter what my words, I am dying. And it is as though all of us are walking in my shadow of death.

This will never do, I say to myself. This is going to be an evening of pleasure and fun. I *fear no evil*, as I have all the confidence in the world that the "kids" will rise to the occasion. I want to shout, "Hey guys, I'm not dead yet." But instead I ask Joanne to say the blessing over the candles, then turn to my daughter Rebecca to get this thing started. And start it she does.

Rebecca *takes a straight path* explaining the meaning of the traditional symbols. Then she introduces two extra symbols: the olive for peace, for respect for Palestinians in their quest for dignity, and in our bond with all who are oppressed, and the orange, to mark our commitment to equality of women. (An Orthodox rabbi reportedly said that the day there will be a female rabbi is the day there is an orange on the Seder table.) With this the table comes to life.

Ben looks to his three-month-old son, Aaron, as if he is to ask the four questions. Of course, silence follows. We wonder where this silence will go. Ben slowly removes his son's handsome top. Emblazoned on Aaron's are the words, "Why this night different?" Everyone laughs and Aaron's broad smile mirrors the happiness we all feel.

Tanya signals us to contain our rambunctious behavior as only a kindergarten teacher can. She distributes iPad around the table. Suddenly the story of the Exodus flashes in front of us in the media of our new age.

Dan crisply moves us from kindergarten to graduate school as he turns the table into a discussion group for advanced Talmud students. With a wry rabbinic smile, he seems to say, "Yes, your answer is a good one, but not quite good enough. How do the ten plagues apply to our contemporary world, what do they say about the scourge of humans' capacity to endanger each other and the planet? And what must we do about it?"

Rachel assigns us to four teams: frogs, lice, locusts, and wild beasts. Each group has to perform a choreographed cheer. Then the teams compete answering questions about Passover, all to gain added seconds, so their team will start the search for the matzah before the others.

I can feel that *all gathered here tonight art with me*: Joanne, my children their spouses, my grandchildren, and those whose spirits I feel but who are no longer physically with us: It is as though an invisible rod and staff guide us. I am thankful for the green pastures that have somehow nourished each child.

I look about the room. Such joy, wit, wisdom and love, such a table before me.

Past the din of surprise and laughter, I step back. I realize: here is my family, together with me tonight as surely as they will be together with me the night I pass from here to there.

Truly, *my cup runneth over.*

Surely goodness and mercy shall follow me all the days of my life. And

I shall dwell in the house of the Lord forever.

– May 30, 2016

W.H.Auden wrote: "Let your last thinks all be thanks."

– May 30, 2016

Oliver Sacks says it this way

"There was an intense emotionality at this time: music I loved, or the long golden sunlight of late afternoon, would set me weeping. I was not sure what I was weeping for, but I would feel an intense sense of love, death, and transience, inseparably mixed."

–June 16, 2015

During my nap today, my older son called about a crisis my grandson is having.

When I learn of the event, I think of Burl Ives strutting the stage in Cat on a Hot Tin Roof, protesting the way his family ignores his dying from the unnamable scourge, cancer. In this day of perhaps excessive truth telling about end of life information, what we face is different. Yet I sometimes feel like Burl Ives. My son explained to Joanne, "I don't want to disturb Dad."

She said "He's taking a nap."

As a result, I am in the dark. In the hours that follow I exaggerate the event as a step towards de-personhood, and picture myself storming about, crying "mendacity, mendacity" (you are treating me as if I am already dead when I am very much alive).

Yet of course, in my storming, I ignore the vast differences between Burl Ives' situation and my own. And I ignore that I am the one who has given the double messages: 'Don't disturb me when I am napping' and 'Include me in whatever is going on.'

I wonder to whom my lusty protest is directed, probably God.

–June 20, 2016

It is not simple. The risk of taking out my frustrations on Joanne, my intimate partner in all this. She is getting cabin fever. She wants to travel. I want to stay at home, to stick with the familiar. I wonder, have I been sitting on the bench too long? Over my gentle protest, we plan a weekend away.

– November 24, 2015

Today marks one year from the date Dr. Cogent advised me I likely had twelve months to live.

The titer in my blood serum of trans-thyretin, the protein that lays down amyloid in my heart, has decreased from 21 to 5. Medically, I seem to be stabilizing. Joanne and I now refer to this as my "new normal."

I am so grateful for this year of living, both for the moments chronicled in the journal and the many more moments not chronicled but experienced more fully than any year I can remember.

As to further entries, who is to predict? The pages remain open

– May 15, 2015

The Task (Tafkeed)

Your youth, my age
Your health, my frailty
Together we meet

Death's mask penetrates horizon
Transfiguring time into sacred space

Unveiling deepest dreams and goals
Choices and directions

Requests for blessing
And for caution

Am I up to the task?
I and Thou?

To listen, Sh'ma
To understand, L'havin
To speak, L'Daber

For life, L'chaim

– January 19, 2016

Today is Joanne's and my 37th anniversary. How grateful we are to mark this day together. Yet, oddly neither of us wants to make a big deal of it. A year ago, every marker in the calendar was the last. This year, though we dare not say this out loud, there may well be more.

My health is stable. I write, I read, I practice the piano. I exercise with Tai Chi rather than tennis. I nap, and I stay in contact by phone with family and old friends. Joanne and I visit our new grandson; we watch Doc Martin and Foyle's War to escape, and Breaking Bad for black humor. I try to go to Literary Club when I am up to it. And we host friends and family who come by to visit. Occasionally I am invited to speak. It wears me out but I feel good about having done it. I am so fortunate to have Joanne by my side.

Life is good.

– March 18, 2016

Today marks one year of taking ISIS 420915. I visit Dr. Quixote. Good news. All the markers indicate my holding steady. No change in thickness of wall of ventricle, of course, moderate heart failure remains.

I can look forward to many more months.

On the night of good news, I dream I am at a picnic. I am dressed in a gray shirt. Mother says that is the wrong shirt to be wearing. My brother Phil is running holding a delicious sandwich. I want some. I run after him but he is too fast. I yell, "Stop, I have a bad heart." I then awaken, screaming at Phil for not stopping.

On reflection, I realize that not only are my mother and brother dead, but also the others in the background of the picnic in my dream, cousins and friends who have recently died. So, the setting for the dream is apparently an afterlife picnic. The "good news" I received yesterday about my medical condition, has evoked a paradoxical disappointment, that, for now, I am to be excluded from joining family and friends in my afterlife "picnic."

We do our best to prepare for what we think will happen next. Then comes life with all its unpredictability.

Edges

This dawn I peek by his window.
Up, alarm already off,
Quickly shaved and showered,
He ignores my presence
He rushes for appointments too important to be pondered
He gulps his breakfast
Guns his car
Attacks problems
Achieves goals
'Til unwittingly he finds no breath
And sudden exhaustion

He looks at me, overwhelmed.
We have been at war this day.
He and I.

Only doing
Has left no room for being

I watch, another day,
He slumbers past my first rays
Awakening naturally.
He sits just outside time
Contemplates dreams not quite remembered

In a haze and in no particular order he
Brushes teeth,
Uses the toilet,
Checks his weight,

Turns on his razor,
Swallows seven pills,
Washes his face.
The haze gradually lifting,
He takes his blood pressure, pulse and oxygen reading
Then sees if he can remember the numbers to write them down.

This day he practices Tai Chi.
I watch as he reaches skyward, breathes deeply, expires slowly
Visits his struggling heart and lungs.

One maneuver begins with hands extended loosely, palms down,
One hand gently circles waist high, then presses down to earth
While the second hand reaches up to sky.
He pauses,
These are the things for now,
One touching earth with its rough texture,
A chore he'd rather postpone,
The other a higher calling,
Something new, to create or give.

These will be the actions of his day
A chore
A poem
A mitzvah

We are friends, he and I,
Each of us not so much doing as being

I complete my paper on the year that was to be my last to live. But it turns out to have been a very special twelve months to live, full of connections, adventure, humor, joy, sadness and gratitude. And as you can see, twelve months became twenty-four. Indeed, I am very much alive two years after learning I had a condition that should have killed me long ago.

It appears I have lapsed into extra innings. Perhaps more on that a later time.

{14}

STOKING THE FIRES

STEWART MAXWELL

"WOULD YOU LIKE TO ACCOMPANY ME to the Literary Club's attic to see one of the earliest and finest mantels of the Federal Style in Cincinnati?" As we sipped drinks in the reception room in November 1996, this question was posed to me by my host and Club member at that time, Professor Walter E. Langsam. Tantalizing a fellow architectural historian with such a question elicited an enthusiastic "Yes!" We proceeded to ascend the two flights of stairs reaching the third-floor attic. On this storage room floor, there it was: a beautifully carved Federal Style wooden mantel.

Painted in an off-white color typical of the 1820 period, its carving exhibited fine craftsmanship superior to other known examples from that time. Distinguishing qualities of this mantel are a pair of Romanesque Revival rounded arched niches at either end, centered above two Tuscan-style columns. The exact purpose of these niches is unknown, but the likely intention was to feature for special attention a pair of *objets d'art* of its owner. For additional enhancement, small globular balls placed in succession, outline each of the rounded arches, as if highlighted by modern-day vanity light fixtures. These same globular balls of a slightly larger diameter also march in alignment across its header, reminding one of a series of cannonballs in a straight line, possibly alluding to nearby Fort Washington. Immediately, these two niches recalled a comparison to the Kilgour Hallway door casings from the late 1815 historic Cincinnati home called, "The White House," sections of which are on display in the Art Museum's Cincinnati Wing. Above each of its door headers can be found a pair of niches in the Gothic Revival Style, featuring pointed arches instead of rounded ones.

The realization of these similarities earned my instant respect, because I had always admired the Kilgour Hallway. However, since I was not a member of the Club at that time, I simply mentally filed the knowledge of the mantel's existence for a later day.

That time came once I was admitted to the Club as a member. Several years ago, Ted Silberstein and I undertook the rehanging of the Literary Club's art collection and the updating of our inventory. It turned out that Ted and others were unaware of the mantel's existence. Peaking Ted's curiosity, we marched our way upstairs to the attic, just as Walter and I had years earlier. What Ted and I discovered was that the mantel had since been installed on a wall, moved from its former placement on the floor.

Not having seen it in many years, time can alter one's impression, either favorably or unfavorably. In this case, my respect for the mantel had only increased, having viewed many others in the interim. Ted agreed that it was of superb quality and much too fine to be relegated to an attic, where no one could appreciate its beauty and significance. Reaching this consensus, we added the mantel to our inventory list, and then pursued with the membership the possibility that it might be donated to the Cincinnati Art Museum, where it could be displayed to the public.

The Art Museum's Curator of Decorative Arts & Design, Amy Dehan, and its Director and Club member, Cameron Kitchin, were equally enthusiastic about the mantel and wanted it for their Cincinnati Wing's earliest display section. Also, it is appropriate that it should be installed there, since former Director and Club member, Timothy Rub, was responsible for the Wing's creation. With the Board of Management's and members' approval, and the generosity of The Decorative Arts Society of Cincinnati, which contributed funds for its conservation and installation, thanks to their skilled crew the mantel made the move to the Art Museum on a warm, sunny day on May 10, 2018.

As the mantel was being removed from the attic's wall, old calling cards and invitations fell to the floor, having slipped between the mantelshelf and chimneybreast at least 140 years ago. Amazingly, these cards must have adhered themselves onto the mantel's back side by means of fireplace heat and the cards' ink, which together, acted as glue. Their survival is truly remarkable, since the mantel was moved in 1930 from the first floor to the attic, and then moved again when it was repositioned from the floor to the wall. For tidiness sake, the Museum's crew was about to throw these cards away. Before that happened, I immediately grabbed them, saving them from becoming a part of the dust heap of history. These calling cards and invitations are a part of the mantel's Cincinnati history, and reveal a bit of the daily lives of the home's occupants. Although some are only in fragments, others survived intact for our perusal. One of the calling cards is that of "McLean & Goodman" — a linseed oil manufacturing company located at Symmes Street and the Miami & Erie Canal, owned by Civil War General Nathaniel McLean, son-in-law of Judge Jacob Burnet. The latter was my great, great, great, great grandfather, who purchased this home on December 15, 1842 for his daughter Caroline and her husband, General McLean. It remained in the family until 1912, a seventy-year timespan. Also of importance is an invitation to a millinery fashion show of Paris creations, dated September 19, 1879, at Bee, Rolfus & Co. of 142 West Fourth Street. This company was unknown to the Art Museum as it was not listed in their late nineteenth-early twentieth-century fashion catalogue, A Separate Sphere. Since the cards have some historical significance and managed to survive all these years attached to the mantelpiece's back side, they, too, have been donated as a part of its story.

These donations led to a new chapter in the mantel's conservation. Having arrived at the Museum, it was placed in quarantine for a few months by their Conservation Department to make certain that no insects, termites, wood worms, or borers had been transported with it. None found, the next step was to do careful scrapings of the mantel's layers of paint to determine its original 1820 color. As the conservators removed these layers, one of them revealed that it had been painted black at some point, probably during the design period of the 1850s to 1870s when to do so was fashionable. As the Art Museum and I had expected, the original color turned out to be off-white or ivory, consistent with the Federal Style.

While this paint analysis and painstaking removal of surface layers were being conducted, Amy Dehan and I were researching the history of the Club's mantel, while also examining other Cincinnati woodcarving examples. One of the most intriguing questions has always been: "Where was the mantel's original location in the Club's home?" Initially, we thought that it might have been designed for the Library, where the current Negro Marquina marble mantel is today. Clearly, this marble mantelpiece is not original to the ca.1820 date for the house; however, its classic clean lines and stone material make it more difficult to ascertain its age. Spanning approximately ninety years of stylistic design creativity from Greek Revival to Art Deco, this marble mantel, we thought, could have been installed conceivably in 1930 by the architectural firm, Elzner & Anderson, who remodeled the home to become our Club headquarters. The wooden one was then banished to the attic. Our thinking was that a more "masculine-looking" Art Deco mantelpiece might have been desired by the architects and the Club for the Library, and that this would have been accomplished during the renovations. If so, the architect's working drawings for the project would note this change. One Monday evening in September, 2018, our Club Librarian, Rick Kesterman and I unrolled these plans, and my eyes immediately focused on the room identified as "Library" on the First Floor. My heart sank, though, when I realized that there was <u>no</u> mention of any alteration to that room's chimneybreast at that time.

About to roll up the drawings in defeat, Rick and I noticed the notes on the plan in the room adjacent to the Library. Consistent with the Federal Style's symmetrical balance for design, there originally had been another room of equal size to the Library, located in the home's northwest corner, which included a fourth mantel (the brick chimney can still be seen on the exterior from the alley). On the First Floor Plan, the notes state "Mantel removed" and "Present fireplace flue continued to Basement". On the Basement Floor Plan, another note was discovered directly below this former room: "Fireplace flue brought down for water heater vent." These notes written on the drawings confirmed the location of the wooden mantelpiece and its move in 1930 to the attic. Furthermore, since there were no notes on the Library's marble mantel during the remodeling, other than for its cleaning and polishing, this meant it was of an earlier vintage, Greek Revival Style (ca. 1840s-1850s). Most likely, the McLean family installed it to be up-to-date with society's taste, when they moved there in 1842. Ironically, the marble mantel replaced another 1820 wooden one original to the house, which may have survived and been reinstalled elsewhere, yet to be rediscovered.

By comparatively studying other Cincinnati mantelpieces and woodwork from residences dating to this same time period, much information regarding our mantel has been learned. Most similar is the earlier mentioned David Kilgour home called "The White House" (1814-1815) with its unique Gothic Revival arched niches in the door headers. In addition to this similarity, there was something else: our mantel has fluting on both sides, rather than on the front face, which would have been the norm. The uniqueness of this detail, therefore, makes it a woodcarver's idiosyncrasy. On the large archway spanning the width of the Kilgour Hallway, there are pilasters with their fluting on the sides, too, rather than the front face. Considering these similarities, the homes' proximity to each other, and their 1815 and 1820 dates of completion, it seems likely that the same woodcarver had done both.

Locally, there are additional examples identified for comparative purposes. The Baum-Longworth-Taft House (earlier named "Belmont", but now known as The Taft Museum of Art — 1820) has in its foyer similar globular balls placed in succession for each of their door lintels, like the ones outlining our mantel's niches and marching horizontally across its header. Globular balls are such an unusual design motif, that it is probable that the same woodcarver had been commissioned to do these as well.

While examining the Taft's woodwork, I also inquired about the whereabouts of their Museum's one remaining original mantelpiece to the house. When posed with this question, the museum staff did not know of its existence. Luckily, photographer Alice Weston with author Walter Langsam had captured its image, when they were compiling their book entitled *Great Houses of the Queen City,* published in 1997. In this photo, the mantel is shown in its former Ground Level Entry Hall location at the base of the staircase. When the Taft underwent its remodeling and expansion in 2001- 2004, the mantel was removed, and its importance lost in the shuffle. The Taft's Deputy Director and Chief Curator Lynne Ambrosini, her assistant Ann Glasscock and I went on a search to find it, as well as two other period mantels not original to the house. They had been differently located before the recent remodeling in the Taft's two front parlors. The original mantelpiece to the house was found in the Docents' File Room and Library on the Ground Level: obscuring the mantelshelf were papers and files, with little surrounding space for its appreciation. Finely carved, it features flanking pairs of Tuscan columns at each end providing classical symmetry, was a supporting header with a sweeping arch spanning from side-to-side. Centered above the fireplace opening is a recessed horizontal elliptical sunburst shell, balanced by two vertical ones over each pair of columns. Along the undulating mantelshelf's edge and chair rail banding, Chinese fretwork was carved into their wood surfaces, adding to its overall sophistication.

The other two mantels in their collection were found in the Basement Storage Room and have a connection with our Club. Former Museum Director and Literary Club member, Walter H. Siple, had purchased both of them, when he was transforming the Taft's residence into a museum. The previous owners of the house, the Longworths, had replaced the original ones (except the one described and rediscovered) with arched white Carrara marble ones of the Italianate Style in accordance with tastes of the 1850s — probably installed around 1857 at the time of the Longworth's fiftieth wedding anniversary. Striving for authenticity, Mr. Siple wanted to find wooden mantels consistent with the ones original to the Martin Baum-era of the home. According to his records and a Literary Club paper, he located mantels, with exquisite quality and style, from the neighborhood and the surrounding Cincinnati area characteristic of this ca.1820s timeframe. Unfortunately, during the most recent reinterpretation of the galleries, these two Federal Style wooden mantels acquired by Mr. Siple were replaced with ones of King of Prussia marble of the later Greek Revival Style (ca.1840-1850s). Contrary to the opinion of former Taft curator David Johnson, the home's original mantels could not have been carved in marble, because there were no stone carvers residing in early Cincinnati, nor was there the means to transport them from the East at that time. Additionally, their one surviving mantel was made of wood: this inconvenient truth was disregarded by Curator Johnson, and so he banished it to the Docents' File Room and Library, where it is off view to the public.

Further insults occurred to the two Federal mantels acquired by Director Siple, which unceremoniously were removed completely from sight and placed in storage. This enabled Curator Johnson to acquire the marble mantels for the front parlors, which he really desired. In the future, hopefully, these three beautifully carved wooden mantels will be placed back on display, since they directly relate to the history and architecture of the house, the neighborhood, and early Cincinnati, whereas the marble ones do not. In review, although

The Taft's wooden mantels are quite handsome, they really did not closely resemble the Club's, thus, may not have been made by the same woodcarver.

In this continued quest to observe, study, and compare mantels of the 1820 period, Walter and I visited a little-known museum in a very surprising place: Woodward High School in Bond Hill. The first Woodward School (and Cincinnati Public School's earliest, while being at the same time the oldest, continuously operating free public high school in the world) was founded by William Woodward in the downtown area. Dating back to 1816, many of the contents of his home and school were saved, when the move to the suburbs occurred in 1953, and a museum was established to celebrate their heritage. Recently, a new Woodward High School was constructed, and this treasure trove of decorative art objects and architectural fragments made the move to a gallery honoring Mr. Woodward. Prominently on display is his 1816 Guest Room mantelpiece, which presents certain similarities to the mantels of both the Literary Club and the Taft Museum. Reminiscent of ours, the Woodward mantel has two rounded arched niches above its flanking columns, but these are open both on the face and the sides. Like the Taft's original mantel, the Woodward one has a large sweeping arch carved into its header. Also, comparisons were found matching it to those located at "Elmwood Hall" (1818) in Ludlow, Kentucky.

As a brief aside, this remarkable house had been built by Thomas Carneal for his family, later purchased in 1827 by William Bullock (brother of the famous London furniture maker, George Bullock). Eventually, the house became the Thomas Candy Co. factory, then acquired by my cousin and artist, Thomas Gaither, who always admired its architecture. This home-turned-factory was transformed into a 2-family residence by him and rented to Walter in one half, the other portion becoming Jack Meanwell's artist studio. In time, architectural historian Patrick Snadon purchased "Elmwood Hall", and he has been respectfully and lovingly restoring it back to its original condition as his single-family residence. Returning to the mantel comparisons, Woodward's is similar to "Elmwood Hall's" with their columns of ringed capitals and tapered shafts, which also closely resemble a game table leg detail designed by Benjamin Henry Latrobe, now in the collection of the Philadelphia Museum of Art. Other similarities between Woodward's and "Elmwood Hall's" mantelpieces are the carved recessed sunburst shells in their headers, but they do not directly relate to the Literary Club's.

What this investigation has revealed is that Cincinnati from its earliest days was blessed with geographical and military advantages, unique to our locale, which led to extraordinary growth and development, with the city's population more than doubling every ten years. At its beginnings in 1788, Cincinnati's superiority over other Midwestern cities can be attributed directly to the protection that the government's military encampment, Fort Washington, offered to settlers from marauding Indians. Although surrounded by steep hillsides, Cincinnati's basin area contains one of the largest sections of flat terrain for building and farming along the Ohio River, another major attraction and advantage. In addition, Cincinnati was the location of a number of mouths of rivers and creeks, providing an early and convenient form of transportation flowing into the heartland of the states of Ohio, Kentucky, and Indiana. Besides the mighty Ohio River, these included the Little Miami, Great Miami, Licking, Whitewater, Mill Creek, Deer Creek, and the Miami & Erie Canal. The latter linked Cincinnati with Lake Erie and the Eastern seaboard, allowing much improvement in speed, ease, and comfort for travelers and farmers' livestock alike. People, products, cattle, and agricultural crops moved with relative rapidity to and from Cincinnati, which further encouraged our city's prosperity, growth, and prestige.

Around 1815, building steamboats was established here, and Cincinnati became one of the nation's principal boat building centers by constructing more than twenty steamboats per year. This industry attracted fine artisans and carpenters, capable of carving elaborate boat decorations, to seek employment in our city.

Many of our settlers were wealthy second oldest sons from the East, who were accustomed to the finer things in life, including the enjoyment of the arts and culture. Moving west to Cincinnati, they reestablished themselves in the fastest growing city in America during the first half of the nineteenth century. Since older brothers had inherited the family business and property, the younger hoped to apply their knowledge and expertise in a new venture to make their own fortunes. If they were not going to live in Philadelphia, Baltimore, New York, or Boston, then they were going to bring their cultured lives with them to Cincinnati. As a consequence, museums, libraries, clubs, historical societies, music, opera, plays, churches, synagogues, and fine mercantile shops soon populated the city, giving it a clear advantage over other cities west of the Alleghenies in attracting people of means. Residents of Cincinnati had discriminating tastes for the very best, which allowed craftsmen to create quality of the highest order. From architecture to furniture, silver, clocks, glassware, clothing, and many other things, they all combined to make a vibrant community, which we still enjoy today.

No discussion of Cincinnati's development and quality of life at this time would be complete without considering Frances Trollope and the publication of her book, *Domestic Matters of the Americans*. This English lady arrived here by boat in 1828 and stayed for two unhappy years. Her frank distaste for America and its inhabitants' manners (or lack thereof) was focused on Cincinnati, since she resided here. At great expense, Mrs. Trollope erected "Mrs. Trollope's Bazaar", a mercantile establishment four stories high, containing eclectic curiosities assembled from all over the world. Designed by Seneca Palmer, he was the first professional architect known to have settled in Cincinnati, its exterior façade was as curious as its contents, with tall slender arched fenestration several floors in height, each separated with columns, and the whole creation recalling the Near East in design. Double curved stairs on the outside led to its *piano nobile*, with a sinuous interior staircase rising from floor-to-floor to a rooftop *rotunda monitor.* Reminiscent of a Turkish bazaar, its roof's undulating crenelated parapet added a playful arabesque touch, in an otherwise conservative city with buildings of a neo-classical style during this period. With her ill-fated business venture, it clearly soured Mrs. Trollope for Cincinnatians not appreciating sophisticated tastes as she defined them. Similar to other failed businesses, she misread her clientele and what they desired. Customers in our city had money and taste, but obviously were not interested in what she was providing. In spite of everything, the fact is that Mrs. Trollope settled here and not elsewhere, so even she believed in the city's potential in exposing its citizenry to exotic, international merchandise. Her shop did not long survive, but her building lasted for many decades as its own curiosity.

In spite of Mrs. Trollope's protestations, it still is not surprising that the quality of architectural detailing and products produced in Cincinnati far exceeds those from other Midwestern cities in the nineteenth century. Confirmation of this can be realized simply by strolling the Art Museum's Cincinnati Wing. The Literary Club's mantel has now been unveiled there for visitors to admire and for us to be rightfully proud of our generosity in sharing in perpetuity this significant piece of Cincinnati history. Its installation will be adjacent to the Kilgour Hallway, where it will reside under the watchful gaze of Judge Jacob Burnet's bust by Hiram Powers. Fittingly, Judge Burnet will be reunited with our mantel from the 500 East Fourth Street home, which he acquired in 1842 for his daughter and son-in-law. Best of all, the triumphs of the as-yet unidentified craftsman, who carved our mantelpiece and likely the Kilgour Hallway, will be featured together — highlighting the outstanding talent available for hire in our Queen City of the West, as it blossomed from its very beginnings.

{15}

THE LANDFILL

FREDERICK J. MCGAVRAN

TECHNOLOGY IS ALWAYS THE ANSWER. Hi. My name is Yardsal ("Yardy") Haines, and that's what I used to tell the school kids bussed out to the landfill for a day in the country. Most kids nowadays have never been to the country and thought they were going to see a cow pasture when we took them up to Lookout Point. Stretched out before them was an inland sea of plastic bags crisscrossed by bulldozers leveling out the bumps.

"Hey, Mr. Yardy!" some kid always asked. "Why's it smell so bad? Is it the cows?"

See what I mean? Those kids couldn't tell a cow from a bulldozer. Anyway, the question gave me a chance to talk about decay of organic matter and give them some terms to describe it besides the ones they already knew. Teachers really appreciated that.

"If it smells like shit, it probably is shit," my friend Bill Bob Leahy, chief of security always added.

Bill Bob is a short man with a beer belly so enormous he has to lean backwards to keep from toppling over. The kids loved him because he spoke their language. Teachers were another story.

I've been chief engineer at Settlers Landfill for twenty-seven years. As a waste management professional, I don't use terms like "dump" or "trash." For us in the industry, waste management is a technological challenge, not a subject for sick jokes. We accepted over two million tons of household and industrial waste every year and spread it out across our 600-acre campus to be layered with soil and blended into the environment. Thanks to reclamation science, we graded and seeded the outer edges just like strip miners grade and seed the outer edges of their pits, so passersby see only rolling green hills from the road.

Inside, however, we had to deal with mounds of plastic bags exploding and out-gassing as their contents ripened in the summer sun. Over the years our sales force was so successful that corporate in Chicago projected the landfill would reach its capacity by 2020. Our neighbors wouldn't sell us more land, and the regulators wouldn't let us use it if they did. Strapped for space, we could not keep layering the waste with dirt to keep the flies and odor down. We had to find a high-tech solution.

Although often criticized in the media, our industry is very sensitive to the needs of our neighbors. We have to be. My wife Cindy and I and Bill Bob and his wife Cheryl live in Settlers Grove, a planned community for employees just outside the landfill. So we were all relieved when corporate announced that it had developed a proprietary solvent that not only made the waste decompose in less than the half-life of a plastic bag, but would also shrink the compost to less than one-third its original size. We learned later that it did this by dehydrating and solidifying the waste into a hardness that could withstand a nuclear blast.

Corporate had thought of everything except the exponential increase in methane gas caused by the enhanced decomposition process. Coupled with a temperature inversion, complaints about bad odors reached a crescendo not even our PR firm and Political Action Committee could silence. School trips were cancelled; grilling out was impossible. I remember wearing an oxygen mask when I cut our grass.

Corporate found another technical solution: a gigantic plastic dome that would cover the landfill and capture the gas. Through an intricate piping system, methane would be routed to our neighbors to heat their homes. The dome was designed by the same NASA engineers who were designing domes for the first colonists on Mars. It made the landfill look like a gigantic terrarium. Offering methane gas at below market rates, we converted criticism into praise and gained many advocates. We even designed clear places in the plastic at Lookout Point so the kids could look in and watch the enhanced decomposition. It was only in the choice of a piping and concrete contractor that we went astray.

Butch Siegel is the best example I have ever seen of why accepting the lowest bid can be a mistake. As the weather changed, leaks developed around the pipes where they passed through the dome due to the different rates of expansion for plastic and metal. Neighbor complaints rebounded reaching as high as the governor's office, and Cindy and I had to cancel our Fourth of July barbecue. I called Siegel to my office in the concrete block administrative building that had been built when the site was used as an ammunition testing ground in the 1940s. He was as confident as ever.

"The pipes are leaking," I said.

"No problem," Butch reassured me.

"How're you going to seal them?"

"Easy," Butch said and winked, holding up a Zippo® lighter engraved "Danang 1968" and a large tube of epoxy cement.

That was the last time I saw him. Bill Bob watched him climb up the dome and light the Zippo by one of the methane pipes. Leahy made it back to our administrative building just before Butch found his first leak.

To my amazement, even our closest neighbors did not hear the blast. When Bill Bob and I went out to survey the damage, the dome was intact, having deflected the blast downwards into the landfill. Only the piping was gone, landing, as we learned later, in backyards and Interstates as far as 20 miles away. After putting in a missing person report on Siegel, we were back in full operation within an hour.

Corporate in Chicago called to ask whether there had been any damage to the waste itself. Obviously, they were thinking of restarting methane gas production as soon as possible. I hadn't thought of that. So we let the dome cool for a day, and then Bill Bob and I clambered up with flashlights to peer through the pipe holes. It was like looking down into the earth through an upside-down periscope.

Not a plastic bag remained. The waste, solidified by the solvent, had been driven deep into the earth like a gigantic bullet, leaving the appearance of a crater on the moon. Now we had space for hundreds of millions more metric tons of waste, enough to serve the prospective needs not only of the city, but also of the surrounding area for decades. We scrambled down to call Chicago.

"Watch out, Yardy!" Bill Bob cried, grabbing my arm and pulling me back just as the concrete base at my feet collapsed, leaving a gap between the dome and the crater below.

"Looks like Butch skimped on the concrete, too," I said.

The explosion had cracked the base all around the dome. Corporate wasn't happy, but who needed a dome now that fifty years' accumulation of methane was gone? The neighbors could go back to getting their gas from the utility company like everybody else. I designed a wire fence on metal stakes to keep workers from falling in, but after a month the ground gave way beneath that, too. Sections of the fence drooped and dangled over the edge until the last stakes gave way and everything dropped into the crater. We had to stop the school tours for good.

We established a protocol that anyone approaching the edge had to wear a safety harness. Every time I got roped up to inspect the crater, I was amazed at how deep it was. Gray, cloudy, with little channels of fire swirling in its depths, it was like looking into the remains of a city hit by nuclear bombs or an opening into hell.

One afternoon the dome started to tilt to one side, like a lid too small for a pot.

"What'll we do if it falls in?" Bill Bob wondered.

"Beats hell out of me," I replied. "Let's hope corporate has the answer."

Corporate didn't care. Aside from a photo of the tilting dome that went viral, no one else cared, either. The day the dome finally slid down into the crater, Bill Bob and I were the only ones who bothered to get roped up to see it. It was lying on the bottom at about a 30° angle, exaggerating the flames beneath it like an enormous magnifying glass.

"Is the dome flammable?" Bill Bob asked.

We soon had the answer to that.

Bill Bob and I had bought houses on the same street in the late '80s when the landfill was just getting started and worked our way up in the company together. Now that our kids were gone, he and Cheryl and Cindy and I were beginning to think about retirement communities where you did not go to sleep to the sound of garbage trucks racing in and out of the landfill, or the crackle of uncontained fires sweeping over mountains of plastic bags.

"You know, I kind of miss the sound of the plastic bags burning," Cindy said the evening the dome fell in while we and the Leahys were grilling steaks on our patio. "It kind of put me to sleep, like a fire in the fireplace on a winter evening."

"What's that?" Cheryl exclaimed.

A rush of wind came from the landfill, followed by the throat-closing stench of burning plastic.

"Get inside!" Bill Bob cried as I took the steaks off the grill. "The dome caught fire!"

The sky over the landfill was clotted with thick black smoke lit orange by the flames beneath.

This time corporate was ecstatic. Once the dome was burned out, we could put in even more waste without it blocking the flow like an upside-down cup over a garbage disposal. Besides, the crater was getting deeper, and Settlers Landfill was about to become the largest in the country. Despite thousands of tons of dirt dumped into the crater, however, the fire burned for three weeks, causing the evacuation of everyone within our out-gassing range. Every TV station in town had drones circling to get real-time action shots, and we were the subject of sarcastic comments by TV talk show hosts and liberal politicians all over the country. Bill Bob and I and our wives had to move across town to an extended-stay motel, cutting short the summer cookout season.

"I don't need all this," Bill Bob said after he had been up all night trying to move protesters out of the access road to the landfill so the trucks could get through. "I'm going to take early retirement."

"Maybe I should, too," I agreed. "Florida is looking better every day."

We weren't the only ones with ideas like that. The only problem was getting our money out of our houses. That's when corporate announced it would buy the house at pre-explosion fair market value of any employee who agreed to stay on until retirement. As usual Chicago thought it would all blow over in a year, and everyone would forget about the offer. Instead, the problem kept expanding.

The crater was getting larger. Even the waste truck drivers noticed that they didn't have to drive as far into the site to discharge their loads. Finally figuring this could be as much a problem as an opportunity, corporate ordered me to find out why.

That's when I met Cleves Warsaw, Ph.D. No one in City University's engineering department knew anything about crater dynamics, so I was referred to physics. Dr. Warsaw was the nation's leading expert on the formation and life cycle of craters. With a scraggly beard whitened by chalk dust and a squint from spending years peering through telescopes, Cleves Warsaw looked more like a janitor than a professor. Bill Bob made him show two sets of government issued identification to let him onto the landfill. Fortunately, he had a current Yosemite National Park pass along with his driver's license, or we would never have learned what was going on.

Like many physicists, Dr. Warsaw was obsessed with data. What was the radius of the landfill when we installed the glass dome? When did we first notice the slippage? Did we measure it? Could we get access to the TV stations' drone films? All this was necessary to determine the crater's coefficient of expansion. Along with all this, he was the most reckless investigator I have ever known. Nearly every day we had to wire him up to inspect the crater's edge, and nearly every day he fell in and was extracted with great difficulty, often with a winch. Did I tell you he weighed over 300 pounds?

Corporate was demanding answers, and some drivers were refusing to enter the landfill for fear their trucks would fall in. When Dr. Warsaw finally announced he had found the answer, I set up a conference call with corporate because no one there would come near the landfill.

"You're not going to like this," Dr. Warsaw told me before he began.

I was just happy that Chicago had not insisted on Skyping. If they had seen Cleves Warsaw, they wouldn't have believed anything he said. As it was, the call was delayed while he fiddled with his laptop and set up a screen to project his conclusions. Bill Bob, who was sitting in out of general interest, was getting edgy.

"Looks like he's about to download his pornography collection," he whispered.

And then Dr. Warsaw turned down the lights and started his presentation. Bill Bob was lost from the get-go, but to me it had a certain logic, like one of those guys at the fair selling tools you could use to chop vegetables and work on your transmission all at the same time.

"So just tell us what's going to happen," our executive VP said over the speaker phone.

It was the first time anyone in Chicago had spoken.

"This is what's going to happen," Dr. Warsaw said, showing a computer projection of the crater expanding until a bulge in its center formed a ball so big the crater disappeared.

"I can't see it," the executive VP snapped. "Yardy, what the hell is going on?"

"The crater is turning the world inside out like a guy taking off a sock," I replied.

"How much did we pay for this?" the VP demanded.

"Dr. Warsaw, what are you telling us?" I asked.

Like so many theoreticians, he could not give a simple answer. In the late 1930s, the Soviet mathematician Dmitri Baklanov had developed a series of equations so elegant and seemingly detached from reality that no one had ever found anything in the universe that corresponded to them. Thinking Baklanov had written a mathematical parody of the Soviet Union, Stalin had him shot. Afterwards the best mathematical minds in the world had searched for some application for the Baklanov equations, much as they searched for something that would change lead into gold or proof of Fermat's Last Theorem.

"And now I have identified the process Baklanov predicted," Dr. Warsaw exulted. "When an explosion occurs with sufficient force directed downward at a particular place on the earth's surface, it sets in motion a process whereby the crater expands and deepens until it exerts a sufficient attractive force on the other side of the globe, which swells downward and engulfs the original crater, causing the world to turn itself inside out."

I have never known Chicago to be quiet for so long.

"How much time have we got?" the executive VP asked.

"Seven years, two hundred and thirty-one days, and two hours," Dr. Warsaw answered.

"At least it's not tonight," somebody else in Chicago said. "I've got to take my kids to soccer practice."

The rest of the call was about keeping everything under wraps so the public would not panic and house prices in the neighborhood would not fall any more than they already had. It turned out that the company was negotiating a class action settlement and had offered its employees the same deal it was offering everyone else, except that the employees had to stay on the job to get it. Dr. Warsaw assured us he would not disclose his work until it was published in the peer-reviewed journal *Crater Dynamics*. Fortunately, *Crater Dynamics* was published bi-annually, and the latest edition had just come out. The world would not know its fate for nearly another two years.

"There's more than enough time for me to win the Nobel Prize after that," he said happily. "The university will have to make me tenure track when I win the Nobel."

"That's right, Professor," the executive VP assured him. "No need to get people all worked up about something when there's nothing they can do about it."

After the call was concluded, Bill Bob and I went to our offices to work on our applications for early retirement. They were granted along with the house buyout after we signed a confidentiality agreement.

Later I asked Dr. Warsaw the last place to be sucked into the earth before the world turned inside out. He said Yekaterinburg, Russia about 1100 miles east of Moscow, where the last Czar and his family were murdered by the Bolsheviks in 1918. Cindy and I don't think a few extra years on the edge of Siberia are worth it.

So Bill Bob and Cheryl and Cindy and I are moving to Key West after the first wave of panic selling hits, and they think they're all going under tomorrow. Being inundated by a tsunami can't be any worse than freezing in a blizzard, even if it comes a little sooner. Dr. Warsaw says we'll have several good years in Florida. That's more than most people get. The end of the world is only a problem if you let it get to you. Come to think of it, maybe somebody will come up with a technical solution for that, too.

{16}

NOSTRUM REMEDIUM

CHRISTOPHER MILLIGAN

GHOST SIGHTINGS IN MUSIC HALL reached a peak in the mid-1980s with regular reports of seeing a female figure in a white gown. I heard such stories myself when I was an intern with the company in 1989 and 1990. A woman with dark hair pulled back in a bun, wearing a white dress and sometimes carrying a candle. She was only ever seen at night when the building was dark and empty—passing in a distant hallway, vanishing into the auditorium from the lobby, or watching from around a corner. My paper tonight is related to these sightings. It's a story that has not been told, and by the end, you'll understand why.

For the sake of clarity, I've organized my paper in ten brief sections. Also, for the sake of clarity, I'll tell this story chronologically, though I learned some of the earlier details much later.

PART 1. NATALIA'S MEDICINE SHOW

The singer's name was Natalia. She joined the chorus of Cincinnati Opera at some point in the 1970s. But, since she never participated in any performances, her name doesn't appear in any of the company's program books from the period. I'm guessing it was either 1977 or 1978 based on those I know who met her.

Descriptions vary somewhat. She was in her 30s and was strikingly beautiful. She had an accent that some say was Croatian. She had long dark hair that she always wore up. She claimed to be a descendent of the Italian composer Giuseppe Verdi. By all accounts, she was an excellent singer.

It was at the third or fourth rehearsal of the season that she became a problem.

She arrived at the rehearsal with a carpet bag. And at the first break, as other singers stretched, compared notes, and drank coffee, Natalia carried her bag over to a table and removed a black leather case, which she opened to display its contents. There were at least two dozen small glass vials. They contained special preparations she had made—cures for common maladies. They offered the promise of reducing hair loss, relieving indigestion, boosting energy, effecting weight loss, and more. She said these were secret family cures passed down from her father, and she offered them for sale.

Soon, there were complaints from fellow choristers, and the management at the time instructed her to stop. At first, she apologized, seeming genuinely contrite. But as it turned out, she just changed tack, approaching chorus members individually with her cures. It was when she began cornering visiting principal singers that she crossed the line. She was fired from the chorus and asked to leave.

Of singers and superstition.

A streak of superstition has long existed among theatrical performers. One must never say the name of Shakespeare's Scottish play in a theatre, you know. And a flawless final dress rehearsal is seen as a bad omen for opening night.

Among opera performers, whose success or failure can depend on a single high note, the belief in good luck, bad luck, rituals, and talismans is common. Luciano Pavarotti, for example, would scan the backstage floor for a bent nail to put in his pocket before going onstage. The obvious placement and careful cleanup of these nails became part of the stagehands' ritual whenever the great tenor was to perform.

Before an opera performance, one never says, "Good luck" or "Break a leg." One says, instead, either "Toi, toi, toi," a reference to spitting three times to ward off evil spirits, or "In bocca al lupo!" which means "Into the mouth of the wolf!" It acknowledges the potentially adversarial relationship between performer and audience, to say nothing of the fact that a theater does look like a voracious maw from the vantage point of the performer. And, similar to how comedians say that they "killed" after a good stand-up routine, opera singers respond to "In bocca al lupo" with "Crepi il lupo" — *I will slay the wolf.*

Almost all singers are very health-conscious. They are acutely aware that congestion or a sore throat threatens their ability to make a living. Many have their own recipes for dealing with common ailments, and they share these with each other. I once received a recipe for a salt gargle that included hydrogen peroxide and sodium bromide.

All this said, Natalia's traveling medicine show went well beyond any normal, occasional sharing of natural remedies. I later learned that her nostrums came from her father, a traveling peddler who would, in his native country, offer tonics and elixirs as cures for what ails you. Whatever you needed, whatever you wanted, he always had the perfect thing or could produce it within a day or two.

PART 2: AN OLD LETTER

The incident with Natalia would have remained in the past, were it not for the discovery of an envelope in 2017. Cincinnati Opera had moved its offices out of Music Hall—temporarily, while the Grande Dame of Elm Street was undergoing an enormous renovation. We set up shop on the 7th floor of the old Cincinnati Club building on Garfield. Performances that summer took place at the Aronoff Center.

Most mornings had a familiar routine. I'd arrive at my office, hang up my blazer, change out the water in my espresso maker, and log in to check email. The first email I would look for as I drank my morning caffeine was the performance report. The Aronoff's house manager was diligent about completing and sending it before she left for the evening. Often, that meant the email came in well after midnight.

There were always incidents—a drunken or disruptive patron, complaints about temperature—from patrons who thought it was too hot and just as many others who thought it was too cold. Some of these required follow-up. As the company's managing director, I was always looking for system issues—things that malfunctioned and needed fixing—double seatings, usher protocol problems, safety concerns. Just as important, of course, were injuries or illness. Every season, we seemed to have two or three patrons who would faint during a performance. The cause was remarkably consistent: they had done yard work in the hot sun, neglected to stay hydrated, and came to the theater, enjoying a chardonnay or champagne when they arrived.

I skimmed the report for June 22, 2017. One ticket-taker was late. One of the video monitors in the lobby was malfunctioning but was scheduled for repair. A patron fell and was treated by the onsite EMT. In the Other Notes section, it was mentioned that one of the stagehands turned in an envelope that had been found in the Music Hall shop as prep work was being done for a new floor. It was hand-addressed to James de Blasis and, remarkably, still sealed. This was odd as Jim had not been with the company since 1996, when he retired after serving as artistic director since the early 1970s.

I was in regular communication with Jim. So, I sent him a quick email, mentioning the envelope and asking for his permission to open it.

About the Renovation

Before the recent renovation of Music Hall, there were many legends and tales about the building. Beyond the oft-repeated ghost stories, the building itself was just curious. There were hallways that ended abruptly, staircases to no- where, and forgotten spaces that went unused for years. In the public areas, there were artifacts older than the building itself. For example, a very fine 15-foot mirror was fastened to the wall in the North Hall. It had been salvaged from the 1850 Burnet House, a grand five-story hotel at the center of 19th-century metropolitan life in Cincinnati. With its flag-topped central dome making it appear like a state capital, this was where Oscar Wilde stayed during his visits to the Queen City in 1882. In addition to attending a meeting of this august group, Wilde also saw a performance of a then-new opera called Aida at Music Hall. Many other famous guests are likely to have taken notice of their appearance before the mirror during their stay at Burnet House, but the most famous was Abraham Lincoln.

Music Hall was also home to numerous statues, busts, and paintings. Of particular interest to this story is the bust of Max Rudolf, the German conductor who led the CSO and May Festival in the 1960s. It was presented in 1968, near the end of Rudolf's tenure with the Orchestra. A curious tradition began around this bronze sculpture.

There is an open chamber at the back of the head, making it possible to reach around and into, well, Max's head. Several years ago, I learned of secret tradition associated with the sculpture from the Opera's longtime historian—our "official unofficial" historian, as he and I liked to say. The tradition was placing notes inside the head. Music lovers would write of their Music Hall memories and place them inside the bust.

PART 3: READING THE LETTER

Within about an hour of my email, Jim replied.

"You're right. That is weird. I've been gone for twenty years! Go ahead and open it. I'm interested to know who it's from, though I'm sure it's nothing. Probably an old invitation for an event twenty-five years ago or more. I wonder if I went! Or maybe it's an apology from a critic who now recognizes my genius. Who knows. Anyway, let me know what it says. Thanks for reaching out."

I turned the letter over in my hand and ran the letter-opener along the envelope's fold. Inside was a notecard with a single line of text:

I have what you need. Look inside the maestro's head.

Pace, Natalia

At first, this made little sense. I read it again, "I have what you need. Look inside the maestro's head. Pace—or Peace—Natalia" Who was Natalia? What did she have? And what might have been in "the maestro's head"? Then it struck me—that tradition of placing notes inside the bust of Max Rudolf.

PART 4: A VISIT TO THE WAREHOUSE

My schedule was clear for the afternoon, so I left my desk for my car. I took I-75 up to Roselawn, where the Opera's warehouse is located. There, sets and costumes from past productions await their ride downtown to Music Hall and the bright lights of appearing onstage. The warehouse is also where the Society for the Preservation of Music Hall was storing some of its artifacts. I hoped to find the bust of Max Rudolf among their items.

The keypad chirped as I entered each of the five security numbers to turn off the alarm. I closed the door and flipped on the light. I made my way through the garage area where we kept our opera truck, past the shop, around the elements of the sets for *Salome* and *Cinderella*. I saw the roping first and then the sign: Music Hall Artifacts/Do Not Access Without Permission. There were framed paintings, old posters, several boxed items, benches, the comedy and tragedy masks from the old South Hall, and gold stanchions with red velvet ropes. Then, there he was. I saw the bronze bust of Max Rudolf partially wrapped in foam rubber and tape. I peered around to the back of the head and reached in. Nothing. I tried again, repositioning myself for a better angle and, reaching up, I could feel with the tip of my fingers a rolled-up piece of paper. I gently pulled it out and carefully unrolled it.

It was a black-and-white photocopy of a photograph. And that photograph showed a sheet of manuscript paper— the kind a composer would use with 20 staves filling up the page. The sheet had no musical notation on it, just handwritten text. Across the middle in large letters was the title and composer: *King Lear* and G. Verdi. Impossible, I thought. This was not supposed to exist. Anyone who knew anything about opera would immediately recognize that what I was seeing was either a forgery or a miracle—and the most significant musicological discovery of the last century.

About Giuseppe Verdi

Opera stages around the world are dominated by the work of five composers—four Italians and one Austrian. The Italians are Rossini, Donizetti, Verdi, and Puccini. And the Austrian is, of course, Mozart. Last year, their operas comprised two-thirds of the repertoire that appeared on opera stages. And of the five, it's Giuseppe Verdi that dominates with the most performances.

Verdi flourished throughout the second half of the 19th century. Most of his operas premiered in Italy—particularly Milan, Rome, Naples, and Venice. But he became an international sensation with commissions for new works in St. Petersburg, Paris, and Cairo.

He wrote 26 operas—beloved works like *Aida, La Traviata*, and *Rigoletto*; and three operas based on Shakespeare: *Macbeth, Othello* and *Falstaff*, based on *The Merry Wives of Windsor.* There was very nearly a fourth Shakespeare opera. It was a work that haunted him. It was the one that got away. Verdi himself had engaged a writer to do the adaptation in 1850. They went back and forth on which characters to keep and which to cut. Soon, the text was completed. But Verdi would live for another fifty years and never set it to music.

There are other such "almost" works in opera. Puccini, for example, had considered an operatic adaptation of Oliver Twist. But the big "almost" work was Verdi's King Lear.

PART 5: AN EXCHANGE WITH EVANS

Evans Mirageas is the artistic director for Cincinnati Opera, a role he assumed in 2005. I called his mobile phone on the way back downtown.

"Hi, Evans. Are you at the Aronoff?" "I'm in the theater." "I'm on my way there. I have something you have to see." I said. I parked on 7th Street near the entrance to the Weston Art Gallery and met Evans in the lobby of the Aronoff. I told him about the note found at Music Hall, my exchange with Jim, and my trip to the warehouse. Then, I handed him the photograph.

"Bloody hell," he said. Evans had spent a good part of his career working in London.

"I know," I said. "I'll connect with Jim as soon as I get back to the office. I'm sure he knows something."

We turned to leave. "You know what," Evans said. "Wasn't there a chorus member years ago who claimed to be a descendent of Verdi?"

Jim, who had recently turned 86, was living in Omaha. I emailed him a photo of the note and the score with the explanation of where I'd found it.

About Jim de Blasis

Jim de Blasis was born in 1931 in New York City. He attended Carnegie Mellon University and, after graduation, taught drama in Syracuse. When he was 37, he arrived in Cincinnati as a stage director for Cincinnati Opera's 1968 Summer Festival. He returned in subsequent seasons and assumed leadership of the company in 1973.

In the 1980s he won the attention of national and international music critics with revivals of two forgotten Italian operas: *Resurrection* in 1983 and *Zazà* in 1985. Both productions were reviewed by the *New York Times*. De Blasis did attempt a third revival but this time went a different direction—a Czech opera with the unlikely title, *Schwanda the Bagpiper*. The *Times* review for *Schwanda* was generally positive, but it was critical of the music, writing that the "cymbals and triangle are positively abused, and some of the orchestral climaxes might make John Williams blush."

Alas, *Schwanda* was not the hoped-for box office success, and leadership change was soon in the wind. One wonders what might have been if de Blasis had been able to follow his two Italian revivals with the world premiere of a lost Verdi opera.

PART 6: A CALL WITH JIM

"Natalia Babic. She was a weird one," Jim de Blasis said when I reached him on the phone. "I heard her audition in New York. She was amazing. I mean, she seemed wacko, but she had a beautiful voice. The kind of voice you hear only every five years, something like that. But, she seemed a little, I don't know, off. Of course, I don't have to tell you—she's a singer; they're all a little crazy."

"You know what happened with her, I suppose. She shows up to rehearsal with some kind of traveling medicine show. I wasn't having it. You can't sell Amway or Avon or whatever during rehearsal breaks. Not in my theater. I put an end to that right away and sent her packing.

"Oh, she pleaded with me. She sent letters. She left messages. Tried to stir the pot with the union reps. She never got over it. She was obsessed. People said they saw her outside Music Hall early in the morning."

I mentioned the score.

"So, this photo you found. Ninety-nine and forty-four one-hundredths percent positive it's bullshit. But try to reach her, if she's still around. You never know. Here's my warning: once you make contact, she'll never leave you alone.

"By the way, we kept that carpet bag. Well, she took the medicine case, but she left the bag. It was gorgeous red and gold. We used it as a prop for years!"

I thanked Jim.

"Let me know what happens!" he said.

We hung up.

On Ghosts at Music Hall

Two elements combine to inspire ghost sightings at Music Hall. First, it's an old Victorian building. Ghosts tend to be from this period for some reason. Second, so much has happened at Music Hall. So many significant performers have appeared there: Enrico Caruso, Richard Strauss, Jascha Heifetz, Sergei Rachmaninoff, Maria Callas, Luciano Pavarotti, among so many others. They appeared before sold-out crowds of thousands. Such vitality and intensity must leave behind some kind of preternatural energy.

Though I myself have not experienced ghosts at Music Hall, I have heard stories. There was the security officer, a retired sheriff's deputy, who was hired to stand guard next to a valuable automobile through the night. In the silence sometime after midnight, he heard whistling. No one was found.

A member of the housekeeping staff witnessed a female figure glide across the lobby and pass through him.

An opera staff person showing his young son the empty and dark theater watched his son wave farewell in the direction of the house left box seats. "Who are you waving to?" he said. "That man who waved to me," he replied. There was no one there.

A former opera employee who worked in the finance department told of coins being disturbed overnight in the locked drawer she used for petty cash. If she stacked them neatly, the next morning she'd find them toppled. If she left them scattered, she'd find them neatly stacked.

Some smelled perfume suddenly or heard the rustling of crinoline or heard footsteps in the distance.

And then, of course, there were multiple stories of a woman in a white dress, silently gliding about the building at night, holding a candle.

PART 7: TALKING WITH CAROLYN

With Natalia's last name from Jim, I turned to my keyboard and typed in the Google search bar: Natalia B-A-B-I-C Cincinnati. I tried a few other spellings and combinations but came up with nothing.

Jim had suggested I reach out to a longtime member of the chorus named Carolyn Martin for more information on Natalia. Carolyn joined the chorus right after graduating from CCM. I reached her on her mobile.

She remembered Natalia and recalled the incident. She said, "It was pretty weird. We called it Natalia's Nostrum Nonsense."

She said Natalia was one of the best singers she'd ever worked with and described her appearance. "She looked like a dancer. Which, of course, all of us other girls hated. And she wore her hair like a dancer—pulled back in a bun. She always wore these flowy cream-colored dresses."

When I asked Carolyn where Natalia was from or if she knew anything about her family, she recalled only one thing—her saying she was related to Giuseppe Verdi and could prove it.

"We never believed it, of course," she said. "But she was pretty intense. I think she married some retired judge, or something like that. I lost track of her."

"Where did she live?" I asked.

"You know, I have no idea," she said. "Somewhere near Music Hall, I'd guess."

About the Hidden Room

Music Hall is a huge building. It's about twice the size of the Biltmore Estate in Asheville, North Carolina. Several years before the building's 2017 renovation, preparation work had begun. This included drawing up a proper set of building plans, which would take months and require a thorough canvasing of every square foot of the building.

In the creation of these drawings, there were a few curious discoveries. One of these was particularly strange: the discovery of a hidden room. Not much larger than a closet, the room was on the same level as Corbett Tower. It was accessed through a closet that had a sliding panel at its back. Though it was small, the space offered a spectacular view of Washington Park. And most surprising, someone had been living there. Among the items found there was a box of battery-powered candles—the kind used in theatrical productions or church services.

PART 8: NATALIA

With the information about Natalia's marriage to a judge, I was able to find her last name. She had married a man named Harold Roth in 1986. He was twenty years older.

Natalia Roth was now in her mid-80s and living alone in Sarasota. After a few attempts, I reached her by phone.

"Natalia, this is Chris Milligan calling from Cincinnati Opera."

"Yes, this is Natalia."

I explained that we had found her note and the photograph. There was a long pause.

"That was a lifetime ago. Did you find the score?"

"No. In fact, that's why I'm calling."

She explained that the score was a gift from her father for her fifteenth birthday. He knew of her love for music. He told her they were, in fact, proud descendants of Giuseppe Verdi and that Verdi had entrusted her grandfather with a secret, unpublished musical score for safekeeping. This was the reason she had pursued opera. And this was how she knew her father loved her even though he had left her mother soon after that fifteenth birthday, never to make contact again.

She was told to keep the score hidden and wrapped until one hundred years after Verdi's death. (Verdi died in 1901.) And she did, opening it only once to take a photo of the title page.

"You know I never did get an apology from the company," she said. "I sent that note as a peace offering, hoping someone would reach out. But, eventually, I gave up. I gave up on opera. I moved on."

I apologized. I explained that we had only very recently discovered the note. And that we, like her, want to make sure the score is properly protected and secure.

"Where did you leave the score?" I asked.

"It was in the bottom of my bag," she said. "Just below the fabric lining. Wrapped in paper and tied with twine."

PART 9: BACK TO THE WAREHOUSE

I remember asking Ashley Tongret, then the company's PR manager, to join me on another trip to the warehouse. I explained the whole thing on the way. At the warehouse, there are shelves upon shelves of props. These include floral bouquets, Madonna statues, crucifixes, spears, swords, daggers, revolvers, goblets, champagne glasses, wine bottles, two roast pigs on chargers, battle flags, and lanterns. There are hat boxes, briefcases, doctor bags, suitcases, trunks, and carpet bags. We found four carpet bags. One of them looked promising.

We took it into the paint shop, an open room with natural lighting. The bag should have been empty, but it felt heavy. I placed it on the table and located a pair of fabric sheers. "OK," I said. "Ashley, I want to record this. Can you film with your iPhone?"

She removed her phone and turned it horizontally. With a nod, she signaled me to begin.

"I am Chris Milligan," I said. "I have here a bag that may contain something very valuable. We just retrieved the bag from storage—a shelf in Cincinnati Opera's warehouse. It is part of the Opera's props collection."

Narrating for the video, I gave a play-by-play for each step. I made a snip by the seam at end of the fabric, lining the bottom. After a few more careful snips, the slit was wide enough. I held up the cut piece with my right hand and reached in with my left. I extracted a large, weighty package tied in twine. I took a deep breath and breathed out.

With Ashley filming the whole thing, I placed the package on the table. I cut the twine, set down the scissors and pushed them aside. With two hands, I slowly turned the package on its face and pulled back the wrapping paper to reveal the backside of the bottom sheet.

"I'm now going to remove the document from its wrapping," I said for the recording.

I grasped the top and bottom of the stack of manuscript papers, lifted it from the wrapping paper, and set it face up on the table. Immediately, we saw the title page. It read *King Lear* and below that, G. Verdi.

"Ashley, are you still recording?"

"Yes, still recording."

I turned to the score. "I'm going to set aside the top page," I said. I did so with two hands. The second page was blank.

Again, same careful grasping, lifting, and placing. Same result: another blank page. And again, the same. The removal of each blank sheet revealed another of its kind. No notation, no lyrics. No overture. No earnest aria for Cordelia explaining to her father that she "cannot heave [her] heart into [her] mouth." No raging baritone Lear on the heath in the storm, "Blow, winds, and crack your cheeks! Rage! Blow!" Ashley turned off the recording. Our hearts sank. We were sad. Sad for opera.

Sad for Verdi. Sad for Natalia.

PART 10: FAREWELL

A few days later, I sent a note to Natalia. Not hearing a reply for several weeks, I tried to reach her, again by phone.

"It's a good day at Villa Palms. This is Maggie."

"I'm trying to reach Natalia Roth. This is Chris Milligan calling from Cincinnati."

"Hello, Mr. Milligan. I have your letter here. I was hoping you'd call. I'm sorry to say that Natalia passed away earlier this month."

"Oh, I'm sorry to hear that," I said. I thanked her for telling me and said she could discard my letter.

As you might imagine, I had carefully considered what to tell Natalia regarding the score. In the end, I simply wrote, "Dear Natalia, I hope to have more news soon. But for the moment, I'll just say, your father loved you very much."

Epilogue

Music Hall has been quiet since the renovation. And our fragile hope of presenting a lost masterpiece has become a distant memory. Nevertheless, whenever it seems our art form has lost some of its vim and vigor, I can't help thinking that a newly discovered opera by Verdi would be just the remedy we need.

The portion of the story related to Natalia is imagined.

{17}
CHALK ON THE WALK

JAMES M. MURRAY

I DON'T KNOW WHY I LOOKED DOWN that early Monday morning and noticed the writing on the sidewalk. I might have been cleaning up after one of my dogs on our daily ritual of an early morning walk or I might have been checking for what I call masons' marks — the imprint of some long-dead concrete contractor who stamped his name and the date in the wet cement. I can tell you where all the surviving nineteenth-century sidewalk is in this town, where I live in one of its oldest neighborhoods. But that morning it was chalk: chalk in two colors — pink and green — clear enough even in that unsteady light, spelling out "LUV U." That's right, four letters, one thought.

I should explain that my neighborhood, called Vine after one of its most prominent streets, was the rich side of town in the nineteenth century, when the industries of Kalamazoo were in their first throes of spewing out products into the world. First there were stoves, hardware, carriages and wagons, then pills and guitars, with a college and then the university providing educational adornment and accompaniment to the moneymaking. The streets of the Vine neighborhood were lined with the domestic product of that exportable production, although the streetscape now showed gaps and elisions, rather like a fine smile ravaged by time's random extractions. Now Kalamazoo no longer made much of anything — its pill and guitar makers were among the last to go, factories sold off, shut up, moved south, anywhere but here in Michigan. Once grand houses were now divided into apartments to house the city's last remaining customers — its college students, imported to drink deeply of the Pierian spring water bottled and sold at the university and Kalamazoo College. As a lover of irony, I should add that the second major item still manufactured here is a particularly potent beer, drunk all-too deeply by both locals and students alike.

The chalk house was one of those formerly grand places, now vivisected into a rabbit warren of small apartments. The chalk message was obviously intended for one of its residents, and judging from the angle, size, and orientation of the message, he resided at the front right of the chalk house.

You might wonder how I knew the sex of the intended reader and guessed something about the message writer? It's quite simple: I am a retired English professor from the university bottler of knowledge, so I can draw on forty-years' experience of post-adolescent penmanship, color scheme, and observation of young love. In literary terms, what we have here is Juliet casting her glance up to her Romeo, but instead of the mellifluousness of Shakespeare, she's left a text message.

"Ah," I sighed, "could there be a more fitting symbol of the decline of modern culture?"

But despite the literary poverty, I was intrigued by the story line. I imagined one of those young girls who descend in the autumn like migratory birds, dragging behind them mothers and fathers, bearing food and furniture, to houses like these, following in the wake of so many predecessors. I confess to looking forward to move-in time, when the old neighborhood throbs with the young once again, and the shopkeepers emerge from their summer-long funk with dollar signs in their eyes. It was a rhythm of life almost tidal in its regularity, with nine months of flood followed by the outmigration every Spring, as SUVs towing rented trailers pulled up once again to rented houses to remove and return what they had once — with such effort — delivered. After the graduation-party boisterousness of the students' last weeks, and the moving frenzy that followed, summer seemed placid and sleepy, with just a few tide pools of young life left to keep things interesting.

Romeo was probably one of those rumpled, slightly paunchy young men, uniformly dressed in t-shirt and baseball cap with the bill reversed, (as if to indicate the general drift of college life) and flip-flops. These lives on the outside seem composed of beer drinking and watching sports with little thought or time devoted to study. Unlike the girls, these boys usually migrated without the help of parents, pulling up in any manner of over-the-hill and decrepit vehicle, often of the four-wheel-drive or pickup variety. Their return was always announced with a scattering of beer cans across the lawns of their rented quarters, and the odor of charred meat emanating from the grills they kept on their porches. Accompanying it all was loud rock, or grunge, or some other cacophony liberally spilling out and enveloping the area all around. How happy their parents must be when they once again four-wheeled back to school!

Yet these chalked messages seemed to reveal to me hidden depths in these young men. Was this Romeo capable of summoning and sustaining the passions his Juliet scrawled in pink and green outside his bedroom window? Where did he scrawl his emotions — did he write her poetry? Deliver orations full of verve and passion? Declare his feelings in the ringing iambs of Shakespeare? Or did he grope her in the backseat of his Jeep Wrangler, which he purchased and maintained partly for the entertaining of young women of more-or-less willing natures? Can I remember what I did at that age?

Whether I liked it or not, the tempests of love and desire had passed to this new generation. Who knows, perhaps scores of Shakespeare's were even now perfecting text messaging as a vehicle for the emotions of love and self-sacrifice. Perhaps this sidewalk chalking was a subset of a vast electronic wave of a sublime textual language of love, set out in staccato form and irregular rhyme scheme. Was there not a timeless swell of longing and loneliness, expressed in the poetry of young men and women of whatever age, falling in love and passion with each other? What difference did it make if the words it assumed were those of Rossetti or scrawled on some sidewalk, or electronic screen? Did I really believe in the "eternity" of Shakespeare's language of love, that in geologic time it was really more significant than the instant message that darted across a screen and then disappeared utterly?

We were in full football season when the change came. It wasn't any of the usual things — not the games with their tailgate preludes and intoxicated postludes, capped by dull athletic contests and bad fan behavior. Nor was it the welcome leaf flame of the maple trees, or gathering leaf piles I corralled with my leaf blower. No, it was written with chalk on the walk: "DULUVME" — "Mentally added the absent question mark to the anguished pink and green question as I looked from the message to the upstairs window where I presumed Romeo lived. The all-in-caps shriek of pain caused me to wince and look away for a moment, as if I had caught a glimpse of something improper.

What had happened? I imagined a party such as those I observed every weekend during the school year with dozens of young men and women revolving and recombining in knots of conversation, beer drinking, and occasional pot smoking. Had R & J been separated in one of these swirls and whirls, he on one side of the room chatting with some other girls, while Juliet looked on in dismay, cornered by some pimply bore with bad breath. Did she accost him later, berating him for his fascination with Andrea's cleavage, that stuck-up bitch, who flaunted her body and money trying to steal other peoples' boyfriends? Or had Romeo lashed out at the attentions of his frat brother, Nick, whose blonde curls and insouciant grace with women had roped in Juliet for a moment, a kiss, or something more?

Thereafter the passions mounted and the messages lengthened, albeit in the curious telegraphy of the text message. "U sd U luvd strng + U lied" In my translation, this is loosely: "You said you loved strong women and you lied."

This looked to me like the point of recrimination, that moment in a breakup when anger and resentment take over. Juliet no doubt pulled hard on the tether that bound her to Romeo — that indiscretion with a friend, or perhaps a weekend trip alone in defiance of his wishes. All couples believe they are inventing love for the very first time and that there's no past, no tradition, or expectation about behavior. I remembered my marriage in its early days, both of us besotted with the Beat culture of 1950s San Francisco, followed by that bohemian year in Paris as Fulbrighters. But once we'd settled down in a tenure-track job, in a strait-laced Midwestern city, we'd become very much like our parents in our expectations of each other. Even as I nursed her through her last illness, as cancer ravaged her body and dementia her mind, I remembered how my mother had helped my father die. I performed the rituals very much as she had, honoring the deepest promise we make to our loved ones: that we will not let them die alone.

"GOOD BYE" I stood for some time over this chalk scrawl, which followed the last by a week or two. It was near winter by then; that time in November of phony fall, before the blitzkrieg of snow and cold descends from the northwest. Juliet had picked her time well; no doubt in a few weeks the sidewalk would be obscured by snow and ice, rendered unavailable for human communication in nature's show of seasonal strength.

I wondered at the words, our shorthand for leave-taking, so unlike the expressions of other languages I knew. Many of those seemed to hold out hope of other meetings; au revoir, auf Wider-eyed, tot ziens, all seemed less definite, less final. What did Good Bye mean after all? Was it one of those remnants from Old English that stubbornly resisted the onslaught of Romance languages like a boulder in the stream, enduring to the point of meaninglessness? For Juliet, it was clear that she had reached the level of acceptance of the pastness of her relationship with Romeo.

The wall that separates us from the past had always preoccupied me. How in memory my wife's face seemed so near, so near that even now I awoke in the morning expecting her warmth to be there beside me, and to open my eyes to the sight of her as the first image of my day. But of course, all that was lost far beyond recovery no matter what tricks my memory played on me. Do we ever fully accept our losses in time's inexorable locking us off from the past?

It was a hard winter that year with a good deal of snow and temperatures cold enough to drive me inside and away from the long walks my dogs and I were accustomed to in other seasons. And the sidewalks were obscured by snow and ice, which no one in our struggling neighborhood bothered to clear before the spring thaw. Many of my friends go south for winter, festooning the coastal towns of Florida, Alabama, and Texas with their Western Michigan and Michigan State t-shirts, while I choose the hats, boots and scarves of the cold season, enjoying the huddled waiting and watching of the dark time.

It was a Saturday in early April and I was at the laundromat bringing out the warm weather wardrobe for a quick preparatory wash. Our neighborhood washhouse is nothing much to look at; it is run by a Korean family who speak little English, but they're friendly enough. Their youngest boy, Kim, is twelve and is the family translator. I can depend on him to help me transfer heavy loads of laundry from washer to dryer. He accepts gifts of chocolate bars in return. It's strange why I come here, for I have a perfectly serviceable pair of laundry appliances at home, standing ready just as my wife left them the day she died. I guess it's the communal aspect, the knowledge that for millennia, human beings have gathered along flowing water to beat, batter, and rinse their clothing together. And most fittingly, it was there I spotted Juliet.

Of course, I didn't know it was she at first — she was just another twenty-something college student wearing the usual t-shirt and jeans with her blonde hair falling down to her shoulders in no particular order. She had the purposeful look of someone whose laundry is pure chore, to be performed as quickly as possible to permit a return to more interesting past-times. I glanced at her just as she was transferring her colored clothes from the plastic basket to the washing machine tub, and right there on top was a pair of jeans with pink and green chalk on the knees.

So, this was Juliet.

I smiled to myself as I went about my own business, averting my eyes as one does to pretend that public spaces are really not "public" — that we are really just alone together as we careen through life. But there at the dryers was a woman capable of great passion and pain, who had given me hope that even if I were no longer young, there were others who had taken over and continued the enormous risk-taking that is falling in love.

Coda: Jump-rope Chant:
Chalk on the walk, chalk on the walk,
funny way to talk with chalk on the walk.
All those colors got to tell others,
the love I feel to make it all real.

Chalk on the walk, chalk on the walk,
girls gyrating, while narrating
hopes and dreams,
while the jump rope screams.

Chalk on the walk, chalk on the walk,
Jump on the right foot,
then on the left,
bow down, turn around,
do a pirouette.

Life is romancing, while we're all chancing,
life and limb,
it's why we're all in,
like chalk on the walk,
that chalk on the walk.

{18}

THE AUTHENTIC ERSATZ CHRISTMAS

A Modest Historical Perspective on the Celebration of the Winter Holidays In Indiana's 93rd County

MARK S. SCHLACHTER

THE MENTION OF INDIANA to the average American conjures images of the Indianapolis 500 or Christmas in Holman, the location of Jean Shepard's classic *Christmas Story*, a reimagined Hammond, Indiana, his boyhood home.

Hoosier Christmases of the 1940s and 50s were much like those in the other forty-seven states but every city had its own special way to celebrate the season, and Griddle along with the rest of Ersatz County was unique. The reenactors at Conner Prairie in Zionsville maintain that there was no typical Hoosier Christmas in the early 1800s. A Calvinist Scots weaver might ignore the date entirely. The local doctor might celebrate with a decorated fir tree and a party, and the smithy might leave a new pair of socks and a cap as gifts for his children.

The 1823 publication of Clement Clarke Moore's poem, *A Visit by Saint Nicholas,* followed in 1866 by Thomas Nast's illustration of Santa for *Harper's Bazaar* created the image we now associate with Santa: portly build, white beard, red suit, and white fur trim. Theoretically the pieces were in place for a coherent American Christmas.

Nothing is easy, and the concept of an American standard Christmas is carved in stone proof. Every city, town, village, and crossroads has its personality, community traditions, civic pride, and public perseverance.

Grindle, Indiana was no exception to the national rule. With founding settler and toymaker Klaus Pringle leading the charge, and brewer, August Schexnaydor offering tactical support, Christmas was a season and celebration of vast potential. Toys were made in amazing quantities sold in the general store, the dry goods store, and even the apothecary. In a fit of inspiration, Pringle and Schexnaydor developed the concept of selling toys at the taverns serving Schexnaydor winter ale. It was genius. After three or four or more mugs of Schexnaydor, the drinker's good mood was exhibited in actions of generosity in the form of toys purchased for the children at home.

By 1868 Grindle had The Mercantile, its first, and still preeminent department store. The "Merc" followed the lead of R. H. Macy and introduced its first in-store Santa in 1875.

But Christmas was not just a merchandising ploy.

Our Lady of Sorrows was the first Ersatz church to offer Christmas Eve services. Father Frank, who long struggled with insomnia, decided that if he was up and about, his flock could join him. The Ersatz Midnight Mass was born. Bishop Washington at the Beulah AME annually relinquished his pulpit, an astounding act, to allow the choir to perform a two-hour gospel celebration of the season. The Little White Church by the Side of the Road, now quite substantial, produced a live nativity every night of Christmas week. Even Grindle's less conventional faith communities were part of the tradition. Members of the Moxitoxic Nation distributed small bags of medicinal mushrooms door-to-door. The Yoders, not to be outdone, enlisted the rest of the Amish community to distribute gifts of eggs, butter, milk, cheese, and pastry. And Amber Koetler, the current crone of the coven, hosted a massive yule log party with food, drink, drumming, and a bonfire.

Christmas in Grindle was eclectic and ecumenical and nearly everyone took part in the Koetler event.

Grindle Christmas appeared to have stabilized. Man, woman, and child knew what to expect and when but appearances are nearly always deceiving.

Radio came to Grindle, Indiana in 1927. Not some static-filled spasmodic transmission from South Bend or Fort Wayne, but bright, clear, distinctly Ersatz transmissions from newly licensed WWEMP. Network radio was just a faint gleam in 1927, so all Ersatz programming was Grindle-born. Filling hours a day was daunting, and ideas for revenue-producing programs were vital. On December 1, 1928 WWEMP invited Grindle's children to send their letters addressed to Santa, to the station's address instead, there to be read on air for all to hear. At first the mail brought few messages for the Master of the North Pole, but soon every child in town wanted his Christmas requests broadcast to all. That first year was a resounding success. Even though it was just a staff announcer reading the letters, The Mercantile bought exclusive rights to the show and the option for sole sponsorship, again in 1929.

1929 found the letters to Santa wrapped up in a whole new package. There was a theme song. There were lots of sleigh bells, and the letters were read by Santa himself, with comments that let the writer know that Santa had personal knowledge of the sender. Santa also made frequent suggestions to improve the sender's gift experience. A red Buddy L dump truck would be much better with a shiny yellow Marx steam shovel. The "Merc" loved it.

World War II had no insignificant effect on Christmas in Grindle. Many young men were missing from the festivities, and war production meant less domestic product on store shelves. Many argued that the less commercial Christmas was a better Christmas. The "Merc" disagreed. Despite the lack of goods for gifts and the missing male contingent, the heart of the holiday was intact. Father Frank said mass at midnight; Beulah AME filled the air with rollicking gospel praise; the Koetler Yule celebration was a blazing glory; and the live nativity at the no-longer-so-little White Church carried on, despite a lack of male participants, occasionally requiring an all-female cast. Grindle accepted a decidedly feminine Joseph and three wise men without qualm or question.

However, the end of the War brought change. Shelves were well-stocked, families were reunited (many of them), employment was high, and joy was heartfelt. After the national commercial example, the "Merc" sent a four-color toy catalogue to every home in the county. The Monday following Thanksgiving, children came home from school to find their usual milk and cookies snack enhanced by twelve pages of wonder: Electric trains; crying, sleeping and wetting dolls; nurse kits; doctor kits; science sets; tea sets; sports paraphernalia of all kinds; and inevitably the classic Daisy Red Ryder BB gun.

WWEMP's Santa now had visual aids as he stoked his young fans' avarice. The "Merc" sold, and sold, and sold. The Depression was over, the War was over, and the world was in order.

Although a small city in a small market, Grindle gained its own television station in 1949. In 1952 WWEMP's radio Santa began simulcasting with WWEMP television. For fifteen minutes every afternoon, Santa and an elf would read letters, make suggestions, and fire the desires of Ersatz County's grade schoolers, all reinforced with frequent cutaway shots to the "Merc's" bible of toys.

It was a perfect storm of merchandising.

For decades, a children's cartoon show hosted by a friendly adult, in character, was an after-school staple on most television stations. National favorites like Howdy Doody, Rootie Kazootie, Captain Kangaroo, and Mr. Rogers defined the genre. Regionally children watched Bozo the Clown, Uncle Al, Stringbean, and Skipper Ryle. In Grindle, Indiana that role fell to Roper Ron. Roper Ron was a Hoosier cowboy; his companion was the comely Pretty Miss Sally, and they both cared for the venerable Dusty Dog, a canine of indeterminate heritage and negligible energy. Roper Ron, a seventh-year student in the Grindle Community College Performing Arts program had been hired on the strength of his amazing good looks. Pretty Miss Sally, a twelfth semester member of the same program, was an economical afterthought. Together they were a team of amazing good looks and insignificant ability. Feeling that the mix was incomplete, WWEMP added canine companion Dusty Dog, an elderly refuge in the Ersatz County dog pound. They were an instant hit.

The show's program was simple: Even Roper Ron, Pretty Miss Sally, and Dusty Dog could do it.

Every day Roper Ron would come on with his two-million-dollar smile, make some noncommittal comment about his morning on the ranch, give a high five to all his "Little Hands" in the studio audience, and cut to the first cartoon. Any third grader could do it, and Roper Ron could, too.

After the first cut to film, Pretty Miss Sally would join Roper Ron. Pretty Miss Sally never said anything more than: "You're our hero" or "Please, help us" or "You're our only hope."

Then, it was Dusty Dog's chance to court audience approval. Dusty Dog was a tired senior when he was saved from the Ersatz County Animal Rescue Mission. On air, he had never moved...never. Roper Ron's single attempt at entertainment and humor was to announce that Dusty Dog had a new trick. At the command to beg, heel, roll over, or speak, Dusty Dog would remain supine. In the fourth year of the show, without command, Dusty Dog expired.

After moments of discussion, management decided that Dusty would be stuffed.

Dusty never missed a single broadcast.

By 1978 Roper Ron and Petty Miss Sally had been signed into the annual Christmas toy campaign. Who was better prepared to bait the audience than a man still in his seventh year of a two-year academic program? Pretty Miss Sally just smiled.

The show got unusually interesting one day in 1979 when, during the Christmas campaign, the duo was given a set of Jarts for on-air demonstration. Roper Ron let fly the first Jart. It landed squarely on the center of Pretty Miss Sally's left foot. Her cries were loud, excruciating, and obscene. In nervous response, Pretty Miss Sally released her Jart, which, without apparent effect, found its home in the upper chest of the recumbent Dusty Dog.

Pretty Miss Sally's loud and profane response to her wound continued. With quick thinking the WWEMP control booth went to black on Roper Ron and cut, ten minutes early, to the next local production.

TV Teacher was usually a relaxed, feel-good show. Miss Cathy, an attractive and energetic single mother of five could, and did cope with anything.

This day she opened her show saying, "Hello students, we've learned some new words today."

The Grindle Christmas traditions continued as remembered for eight more years, until Charlie Feaster and a half dozen co-workers from the Ersatz and Moot Point backshop made their nightly stop at the Rip Track. All seven of the instigators lived in identical homes in the Pullman Estates. Built with economy in mind, there was no variation home to home. Years after construction it was found that all 218 homes in the development could be accessed with the same front door key. There had been a quantity discount on like locks.

Christmas Eve afternoon, Charlie and friends were enjoying a seasonal round or three or four, when the idea to have their children's presents delivered, in person by Santa, crept into the conversation and soon took center stage. The only things standing between concept and performance were a Santa and a suit.

The Santa solution was obvious. There at the end of the bar, occupying stool three, was Shorty. Shorty was Grindle's equivalent to Sugar Bear —

roundish, shortish, affable, and ready to help at the drop of a Schexnaydor. Shorty was generally acknowledged to be E&MP President Roy Lee Roy's brother by another mother. On his twenty-first birthday he had left home, walked to the Rip Track, mounted stool three, and ordered his first legal beer. Shorty adopted stool three as his home, and the Census Bureau and the United States Postal Service both consider it his legal address. Shorty was the perfect Santa.

The suit was another issue.

Rip Track proprietor Thelma Snell turned on the bar's television, and there for all to see was Roper Ron, singing the jingle for sponsor Grindle Bottling… "Makes you happy, makes you smile, drink it in, and wear a grin, drink, drink, drink Grin-Cola." Standing between Roper Ron and Pretty Miss Sally was Santa. Fresh from duty reading the day's gift pleas, Santa was about to enjoy his own Grin-Cola.

Charlie Feaster's brother Bud was the operator of camera three on the Roper Ron Show and had the distinction of having been lassoed eighteen times as Roper Ron gave his inept daily performance of rope tricks for the studio audience of "Little Hands." On other occasions Roper Ron had lassoed Pretty Miss Sally (five times), Dusty Dog (nine times), a studio monitor (four times), and the mother of a "Little Hand" (twenty-three times). He seldom managed to get the lariat around the neck of the stationary, stuffed cow provided as a target but no one cared because he was so good looking.

Bud also had children, also lived in Pullman Estates, and would have no problem getting the suit out of the station and down to Shorty at the Rip Track. All Bud required in exchange was a home delivery from Santa for his own youngsters.

In short order Shorty was suited up and on his way to Pullman Estates. Each targeted home was marked by a large gift-filled bag left at the end of its driveway. Shorty was to go to each house, pick up the bag, go to the door, and announce his presence by jingling sleigh bells. The first stop went off without a hitch. To show appreciation resident Herb Poston offered Shorty a beer. Shorty had never been known to refuse the offer of a beer.

This scene repeated itself six more times, until Shorty unsteadily headed to his last stop. Shuffling up Charlie Feaster's drive humping a large sack containing only Santa-knows-what, the steadfast Shorty realized he was at the end of his tether. He opened the door to the 1953 Studebaker Commander Charlie had on blocks for restoration, climbed in, and passed out.

Time passed. At 11:48 Shorty awoke, realized there were gifts to deliver, and made a final lunge for the Feaster front door. He shook sleigh bells, yelled, "Ho, ho, ho" at the top of his lungs, and gave three massive kicks to the door. Eventually Charlie opened the door. Wife, Joy, roused the children, and when all were assembled, Shorty slowly spoke in only slightly slurred words, "Merry Chrismuss. Here's your stuff."

Charlie offered Shorty another beer for a job well done. Shorty astounded all by refusing.

Some final thoughts. Shorty as Santa became a part of the Ersatz Christmas tradition. The Mercantile has legally changed its name to The Merc, and in 1986 in an effort at inclusion, The Merc advertised not one or two, but three diverse Santas: white, black, and indigenous. While the white and black Santas continued to give each child a candy cane, the indigenous Santa, played by Chief Mellow Fellow's youngest brother, Lovie Bear, gives each supplicant a medicinal mushroom. His line is always longest.

{19}
MY FIRST TIME

JOSEPH TOMAIN

GENTLEMEN, let me admit to no small amount of nervousness as I share with you my first time. Hopefully, you will sympathize with me taking this story public at the risk of exposing my ignorance; my youthful incomprehension; exposing my tender conscience.

As fathers do, my father recommended a place to me. I was fourteen, maybe fifteen, and it would mean going into The City. I recruited my friend, Pat Federici to go along and, as it happened, his father, another similarly disposed Italian Romantic, had made the same suggestion. We boarded a Greyhound, which deposited us in the bowels of the New York Port Authority Bus Terminal, then we hoofed it across town and found our destination. The building was a few stories at best. We manly entered and began exploring to find it almost empty.

The rooms were oddly configured. Few were square rooms with normal entries and exits. The rooms were all shapes and sizes including curved rooms and rooms that were more hallways than enclosures. We wandered through this funhouse with no plan, no expectations. At some point, we found ourselves in an unfamiliar space. As I turned to my left, I faced five tall, naked women. More arresting than their nakedness were their stares; stares that were challenging and came with an invitation that was as troubling as it was threatening. Noticeable, disturbing even, were the looks of the three women on the left that were intentionally, consciously directed at me.

The first woman on the left was powerful, had long dark hair and as she entered the room to join the others she walked purposefully, determined. The two women to her right, and center stage, had brief cloths covering a patch of a hip or a thigh with their arms raised and their pink breasts tantalizing against a pale blue background. While, at first, their gazes were harsh; there was also a softness about them, a youthfulness, an innocence perhaps. Perhaps an invitation to love. To their right, one woman squatted with her back to me, elbows akimbo. She turned. Was that her face? Was she wearing some odd makodd makeuposseupmakeup? Her gaze was quizzical. Who was I? Why was I here? Why was I bothering her, bothering them? The last woman on the far right was opening a curtain and although she had an eye on me, she gave the other girls a look that said the break is over, it's time to work.

What had I walked into? Where was I? What was I to make of those several invitations made by these staring women? Was I being invited to join them? It seems that I was being asked to enter their setting; the world in which they lived; the world that was being made and the world that was to be; and I was being invited to look at myself. I was being challenged to confront power, fear, women, sex, and for the faint of soul — an invitation to sin; to surrender to the temptations of the flesh, of desire, of the secular world. What was a poor Catholic school boy to do? Accept the invitation and succumb? Or, reject and regret?

Those five young women were sold in 1937 for $28,000 to the Museum of Modern Art. Alfred Barr, MoMA's first director, said that *Les Demoiselles d'Avignon* was "one of the few pictures in the history of modern art which can justly be called epoch-making." He added, "In few works of art is the arrogance of genius so powerfully asserted." Those ladies, those coquettes, those prostitutes, those whores, those *jeunes filles*, have been in MoMA's collection ever since.

If you will allow me an abbreviation, *Les Dems* has a remarkable dual history. The history of its painting and its release to the world is itself fascinating. The history of its critical reception is, I believe, even more so.

Picasso may have begun painting *Les Dems* in 1906 after his fertile Blue and Rose periods that ignited his career and put a few francs in his pocket, enough to enjoy a modest meal at the Lapin Agile. After several months of work, Picasso finished *Les Dems* in 1907 in his Bateau Lavoir studio in Monmartre; the heart of bohemian Paris; the heart of the European, of the world's, avant-garde. The grimy Bateau, and it surrounds, hosted an assortment of artists, models, hangers-on, vagrants, and hookers. Hookers?! (Excuez-moi, I meant girlfriends.) This band of merry fools enjoyed the dives and brothels, the circuses and cinema, the jugglers and acrobats that inspired them as much as their shared dinners, cheap wine, and available opium.

For all of his notoriety as the preeminent "painter of modern life" (as Baudelaire would have it), Picasso did not create *Les Dems* in a burst of artistic genius and energy. Rather, he brooded over the painting that has been called the "most deliberate, the most carefully plotted of his career." On the way to completion, Picasso filled sixteen sketchbooks with hundreds of preliminary studies, the quantity of which was not only unique to Picasso, but "without parallel . . . in the entire history of art." Understandably, the sketchbooks have become central for art critics.

Toward the end of 1907, Picasso showed *Les Dems* to a few friends, art dealers, and fellow artists. He knew that he was onto something, something with which he could compete with his rival Matisse. He wasn't, though, quite sure about what that something was. Neither were the first viewers quite sure of what they were seeing.

Leo Stein, Gertrude's brother, thought that it was a "horrible mess." Others laughed. His dealer Daniel-Henry Kahnweiler thought that it was obviously unfinished. His artist friend, André Derain, predicted that Picasso would be found hanging behind his own canvas for its affront to art. Among the first to see *Les Dems*, was Picasso's future partner-in-crime against classical representation — George Braque. On seeing the picture, Braque exclaimed "It was as if someone was drinking kerosene so he can spit fire." To Braque, *Les Dems* exploded the very conception of what had then been understood as modern art.

Braque later recalled that when he saw the painting with Apollinaire he felt that this was his first true meeting with Picasso in which he saw Picasso's "unswerving determination, and extraordinary yearning for freedom asserted with a daring." Apollinaire later recounted that he "saw [Picasso's] new painting: even colors, flesh pinks, flowers, etc. . . . women's heads, all the same and simple, and men's heads too. A wonderful language that no literature can express . . . ." The poet Apollinaire tipped his hat to, his friend, the painter Picasso.

Gelett Burgess, an American author and humorist visited Picasso at the Bateau-Lavoir and wrote:

> "The terrible pictures loomed through the chaos. Monstrous, monolithic women, creatures like Alaskan totem poles, hacked

> out of solid, brutal colors, frightful, appalling. How little Picasso, with his sense of humor, with his youth and deviltry, seemed to glory in his crimes!"

The 26-year-old Pablo quite liked that review.

When Matisse saw *Les Dems*, he immediately understood not only the meaning of the painting but also the artist's intention. He saw it as a mockery of all that he had been working toward. *Les Dems* could not be further from Matisse's dreamlike figurative paintings and his Arcadian landscapes of nymphs at play in Fauvist colored gardens. Matisse used color to define and dominate form. Picasso expropriated form by jettisoning color.

These initial reactions were hardly auspicious and hardly prefigured claims like Barr's that *Les Dems* was "epoch-making" or John Golding's 50 years later that it was the "most important single pictorial document that the Twentieth century has yet produced."

The painting was first publicly shown in 1916 at the exhibition *L'Art Moderne en France*. There the painting acquired the name by which we know it much to Picasso's annoyance. Picasso wanted to call it a bordello; that's what it was, that's what it represented, and that was his vision. To Pablo, *Les Demsoiselles d'Avignon*, as his friend André Salmon christened them, were not strolling on some placid Barcelona Street; they were working girls. But the name stuck. From there, the painting went into seclusion until it was privately purchased in 1924 for 30,000 francs and then acquired by MoMA where it was exhibited two years later.

The reemergence of *Les Dems* in 1939 opened it to the viewing public and to the critical world as well. It is when the painting's critical history began and continues.

How did the painting come to be? What does it mean? Here is where the now famous sketchbooks (and the critics) enter the drama. And, here is where things get a bit tricky. First, the initial assessments of *Les Dems* were made without full access to the sketches. Then come the critical assessments with them. And, just to add a complicating (and troublesome) touch, the practice of criticism changed dramatically at the end of the 20th c. with the intended consequence of altering the way *Les Dems* was to be open quote — read — close quote.

Although the finished work contains only the five women; the studies show two male figures — a sailor and another later identified as a medical student. A sailor in a brothel is a common enough trope. But why a medical student? In early sketches, the student is carrying a book and later he is carrying, or contemplating, a skull. With naked women, clearly Eros makes an appearance. With the skull, does Thanatos appear as well? The critics have had much to say about these two now vanished gentlemen.

Now, let's not dismiss the idea of two men in a brothel, two men in *Les Dems*, too quickly. After all, Pat and I were standing in front of it. Over its critical history, these two men take the place of us, they represent us. In Leo Steinberg's words "the unity of the picture . . . resides above all in the startled consciousness of a viewer who sees himself seen." The whole experience of the picture, Stein continues, is "centered on the beholder." We, the viewers, are as much a part of the painting as the Demsoiselles themselves.

The sketchbooks also contain a line drawing of Picasso's live-in lover/model Fernande Oliver. The drawing shows that her portrait was originally intended for a carriage scene with Fernande holding a parasol promenading through the Bois de Boulogne. In the finished painting, Picasso transforms Fernande from a society woman to a whore; a transformation that he later joked about with friends.

There are two groups of women in *Les Dems* — three on the left and two on the right. The groups are distinct and those on the right are particularly exotic as the result of three experiences. First, as told by Gertrude Stein and confirmed by Matisse and Max Jacob, Matisse introduced Picasso to African sculptures. He had brought two small fetishes to dinner at the Steins and showed them to Picasso who held them all evening and sketched them that night.

The second experience is a shady, questionable dealing with a Belgian con man named Géry Pieret. The shady part is that Pieret stole two ancient stone Iberian heads from the Louvre that he allegedly "sold" to Picasso. The questionable part is that the theft was instigated by a remark Picasso made at a dinner party. Regardless, Picasso had the heads, was fascinated by them, and they triggered his interest in primitive art that was deepened by his third experience, his visit to the ethnographic museum in Paris, now the Museum of Man. There he was mesmerized by African exotica and, as the story (or as the legend) goes, this visit changed his view of art.

Years later, he told Andre Malraux, that:

> When I went to the old Trocadéro, it was disgusting. The

> smell. I was all alone. I wanted to get away. But I stayed. I stayed. . . . The masks weren't just like any other pieces of sculpture. They were magic things. . . . The Negro pieces were *intercesseurs,* mediators . . . They were against everything . . . I understood; I too was against everything. . . . I understood what the Negroes used their sculptures for . . . . The fetishes were . . .weapons. . . . *Les Demsoiselles* must have come to me that very day. It was my first exorcism painting.

Yet on another occasion, Picasso adamantly denied any connection between *Les Dems* and "l'art nègre," "the art of black Africa." He said that he did not visit the museum until after the painting was finished. It's difficult, impossible really, to accept his disclaimer. The women, in various degrees, wear tribal faces that are one source of the painting's magic and its mystery.

So, while there are a few stories about the creation of *Les Dems*, the stories from the artist are vague, when not contradictory. Some of the sketches may or may not have been of Fernande. Picasso did or did not visit the Trocadero before or after painting *Les Dems. Les Dems* is a finished work of art or it was left intentionally, or unintentionally, incomplete. Picasso called the painting either jokingly *El Bordel Philosophique* or *The Brothel of Avignon.* The Barcelonan street either housed a brothel or it did not. Matisse may or may not have given Picasso fetishes that Picasso did or did not return. All may be true. All may be apocryphal. Most likely both. Or, we can believe the man himself who said "You must not always believe what I say. Questions tempt you to tell lies, particularly when there is no answer." Picasso, simply, is an unreliable narrator of his own life. Then again, aren't we all unreliable narrators in our own mythmaking?

What influenced or inspired *Les Dems*? There is no shortage of candidates and attributions change according to the critic. Influences range from El Greco and Baroque group portraits to Cezanne's *Three Bathers* and Gauguin's primitives. The more convincing argument, though, is that the painting was an inspired answer to his antagonist Matisse.

In 1906, Matisse, 10 years Picasso's senior, had exhibited Joie *de vivre* at that year's salon. Although Picasso did not show at the salons, he was fully aware (and jealous) of Matisse's accepted reputation. Their pictures could not be more different. As John Golding writes "Unlike the *Joie de vivre,* which was intended to soothe and delight the eye, the *Demoiselles* can hardly have been calculated to please. Whereas Matisse's painting is . . . wonderfully joyful and full of rich color and sensuous rhythms, the *Demoiselles* is angular, harsh, and grating." Regarding color and form, these two artists were painting on different, separate canvases yet both coveted the same championship title of The Modern Artist.

The first criticisms of *Les Dems* were not about its subject matter. Ladies of pleasure had been done before. Ingres painted his *Grande Odalisque* in 1814. Manet's *Olympia* was painted in 1856 and both were paintings of prostitutes. Or, we could go back to Greek sculptures or the frescoes at Pompeii for such delights. Nor was the criticism that *Les Dems* had the effrontery of confronting the viewer. *Olympia* had broken the fourth wall decades earlier as had the court characters in Velázquez' *Las Meninas* two centuries before that. The criticism was not about it subject; it was about its style.

Courtesans of yore were classically posed as reclining nudes and, while they had seductive, come hither looks, they were also portrayed with an element of high romanticism. In a search for the classical, some critics see a reclining nude in *Les Dems* and say that Picasso in fact painted one; he just painted her vertical.

Nor was the criticism that *Les Dems* was particularly erotic. Gustav Courbet more than owned that territory with *The Origin of the World.* Rather, the early criticisms were based on rejection; Picasso's rejection of the erotic in favor of the exotic; of classical representation for something new and unfamiliar; and of space, depth, and perspective for something flat and cropped. One might imagine that the idea of the conflation of space and time was in the air given that 1905 was Einstein's year of special relativity. *Les Dems* stops and fuses space and time. For all of its angles, the surface is flat. For all of its figures, motion is suspended. And, if there is a story to tell, it is told in a glance; there is no narrative. It is all impact.

MoMA Director Barr wrote the catalog for the 1939 exhibition. He thought the painting "was a transitional picture, . . . a work of formidable, dynamic power unsurpassed in European art . . . [and] together with Matisse's *Joie de Vivre* it marks the beginning of a new period in the history of modern art."

Barr thought that the medical student was carrying a skull and that the skull referenced death and constituted a "moralistic contrast between virtue (man with the skull) and vice (man surrounded by food women)." He then described it as "a kind of *momento mori*" or as an allegory about the "wages of sin." For Barr, this scene was a conflict between sex and death, between good and evil, between human desire and human weakness. Such a morality tale makes some sense. Consider Picasso's background — close knit family, Catalonia, Catholicism — what better way to challenge, if not reject, the authority of those influences than by welcoming, and in no small part, inventing modernity.

The next major study of *Les Dems* was published in 1959 by John Golding. He insightfully discussed the influences of other painters, the importance of the Iberian sculptures, and Picasso's visit to the museum in the Trocadero. Importantly (and, I believe, correctly), he downplayed the significance of *Les Dems* in the development of Cubism.

> "Cubism was an art of realism, and insofar as it was concerned with reinterpreting the external world in a detached, objective way, a classical art. The impression made by the *Demoiselles* . . . is one of violence and unrest. Indeed, the savagery of the two figures at the right-hand side . . . would justify its classification as one of the most remarkable products of 20th century expressionism."

Writing shortly after Golding, the critic Robert Rosenblum expanded on the notion of savagery:

> "The 'savagery that dominates the painting' [is demonstrated by] the 'jagged planes that lacerate torsos . . . harsh junctures . . . [and] the furious energies of . . . collisive, cutting angles'; the 'demonic' eyes of the crouching demoiselle [has] 'magical force.'"

After Golding, Leo Steinberg's important 1972 essay, "The Philosophical Brothel," adopted the early joke name for the painting. Steinberg had access to many of Picasso's notebooks together with 19 full studies. He set out to answer some open questions: How was the painting composed? Why were the two men there then gone? Did the women have to be prostitutes? Why the African masks? Why the several styles? And, why the staged setting? Opening the essay, he announces his conclusion: "No modern painting engages you with such brutal immediacy."

Steinberg breaks the picture down into its particularities. Each figure is studied individually as is the sequence in which each woman enters the frame. Each pose is analyzed. Each facial expression. He comments on details such as the placement of the fruit, the table, and the curtain. Steinberg dissects the lines and edges of the painting; its colors and shadows; and its very shape. The canvas is large, a roughly 8' x 8' square; a square that compresses the figures as if they are being viewed through a window.

Regarding the two male figures, Steinberg asserts that even with their elimination, they remain a "shadowy presence" and we, the viewers, become the shadows of those figures.

Considering *Les Dems* as a group portrait, he said that each woman stands alone. It is a discontinuous group. There is no obvious communication among them. Instead, they direct their attention outward thus giving Les Demoiselles girl group power through a seduction that brings the viewer into the scene; into art; and into the modern world. The five figures are five versions of the subject, and they are five versions of the artist, and of the direction of art.

The women of *Les Dems* are primitive and tribal precisely to tap into the preternatural power of sex; to tap into the energy of the life force. These nativistic creatures have been trafficked into an urban brothel as a means of importing the pre-historic jungle into the city and infusing the origins of passion into modern consciousness.

Steinberg debunks Barr's *memento mori* conceit, a conceit that even Barr did not hold onto too tightly. A skull is in a preliminary sketch or two; in others, the figure is holding a book; and, and still others, he is holding nothing at all. Maybe the skull is nothing more than a simple prop. Sometimes a skull is just a skull.

Still, Barr's *momento mori* interpretation was later embellished by other critics who argued that the student with the skull represented Picasso's fear of death and, since the scene is taking place in a brothel, Picasso's fear of syphilis. Maybe, though, Picasso disappeared those two guys because they added two too many to the women's party. Isn't it more likely that Picasso was aiming at other, larger, more artistically and historically impactful quarry than another tale about good and bad?

Steinberg's 1972 essay arrived at a maybe peculiar is a better word, time in intellectual and art history. For about a decade or so before then, New York art critics, led by their high priest Clement Greenberg, were asking: "Did Picasso still matter[?]" "Didn't Picasso's artistic genius end with Cubism?" And since then, "hadn't he dissipated his gifts on minor works?" Odd questions indeed. Cubism's sell by date was 1916 and Picasso's 1937 *Guernica* can be called many things; minor is not one of them. Still, the whole Picasso oeuvre was not universally admired.

In another advertisement for himself, Norman Mailer weighed in on *Les Dems.* He began focusing on differences between Matisse and Picasso. "If Matisse was rousing prodigies of attention among his fellow artists and critics by what he could accomplish with color, Picasso now had to show what could be done with form — even more, the destruction of form, at least as everyone understood it." Mailer had done his homework; but the artistic conflict between color and form had been mined earlier.

Mailer may well have been infected by the Greenberg School of Picasso criticism. He writes of *Les Dems* that although it is an artistically pleasing work: "We are looking at nothing less moving than a prodigiously important historical artifact — for those who are aesthetically devout, it is quite equal in modern art to the relics of the saints." He goes on to call it a repellent work "not unlike an obscure poem that will never repay one's attention without a solemn search into the poet's notes, ambitions, and themes." For Mailer, *Les Dems* is modern in a way that it cannot be enjoyed on its own without expert commentary. *Finnegan's Wake* anyone?

Mailer concludes that *Les Dems* is a "notable event" on Picasso's journey to Cubism. Well, so much for Mailer as art critic.

The young ladies left New York City for Paris in 1988. They did not visit the Bateau Lavoir in Monmartre; instead, Les Demsoiselles went to the Marais and stayed at the Hôtel Salé, recently converted to the Musée Picasso. As a brief aside, I also remember my first time at the Musée when the special exhibition was a voluminous display of Picasso's pornography. Oops, I did not mean pornography, I meant his erotic art.

I have since regretted not buying the exhibition catalog; you know how heavy they are and it was in French. Still, I should have bought it. After all, I didn't want to read it; I only wanted to look at the pictures. In my mind's eye, those pictures were more startling, by far, then *Les Dems.* Regarding them, let me just say that Picasso was not afraid of menstrual blood.

The 1988 exhibition catalog, two volumes of over 700 pages, republished

Steinberg's 1972 essay together with all of the sketches and additional critical essays. Notably, the 1988 exhibit, and the surrounding criticism, occurred at the height of Postmodernism in academic Europe and America.

By way of example, one interpreter sees Picasso's use of African motifs as an example of colonial appropriation:

> *Les Demsoiselles* and the primitivising work it generates necessarily constituted both an act of valuing the products of African culture and an allusion to French brutality that contradicted the nation's image of itself as a 'civilizing' force, pointing up this 'hypocrisy' and 'bankrupt' cultural traditions at a charged period of political debate.

From such an altitude, art criticism takes a left turn away from art appreciation directly into cultural criticism. Typical of that period is the focus on the sexuality in the painting as a way to critique sexuality wholesale. In an essay entitled "Painting as Trauma" Yve-Alain Bois says that with *Les Dems*, Picasso "meant to take on the whole history of painting," including his own work and that the painting is intentionally "self-referential, even onanistic." Continuing, he writes:

> The *Demoiselles* creates a fundamental break with the symbolist tradition, and that break may be linked to an investigation of what Lacanian psychoanalysis calls the symbolic (i.e., the order of the law — governing the Oedipus complex and it's correlative, the castration complex — that structures of personality give access to every construction of opposition, to language, society, or, even, art).

Whew! Masturbation, castration, deconstruction, Picasso's Oedipal killing of the father? Who could have guessed?

If Lacanian psychoanalysis can enter the critical world of *Les Dems*, can feminism (and the dreaded male gaze) be far behind? Not according to Tamar Garb who opines:

> But about one thing there is universal agreement . . . *Les Demsoiselles* was intended to be viewed by men — virile, heterosexual men of European origin. . . . The fact of the matter is that most of the men who first looked at the painting in the privi-

> leged conditions of Picasso's studio could not recognize themselves . . . . They could not fathom its formal disjunctions, its incoherence, its peculiar iconic hybridity. Neither did it speak to their sexual fantasies, their dreams of dominance or fears of castration. They could not 'penetrate the picture' . . . Only much later, when it's pictorial transgressions had been tamed by formalist teleologies and its secret history had been revealed by careful tracking of studies and sketches, could this picture provide the narrative spur to scintillating tales of sex and seduction

I apologize for the lengthy quotations but postmodernists can get windy. Note that again, we have, penetration, male privilege, teleology, reduction; there is something afoot here other than the study of a particular work of art or of an artist.

In an attempt to get away from the condemnation of male sexuality and domination, Garb, to her partial credit, recognizes that one of the painting's first admirers was a woman. In the world according to Garb, Gertrude Stein appreciated the power of the painting and the power of the artist's vision. Stein drew inspiration from Picasso for her own work. Just as *Les Dems* was an assault on previous artistic conventions, it also allowed her to reject traditional narrative and linguistic models. Garb notes: "What the painting represented to [Stein] was an attack on a genre, not an attack on women. She identified with the artistic agency thematised in it, rather than the image of femininity brutalized by it."

Unfortunately, Garb gives with one hand and takes with the other. She continues: "Perhaps . . . [Stein] was so identified with masculine models of agency that she failed to notice the potential for her own symbolic objectification here." Apparently, Gertrude was not man enough to acknowledge her own gendered subjugation. Peut-être. Maybe Picasso's attribution of the erotic to women is not to objectify them but to venerate their power, their awe, their majesty, their mystique.

Yet there is Picasso's misogyny. A critic writes: "I am fascinated that no one I have read seems to have noticed that the literature on Picasso continually turns grown-up women into girls." And, more, the very name "'Picasso' has come to signify a heroic myth of greatness — an agonistic narrative of influences and stylistic revolutions — that coincides with the sequence of women and their consequent ouster from favor: Picasso as Henry VIII." This criticism is not far off. Picasso did use women as models and as lovers and he did move on from one to another. Is it possible, though, that his art is infused with sex to the point where sex and art form a unitary and essential dimension in his art as in his life? Or, does that interpretation just perpetuate the heterosexual male impulse to relish sexual privilege and erotic power?

With another critic, the curtain is pulled back from Po-Mo think to expose its true target. After recognizing that *Les Dems* has been "read" as "incipiently sexist, heterosexist, and neocolonialist," Anna Chave confesses that "neither Picasso's own intentions . . . nor his susceptibility to [those] biases" are the targets of her investigation. Instead, she continues, "poststructuralist and reception theories have shown that all publicly circulated images accrue new meetings beyond their maker's intent and control. . . ." Here she has admitted that the role of the critic is to "interpret[e] art works [to] shape their significance by shaping how and what the public sees." Ah-ha, in the Po-Mo world, the art and the artist disappear, and they are replaced by the art critic just as art appreciation is replaced by politico-cultural interpretation.

Next, William Rubin's 1994 monograph *The Genesis of* Les Demsoiselles d'Avignon, moves in a slightly different, and a bit more familiar direction. Rubin's study returns to the painting and the sketches and for him *Les Dems* "created an historical fault-line" for modern painting. He thought that Picasso was painting a "terrifying night journey of the soul."

Rubin explores Picasso's state of mind at the time such as his troubles with Fernande, their adoption of the 13-year-old orphan Raymonde, and her return to the orphanage shortly thereafter. He also discusses Picasso's "deep-seated fear and loathing of the female body, which existed side-by-side with his craving for and ecstatic idealization of it." And yet, can it not be the case that this common Freudian, male attraction/repulsion meme is transcended in *Les Dems* to attain something more universal, more amplified, more encompassing?

Rubin also argues that the painting's diverse styles reveal Picasso's "underlying polarities:" "Eros and Thanatos, beauty and ugliness, human and animal — all of which can and do become reinforced on the stylistic level by means of Picasso's revolutionary departure from the traditional 'unity' of figuration." But isn't art always about form and content and their ever-changing relationships?

Rubin's detailed study describes the development of each figure; the sequence of the women in the picture; how their poses change over time; the disappearing act of the two men; and even the placement of the objects in the square. He also discusses the influences on Picasso and is skeptical of claiming too much. He recognizes Cézanne's contribution to Cubism but less so to *Les Dems.* Instead, pride of place goes to El Greco particularly his *Apocalyptic Vision* and his *Vision of St. John.*

Let's return to MoMA for a final viewing. In *Les Dems,* as in literally all of his paintings, Picasso has inserted himself not only as artist but as participant. Whether he represents himself by his coal black eyes or by the mythic figure of the Minotaur, Picasso is there. He is staring at you, daring you, inviting you, challenging you.

In *Les Dems,* each woman has Picasso's eyes. The male gaze, so much criticized by the PoMo school, is there in the painting but it is not the gaze of the male ogling naked women. Instead, it is the gaze of the painter contemplating (and challenging) you, the viewer. And, Picasso's male gaze is neither reproving nor prurient; rather, it is a gaze of wonderment and amazement, and of declaration and authority. "I did this," he says. "I am the master." "My eyes can be seen in the women I paint not because I am expressing the feminine; No, I am Eros, the source of all sex; I am the seducer of art, of life." No one has ever doubted Picasso's sense of self or his ego.

Art criticism changes from time to time and from critic to critic. At times, it is informative; and unreliable at others. There is much to learn from the history of a painting and reading the history of its criticism. One danger, though, must be avoided and, let me return to Steinberg. We cannot, he says, let "source-hunting forays" into the picture "remove our gaze from the picture itself."

There are other, reliable ways to look at art. About the turn of the last century, the young Anglo-American Iris Cutting, later the Marchese Iris Origo, was living in the English enclave in Florence when she asked her mother's friend Bernard Berenson to teach her about art. BB's reply? "Use your eyes." Indeed, when we use our eyes to see — what do we see? With thoughtful, reflective viewing our eyes will tell us.

After the museum and before returning to the Hades of the Bus Terminal, Pat and I walked a block to the Tiki Bar in the Hilton Hotel on Lex for our first Mai Tais those sophisticated drinks in coconuts with umbrellas, cherries, and pineapple slices! I remember those drinks; I remember the bar; and when I use my eyes to see, I most certainly remember the other new friends that I met on that visit to MoMA; those friends named Brancusi, Giacometti, Modigliani, Monet, Revelson, and many others and, of course, I remember *Guernica* and I remember those *Les Demsoiselles.* You never forget your first time.

Bibliography

ALFRED BARR, PICASSO: FORTY YEARS OF HIS ART (1939).

Yve-Alain Bois, *Painting as Trauma* in CHRISTOPHER GREEN (ED.), PICASSO'S LES DEMSOISELLES DAVIGNON (2001).

Anna C. Chave, *New Encounters with* Les Demsoiselles d'Avignon: *Gender, Race and the Origins of Cubism*, 76 THE ART BULLETIN 596 (1994).

Judith Cousins and Hélène Seckel, *Chronology of* Les Demsoiselles d'Avignon in WILLIAM RUBIN, HÉLÈNE SECKEL AND JUDITH COUSINS, STUDIES IN MODERN ART 3: LES DEMSOISELLES D'AVIGNON 145 (1994).

Tamara Garb, *"To Kill the Nineteenth Century": Sex and Spectatorship with Gertrude and Pablo* in CHRISTOPHER GREEN (ED.), PICASSO'S *LES DEMSOISELLES D'AVIGNON* 55 (2001).

John Golding, The *Demoiselles d'Avignon*, 100 BURLINGTON MAGAZINE 154 (May 1958).

John Golding, Demoiselles d'Avignon *and the Exhibition of 1988*, in CHRISTOPHER GREEN (ED.), PICASSO'S *LES DEMSOISELLES D'AVIGNON* 15 (2001).

John Golding, *The Triumph of Picasso*, N.Y. REV. BOOKS (July, 21, 1988).

SIRI HUSTVEDT, A WOMEN LOOKING AT MEN LOOKING AT WOMEN: ESSAYS ON ART, SEX, AND THE MIND (2016).

Patricia Leighton, *Colonialism,* l'art nègre, *and* Les Demsoiselles d'Avignon in CHRISTOPHER GREEN (ED.), PICASSO'S *LES DEMSOISELLES D'AVIGNON* 77 (2001).

NORMAN MAILER, PORTRAIT OF PICASSO AS A YOUNG MAN (1995).

JOHN RICHARDSON, A LIFE OF PICASSO: VOLUME II 1907-1917 THE PAINTER OF MODERN LIFE (1996).

SUE ROE, IN MONTMARTRE: PICASSO, MATISSE AND THE BIRTH OF MODERNIST ART (2015).

William Rubin, *The Genesis of* Les Demsoiselles d'Avignon in WILLIAM RUBIN, HÉLÈNE SECKEL AND JUDITH COUSINS, STUDIES IN MODERN ART 3: LES DEMSOISELLES D'AVIGNON 13 (1994).

Hélène Seckel, *Anthology of Early Commentary* on Les Demsoiselles d'Avignon in WILLIAM RUBIN, HÉLÈNE SECKEL AND JUDITH COUSINS, STUDIES IN MODERN ART 3: LES DEMSOISELLES D'AVIGNON 213 (1994).

Leo Steinberg, *The Philosophical Brothel*, 71 ART NEWS (September/October 1972).

MILES J. UNGER, PICASSO AND THE PAINTING THAT SHOCKED THE WORLD (2018).

{20} TOUR EN FER

ROBERT VITZ

MOST CITIES have their peculiar and singular architectural or engineering structures, and Cincinnati is no exception. Now, we are all familiar with the Queen City's most prominent structures. Unfortunately, the Roebling Bridge belongs to the Commonwealth of Kentucky; our tallest buildings cannot compare to New York's or Chicago's; and our magnificent Union Terminal reflects the city's procrastination in constructing a central railroad station. Still, we do have our own not-so-well-known curiosities.

Up I-75, about halfway to Dayton, was the Solid Rock Church's "King of Kings" statue, known to many disbelievers as either "Touchdown Jesus" or "Jesus in the Quicksand." To those with lingering memories of state fairs, its off-white coloring suggested a blue-ribbon entry in the butter-carving competition. This massive sculpture, which rose from the grounds in front of the non-denominational Solid Rock evangelical church, with its arms uplifted, burned after being struck by lightning a few years ago. Its replacement, a fifty-two-foot full-figured Jesus, considered to be fireproof, is perhaps less imposing, but still represents either an awesome religious icon or a tasteless example of man's hubris.

Reversing our direction, just south of the Ohio River sits the world's smallest chapel. At least that was the claim made in "Ripley's Believe It or Not" some years ago. Officially called the Monte Casino Chapel, this 6' by 9' stone structure was built in 1878 by monks of the Benedictine monastery in Covington. After the monks departed the region, the chapel was restored and moved to the then-new Thomas More College campus, where it is open for personal meditation . . . and Munchkin weddings.

A very different architectural structure is the well-known Loveland Castle, the brainchild of one Harry Andrews. Andrews, who was declared dead from spiral meningitis during the First World War, returned to the United States — very much alive — with a profound dislike of modern warfare and an overly romantic understanding of medieval life. In the early 1920s he organized a Boy Scout troop, and out of this came an organization called The Knights of the Golden Trail. Harry Andrews soon became Sir Harry Andrews. The knighthood was self-imposed and no doubt Queen Elizabeth remains unaware of this particular branch of the lesser nobility.

Having absorbed the early Boy Scout emphasis on developing manly character, Andrews often took his boys hiking and camping along the banks of the Little Miami River. So often, in fact, that they constructed two stone shelters to house their gear, and from this modest beginning rose the great castle-like structure called Chateau Laroche, the eventual product of several generations of local boys. Andrews, a graduate of Colgate University, died in 1981, at the age of ninety-one, but the Castle and the Knights of the Golden Trail remain.

Just a few miles north of Chateau Laroche sits a fourth local curiosity, the centerpiece of King's Island. I am referring, of course, of the Ohio version of the Eiffel Tower. Why this was deemed a fitting symbol for an amusement park remains a mystery to me, although no doubt it seemed logical at the time as part of the original "International Street," an area of kitschy European restaurants and shops. This replica, approximately one-third the size of the original, continues to serve as the amusement park's own iconic image.

For centuries, cities around the world often have been signified by unique physical structures. Rome has its Coliseum, Sidney, its Opera House. The onion-topped Saint Basil's Cathedral identifies Moscow; Rio is instantly known by the imposing statue of Christ the Redeemer; and London has its Bridge (except that the London Bridge is now in Arizona). Oh, well, it has other bridges, along with Big Ben and, more recently, a huge Ferris wheel. One could place the Empire State Building in the same category, although it has to compete with too many other New York skyscrapers. As for Paris, nothing represents that city, or for that matter France itself, so well as the great iron tower constructed for the World's Fair of 1889. Indeed, the Eiffel Tower may be the world's penultimate urban image. But this brief tour led me to the realization that I knew more about Sir Harry Andrews than I did about the designer of the great tower, Gustav Eiffel.

Eiffel's great-great-grandfather emigrated from Germany to France early in the eighteenth century, where he changed the family name to Eiffel from Boenickhausen, the region in Germany from which they had come. This was a fortunate decision on his part for few would want to visit the Boenickhausen Tower. After two generations of upward economic mobility, Gustav's father left the ranks of the petit bourgeoisie to join the ranks of Napoleon's army, and after Waterloo he was assigned to the barracks at Dijon. Here, he married the daughter of a prosperous merchant, and Gustav was born in 1832. After a normal provincial boyhood, he attended the Central School of Arts and Manufactures in Paris, where he studied chemical engineering, graduating in 1855. He aspired to a position in an uncle's vinegar distillery, but his uncle, a staunch republican, violently disagreed with Gustav's parents' Bonapartist views, and that ended Gustave's future in vinegar. Left to his own resources, he took a position with a company that designed railroads. Hired initially as the assistant and private secretary to the company director, he eventually was placed in charge of research. In 1858, he was part of a team sent to build a cast iron railroad bridge across the Garonne River in Bordeaux. After several engineers quit the project, Eiffel found himself in charge. The company's officers quickly learned what a valuable asset they had.

During the 1860s he developed a formula for determining the elasticity of wrought-iron, a formula that allowed him to do away with the costly trial-and-error method so commonly used, and in 1867 he used his formula to construct Machinery Hall at the Paris Exposition of that year. This structure, a 1,600 by 1,266-foot iron-framed ellipse was the largest structure of its day, exceeding the size of London's Crystal Palace, built sixteen years earlier for the first world's fair. In France, this was considered a great victory over the despised English.

The second half of the nineteenth century might well be called the "age of engineering." Iron replaced masonry. Steam power replaced animals. Height, speed and distance records were established and then re-established. James Eads built his great bridge across the Mississippi; the Roeblings built their suspension bridges over the Ohio and then the East River; and Eiffel's Machinery Hall pushed his name to the forefront of French engineering. Victoria's Prince Albert had caught the essence of the era when he wryly commented that, "If we want any work done of an unusual character and send for an architect, he hesitates, debates, trifles; we send for an engineer and *he does it.*" Eiffel, himself, while looking at bad designs, on occasion was heard to mutter, "Stupid as an architect."

Between 1867 and 1886, the newly formed Eiffel and Company constructed, in France alone, forty-two railroad bridges. Because suspension bridges were still considered dangerous— and the tragic collapse of Scotland's Tay Bridge in 1878 underlined that concern — Eiffel 's trademark became the trussed arch which he had used for the Bordeaux bridge and later to such good effect for bridges at Oporto, Portugal, and over the Truyère River in eastern France, the latter a four hundred foot high "monster" that took five years to complete His work also included the train station in Pest, Hungary, numerous bridges in Indochina, the framework for the Bon Marché department store in Paris, various structures in South America, and the skeletal support for the Statue of Liberty.

His work on the Statue of Liberty must have reinforced his views about poor design. The sculptor Frederic Bartholdi had designed the statue, a 151-foot-tall Amazon, with an upraised arm that itself was forty-two feet long and twelve feet thick. The head was to be seventeen feet from chin to cranium, and an index finger to extend eight feet. It was to be, and remains, the tallest human figure in the world. Unfortunately, Bartholdi had not a clue how this massive sculpture could be supported, particularly with the tricky winds of New York harbor. He turned to Monsieur Eiffel. Eiffel chose to construct an interior iron skeleton for the hollow lady, and for the inherently weak arm holding the torch, he used iron beams to support it and then extended them across the back to the left side, thus creating a practical counter balance. It was Eiffel who also suggested that "Liberty" be clad in a protective sheaf of copper attached to its iron framework. The final product is more engineer than artist.

Massive buildings, soaring bridges, the Statue of Liberty, all of this made Gustave Eiffel the logical person to construct a tower that would be the centerpiece of the Paris Exposition of 1889. World's Fairs, of course, had been around since 1851 when Great Britain, pushed by Prince Albert, conceived of the idea of holding a great exhibition to showcase industrial advances around the world, many of which, of course, reflected Great Britain's place as the world's leading industrial nation. The Crystal Palace exhibition, as it was dubbed, was a great success. Not to be upstaged by a nation of shopkeepers, France held its first Exposition Universelle in 1855, to be held on the Champs de Mars. London countered seven years later with its second industrial exhibition. Paris again responded, in 1867. Eventually Vienna and Philadelphia joined the mix. But 1889 was a special year for France. The country wanted to celebrate the 100th anniversary of its revolution, and a fair would allow the none-too-stable Third Republic to strengthen its position against clamoring Bonapartists and leftover Communards. It was also an opportunity to show the world that France had cast off its humiliating defeat by Prussia in 1870, and was once again the leading nation on the continent. This was to be the opening of France's "La Belle Èpoque."

Eiffel was not the first to envision a colossal tower. As early as 1833, a British railroad engineer had suggested erecting a one-thousand-foot cast-iron tower in London, situated on a one-hundred-foot-wide masonry base, with the tower gradually narrowing at the top to ten feet and surmounted by a large statue. The project was never attempted and later engineers found the design fatally flawed. Nevertheless, the 1000-foot tower became something of an obsession on both sides of the Atlantic, although some considered it unachievable, like climbing Mt. Everest or running the four-minute mile in the next century. Two American engineers wanted to attempt such a tower for the Philadelphia Centennial Exposition in 1876 but their plans remained on the drawing board. By 1889, man's loftiest achievement remained the all-masonry, 555-foot Washington Monument, completed in 1884 after a gestation period of 36 years.

As soon as the French government announced plans for its third exposition, with a dramatic centerpiece, two of Eiffel's engineers began planning a thousand-foot tower. Indeed, even before the required specifications were released, Eiffel had published a general description of this plan, a plan much admired by Edouard Lockroy, minister of commerce and industry and the guiding force behind the Exposition, and there is considerable evidence that the official specifications were largely based on Eiffel's preliminary work. Thus, it should have come as no surprise when Eiffel received the contract. Of course, controversy followed immediately. Competitors claimed foul, although many of their designs ignored the required specifications or were completely unrealizable. One entrant envisioned a tower with a gigantic water sprinkling system that would alleviate any future summer droughts. Another displayed a large guillotine to evoke the event being honored. Jules Bourdais, architect of the famed Trocadéro Palace, designed an all-granite tower with a huge electric searchlight at the top, surrounded by parabolic mirrors, which would banish night from every corner of Paris.

More importantly, France saw itself as the center of culture, and the art world resisted the concept that industrial materials and processes could result in an appropriate aesthetic symbol for the nation. One of the first criticisms came from the editor of the architectural journal, *La Construction Moderne.* He denounced Eiffel's plan as "an inartistic . . . scaffolding of crossbars and angled iron" with a "hideously unfinished" look. Others denounced it as "a useless and monstrous" tower. Forty-seven of France's best known and most powerful artists and intellectuals published a joint letter which described the proposed tower as a dishonor to Paris. "For the next twenty years we will see cast over the entire city . . . cast like a spot of ink, the odious shadow of the odious column of bolted metal." Although many of these critics eventually changed their minds, the writer Guy de Maupassant retained his dislike. Some years later, when asked why he so frequently ate in one of the tower's restaurants, he famously responded that it was the only place in Paris where he did not have to look at it.

The slings and arrows of aesthetic criticism proved to be only the beginning of Eiffel's worries. A new line of attack soon surfaced. In June 1886, a virulent screed titled, *The Jewish Question,* accused the engineer through his German ancestors of being Jewish, and it labeled the proposed tower as "*une tour juive*." Coming just eight years before the infamous Dreyfus Affair, Eiffel felt called upon to defend himself in the republican paper *Le Temps*, by firmly stating that he was born of French Catholic parents. And he didn't even have to produce his birth certificate. After parrying this surprising allegation, Eiffel was anxious to get started in order to meet the Exposition's opening deadline, but more serious problems quickly surfaced.

Eiffel estimated the cost of the tower at five million francs, or about forty million dollars in today's currency. The government had originally implied that it would pick up the entire cost, but now fiscally conservative politicians backpedaled, and finally it was determined that the government would underwrite only one and one-half million francs, or just thirty percent of the estimated cost.

This left Eiffel with the personal responsibility to raise the rest. To attract investors, he was permitted to keep the tower in place for twenty years and retain all the profits from entry fees and restaurant concessions during that period.

While politicians debated the financing, the COMESA de Poix, who lived on the boulevard that ran alongside the Champs de Mars, filed a law suit to block construction, claiming that the tower was not only a menace to her house but "that it will block up for many years the most agreeable part of the Champs de Mars . . . in which [I have] been accustomed to take [my] daily exercise." There was also concern that the iron tower would function as a giant lightening rod and draw dangerous storms to the area. With weeks turning into months of dithering, Eiffel contemplated dropping the entire project. Finally, in a bold move, he accepted personal liability for any damage to neighboring homes if the tower should fall. However, nothing was resolved concerning the Comtesse's exercise regimen.

On January 28, 1887, some eight months after receiving the bid, Eiffel and Co. broke ground. From this time on, his problems would be engineering ones, not political or personal. His original plans had been drawn with the idea that the tower would sit more or less in the center of the Champs de Mars, but opposition from the army, which used the area for training exercises, pushed the tower to the very edge of the Seine River. Two of the foundations four legs would now be on the unstable alluvial soil along the Left Bank. This required not only deeper excavation but the need to use compressed air inside sunken caissons to protect workers from water seepage while they removed the soil. By the end of June, however, the great masonry foundations had been completed and the iron tower could now start its ascent. Since even a very small deviation from the horizontal plane could throw off the tower's balance, Eiffel designed an ingenious system for fine-tuning. In the base of each leg, where they joined the foundation, he installed four hydraulic jacks which would permit minute adjustments as the iron beams moved upward to the first platform.

During these early months, Eiffel and Co. had been busy manufacturing the thousands of iron beams that would make up the actual tower. Each of the 18,000 pieces was designed separately, numbered, and holes, calculated to within one-tenth of a millimeter, drilled for the rivets. According to *The Atlantic Monthly*, this required a total of over seven million holes. Steam-powered cranes traveled up and down the framework hoisting the beams for installation, and like a gigantic Erector set the tower climbed upward. By mid-October, Parisians out for a stroll could see the four legs stretching up some ninety-two feet; five months later the tower approached 200 feet. The world had never seen anything like it.

By March 26, 1888, the first platform was securely in place. To celebrate the occasion and to curry favor with the press, in July Eiffel invited eighty of the city's most influential journalists to a banquet to be served on the first platform. Wearing a formal frock coat and top hat, Eiffel led his guests up the stairs to the platform where they all dined off trestle tables, almost 200 feet in the air. Above them, they could see and hear workmen riveting the spidery latticework that would lead to the second platform. Below them lay the sprawling city, a view previously seen by only a few intrepid balloonists. Already the tower was the tallest structure in Paris, eclipsing the dome of Les Invalides. On July 14, Bastille Day, a fantastic display of fireworks illuminated the rising giant. By now, no one doubted that the great tower would be finished.

At this point, a problem that had been bothering Eiffel for some time had to be addressed. How were the curious masses going to reach the top of the tower? Elevators, of course, but no one had yet designed elevators for such an unusual structure. The simple solution was to run a shaft up through the middle of the tower, but to Eiffel this would spoil the symmetry and simplicity of the tower's elegant profile. Instead, he devised a plan for three sets of elevators, each set requiring different specifications, and he employed a French engineer named Backmann to design them. However, just twelve months before the Exposition's scheduled opening, Backmann still struggled with plans. To reach the first platform from the ground was not a problem. The width of the legs and the slight degree of curvature meant that a straight track could be employed. To safely and swiftly carry passengers to the second platform, however, proved much more difficult. Here, the curvature was much greater and presented a serious challenge in a time when most elevators ran on hydraulic pressure. Then, of course, there was the need to reach the top platform, which would have to be done in two stages. To complicate the matter, the government required that all elevators be built by French companies.

A French company installed a somewhat noisy, but reliable articulated chain-link operation to carry passengers from the ground to the first platform. For the two-part third stage, the primary obstacle was the sheer distance to be covered — 525 feet. Backmann was dismissed and Léon Édoux, who had installed a successful 230-foot elevator in the Trocadéro Palace, neatly solved the problem. He used two cars, running simultaneously. As the lower car began its ascent from the second platform to the interim transfer point, the second car would descend from the top. They would counterbalance each other, with the help of hydraulic pressure brought from a holding tank at the top of the tower.

But it was the elevators in the middle, those that would connect the first platform to the second, which continued to baffle Eiffel. When bids went out, no French company even responded, only the Paris branch of the American Otis Brothers and Company submitted a design. After a second call for bids, the government reluctantly waived its rules and gave the contract to Otis. Otis had gained a strong reputation in the United States for the safety of his equipment, and he had perfected elevators that moved by cables from the top, with the energy provided by water pressure that moved large pistons. A safety system involved strong leaf springs that forced brake shoes to grip the rails, slowly bringing the car to a halt. In Europe, most elevators used a system similar to cog railroads, a system that was both noisy and limited the speed of elevator movement. But Eiffel didn't trust the Otis method. After all, both his reputation and his financial liability hung in the balance.

Although the Otis Company installed its elevators, the situation was not finally resolved until three weeks after the Exposition opened when Otis's chief engineer came to Paris to demonstrate with a test run. He loaded approximately 7,000 pounds of lead in the cabin; secured the elevator with thick ropes; and then disconnected the steel cables. In front of thousands of spectators, two workmen, armed with axes, then walked up the narrow spiral stairs to the second platform. With both Eiffel's and American manufacturing prestige at stake, the signal was given. The ropes were cut and the fifteen-ton Otis cabin began to fall, but then as the brake shoes grabbed, it gradually slowed, swaying gently, and stopped just thirty feet above the first platform. When Eiffel inspected the cabin, he noted that "not a pane of glass . . . had been broken or cracked." The next day the elevators were made available to the public.

When the exposition opened on May 6, 1889, many of the exhibits were not yet ready, including the much-anticipated tower, which was still receiving a handsome coat of bronze-red paint. Nine days later, and with the elevators not yet tested, some 12,000 people became the first visitors to walk through it, although the great majority of them, after climbing the 350 steps to the first platform, chose to forgo the 380 step climb to the second platform. If Eiffel felt uncomfortable about the delayed elevators, he did not show it. This was his day. Congratulatory telegrams came from around the world. French newspapers touted his skill, his fortitude, his attention to detail, and even many of the tower's early doubters now came around. The four restaurants on the first platform became the most popular places in Paris for dining, especially during soft summer evenings when the daily fireworks went off.

For the next five months Eiffel was the toast of Paris. Honored at frequent banquets and praised around the world, he modestly accepted various awards in the name of French engineering. He received foreign decorations ranging from the Austrian Order of the Iron Crown to the Japanese Imperial Order of the Rising Sun, and French President Carnot awarded him the rank of officer in the Legion of Honor. Although most European monarchies had chosen not to set up their own exhibit halls because of the fair's association with the French Revolution, many "royals' could not stay away, and Eiffel was happy to escort them personally up his tower. The future Nicholas II of Russia and the former Queen Isabella II of Spain made their appearances. So did the Prince and Princess of Wales, the Duke of Edinburgh and King George of Greece. Russia's Grand Duke Michael showed up in resplendent uniform. The King of Senegal, the Shah of Iran, and the Kedive of Egypt arrived, surrounded by their many retainers. Even the German ambassador came, although unannounced and hoping to avoid publicity. But Eiffel spotted him . . . and then gleefully notified the press.

At the height of his reputation and just fifty-seven years old, Eiffel had no premonition that the tower would be his last work. Less than four years later he was a criminal defendant in a Paris courtroom desperately trying to hold on to his reputation. Paralleling the great Exposition Universelle, French engineers had undertaken to construct a canal across Central America, a project that, when completed, would secure for the nation much wealth and admiration. The original plan, designed by Ferdinand de Lesseps, the designer of the Suez Canal, called for a sea-level canal without any locks. When this plan was unveiled, Gustave Eiffel had opposed it, believing it to be unfeasible. By 1887, and some $280 million dollars later, Eiffel's fears had come true. Still, when de Lesseps turned to him for help, he could not resist. He quickly designed a plan for a series of locks and started their construction but it was too little, too late. Just months before the opening of the World's Fair, work on the locks ground to a halt. The Panama Company filed for bankruptcy and thousands of investors wanted to know how their money had vanished in the jungles of Panama. The ensuing investigation revealed the unworkable original plan, several years of waste and mismanagement, and the use of almost $five million dollars in bribes to members of the National Assembly and members of the press. Along with the company officers, Eiffel found himself on trial for fraud. Although he had been only a contractor and had had nothing to do with either the financial or management side, the fact that he had profited by over six million dollars on his lock contract made him a culprit in the eyes of the public. In the highly-charged political atmosphere the judge pronounced him guilty of misusing funds and sentenced him to two years in prison. A week after Eiffel entered prison, a higher court voided his guilty verdict on a technicality, and a later investigation by the Legion of Honor found him innocent of all charges. Still, the damage to his reputation was done.

Eiffel retired from active engineering, and even had his name removed from his company. However, his personal wealth allowed him to experiment with a subject that had long interested him — weather. The Eiffel Tower already contained a weather station that monitored wind speed and direction, temperature, humidity, and precipitation. Over the next quarter century Eiffel set up some twenty-five such weather stations all across the country, published daily weather information, produced a weather atlas, and established the foundation of meteorology in France. Always cognizant of the power of wind, he worked daily in his office at the top of the tower and, ever the meticulous researcher, experimented with air resistance by dropping objects of various shapes and measuring the time it took them to reach the ground. Eventually he constructed a large wind tunnel at the base of the tower and conducted experiments based on his early recognition of the importance of aerodynamics. His published observations furthered developments in both aircraft lift and in the design of efficient propellers. In 1913, the Smithsonian Institution awarded him its prestigious Langley Gold medal.

With the development of radio, Eiffel eventually persuaded the French military to install a telegraphy unit at the top of the tower, which it did but only because Eiffel agreed to pay for it. In the meantime, his twenty-year lease on the tower would soon expire. Although it had remained as the part of the Paris Exposition of 1900, there were many who happily contemplated its removal, including, no doubt, the Comtesse de Poix. In the usual way of governments, a committee was established in 1903 to explore the issue, and it concluded that the combination of scientific experiments and anticipated adverse foreign opinion justified doing nothing at that time. In 1906, just three years before his lease would end, the City of Paris grudgingly granted an extension to 1915. "Since it is there, let it stay a little longer," seemed to be the Gallic attitude. Eiffel's worries about the future of his tower ended when the French War Department finally installed a radio antenna on it which could receive messages from as far away as North Africa. In 1914, the tower proved its military value when its receiver captured a radio message that the German army bearing down on Paris had run out of food for its horses. This convinced the French General Staff to launch a counterattack at the Marne River. Paris was saved and the tower was then closed to the public for the duration of the war. But the war had saved it from the scrap heap.

When peace again reigned over Europe, the eighty-six-year-old Eiffel took great pleasure in noting that once again thousands ascended its heights each year . . . and it was still the tallest man-made structure in the world. When he died in 1923, at the age of 91, his only lament was that the tower led people to think that it was his only work. Six years later, the Chrysler Building, which topped out at 1,046 feet, finally exceeded the height of Eiffel's *Tour en Fer.* No doubt, Eiffel himself would have discreetly smiled at the fact that it took forty years for a structure to surpass his namesake; and he would have taken just as much pleasure in knowing that it had become his country's most recognizable symbol. There is no way to know what he would think of its King's Island offspring.

LUCEAT LUX VESTRA.

www.ingramcontent.com/pod-product-compliance
Lightning Source LLC
Chambersburg PA
CBHW060626310726
48982CB00003B/686

* 9 7 8 1 9 4 7 9 3 4 1 1 5 *